Steven Berkoff

One-Act Plays

I Wanna Agent
Actor's Lament
Purgatory
Mediocrity
Howl
This is an Emergency
Six Actors in Seach of a Director
Adam and Eve
David and Goliath
Samson's Hair
Moses
How to Train an Anti-Semite
Roast
Line-Up
Pound of Flesh
Gas
Guilt
'Ere
Exit

Praise for *Decadence*

'A thrilling tour de force. Berkoff lays into the ruling classes . . . with all the bile, bitterness and technical expertise he can muster.'

— *London Daily News*

'The impact of Berkoff's work is visceral; and excess, and the pleasures of hatred are the essence of the show. It works marvellously because Berkoff is matchlessly equipped to transform the gut reactions of the outsider into material of high art.'

— *The Times*

Praise for *East*

'Berkoff transforms the ugliness of his material by his presentation: the language is an ironic mix of Shakespearian phrases and East End argot, the style ranges through song, dance, mime and dramatic confrontation.'

— *Spectator*

'[The characters'] speeches, specific in naming people and places, but lyric as in a memory of changes on the 38 bus route, bring to the bombast and violence a sense of history. It is quite an achievement.'

— *The Times*

'A violent, scabrously eloquent strip cartoon of the grimy underbelly of East End working-class life . . . a piece of obscene reality observed from without and within. The shockable and politically correct are advised to make other arrangements. The rest should book before it is too late.'

— *Sunday Times*

'A great blast of invigorating energy and rudery.'   — *Time Out*

Praise for *Kvetch*

'A study of lives of quiet desperation with the sound turned up to an almost unbearable volume . . . as funny as it is painful.'

— *Daily Telegraph*

'The anguish of repressed, or not repressed, hysteria that Hamlet would consider excessive applied to his own dilemmas'   — *The Times*

'Every confessional delay is integrated in the powerful comic rhythm, and physically articulated to project the group's racing fantasy life.'

— *Independent on Sunday*

STEVEN BERKOFF

One-Act Plays

*with a preface by the author
and an introduction by Geoffrey Colman*

B L O O M S B U R Y
LONDON • NEW DELHI • NEW YORK • SYDNEY

Bloomsbury Methuen Drama

An imprint of Bloomsbury Publishing Plc

50 Bedford Square	1385 Broadway
London	New York
WC1B 3DP	NY 10018
UK	USA

www.bloomsbury.com

Bloomsbury is a registered trade mark of Bloomsbury Publishing Plc

First published 1992
Reprinted 2013

British Library Cataloguing-in-Publication Data
A catalogue record for this book is available from the British Library.

ISBN: PB: 978-1-4081-8247-5
ePDF: 978-1-4081-8249-9
ePub: 978-1-4081--8248-2

Library of Congress Cataloging-in-Publication Data
A catalog record for this book is available from the Library of Congress.

Typeset by Country Setting, Kingsdown, Kent CT14 8ES
Printed and bound in Great Britain

Steven Berkoff was born in Stepney, London. After studying drama and mime in London and Paris, he entered a series of repertory companies and in 1968 formed the London Theatre Group. His plays and adaptations have been performed in many countries and in many languages. Among the many adaptations Berkoff has created, directed and toured for the stage are Kafka's *Metamorphosis* and *The Trial*, *Agamemnon after Aeschylus* and Poe's *The Fall of the House of Usher*. He has directed and toured productions of Shakespeare's *Coriolanus* also playing the title role, *Richard II*, *Hamlet* and *Macbeth*, as well as Oscar Wilde's *Salome*. Berkoff's original stage plays include *East, West, Messiah: Scenes from a Crucifixion*, *The Secret Love Life of Ophelia, Decadence, Harry's Christmas, Massage, Acapulco* and *Brighton Beach Scumbags*. He has performed his trilogy of solo shows, *One Man, Shakespeare's Villains* and *Requiem for Ground Zero*, in venues all over the world. As an actor, Berkoff's appearances include *A Clockwork Orange, Barry Lyndon, Octopussy, Beverly Hills Cop, Rambo, Under the Cherry Moon, Absolute Beginners* and *The Krays*. He directed and co-starred with Joan Collins in the film version of his play *Decadence*. Berkoff has published a variety of books on the theatre such as the production journals *I am Hamlet, Meditations on Metamorphosis* and *Coriolanus in Deutschland*. Berkoff's work has led him to traverse the globe, and his love for travel is apparent in his book *Shopping in the Santa Monica Mall: The Journals of a Strolling Player*.

Geoffrey Colman is Head of Acting at the Central School of Speech and Drama, London.

Contents

Preface

A one-act play is like a confession, an outpouring to your father confessor. It's usually swift, pungent and to the point, needs few extraneous characters or scene and set changes. I have a particular fondness for the one-act play since it seems to convey the essence of the playwright's mind, undiluted so to speak, and in some strange way is often more personal and intimate than a full-length play. Also, without trying to strain analogies overmuch, the one-act play is like what in film would be a 'close-up' – where, as we draw away, we do see more of the background and environment.

As an actor, my first one-act play was Edward Albee's intense thriller *Zoo Story*. It was a terrifying piece to learn and play with its central twenty-minute monologue about the alienated young man's relationship with a ferocious dog. The intensity of *Zoo Story* could not have been prolonged beyond its forty-minute time scale, but the effect was harrowing.

Tennessee Williams is probably the master of the one-act play, as are Anton Chekov and Samuel Beckett. I shall never forget Tennessee Williams' extraordinary evening of one-act plays at the Arts Theatre called *The Garden District*. One of them was *Suddenly Last Summer*, with the late, massively talented and much missed Patricia O'Neill and the remarkable Beatrix Lehmann.

I began writing one-act plays in my early days of writing before advancing to full-length plays and I have come back to them. There are certain stories that need to be told but do not have to be told over an entire evening and in fact would lose their power if they were deliberately over-extended. I have written about what I am mostly familiar with and wanted to give voice to.

In many of the plays I deal with the vicissitudes of our extraordinary profession, the theatre. It is sometimes quite demanding, and what agonies actors will go through before they are satisfied; and even then the very act of baring themselves on stage, not via an instrument but by being the instrument, is a traumatic experience. But what the hell, you grit your teeth and bear it.

I was tempted to write a contemporary version of four of the most famous biblical myths as the myths are so pungent, so powerful in the stories they tell, with their strong underlying moral code, that they just cry out for reinterpretation. These are ancient Hebrew legends and in the curious way the mind works I was provoked into examining them by a rather unwholesome flurry of anti-Israel sentiment that surfaces from time to time. Of course one must not equate just criticism with anti-Semitism but there can be no doubt that those with a certain 'bias' will always seek an opportunity to condemn Israel.

This also tempted me to write *How to Train an Anti-Semite*, a rather provocative one-act play giving guidance to those writing gently insidious anti-Semitic tracts to really get to it!

I have developed quite an affection for the characters in these plays and I hope the reader will too, and that actors will be encouraged to perform them.

STEVEN BERKOFF
2012

Introduction

In a late-1980s black-and-white publicity photograph for a National Theatre production of Oscar Wilde's extraordinary biblical tragedy *Salome* we see Steven Berkoff: white-faced, eyes like a Cleopatra – decorated and shining, poised and dressed in a long, antique dinner jacket, cuff-covered hands curled into what looks like a fist. Standing with him are an arrangement of other like-faced actors, all in a similar state of frozen, near-morbid funereal display. Berkoff, the controller and clown; Berkoff, the showman and priest; Berkoff, the nineteenth-century time-lord actor-manager at his most ridiculous and haunting. Work of such grand poetic majesty does not share a set of exclusive Stanislavskian rehearsal approaches nor is it routed via the more usual camera-real skills of actors in the subsidised or commercial theatres. This is the slowly found stage greatness of an artist and exile.

Born on 3 August 1937, Steven Berkoff has been in a perpetual state of exile for most of his personal and professional life, which has sometimes prevented his work as an actor, writer and director from being accepted by the mainstream. His personal exile has been not simply that of a working-class Jew grasping for placement but, additionally, that of an artist searching for an aesthetic. In the 1940s, Berkoff's early childhood did not provide the map for later greatness, but accidentally encoded it. Was it the devotion of his forbearing mother, Polly, who – rejected by the fantasist husband Abraham she loved – was herself so rich in unconditional love? Or was it perhaps the silken hem of a beautiful Hollywood ice-skating star named Belita who signed boy Berkoff's autograph book at an accidental encounter she had with him when slumming it on the ocean liner the *Queen Mary*, with the failed and penniless post-war families being deported back to Southampton from America, their imagined new beginning in tatters? Was Belita the mythical good fairy that appears only once in a person's dreams and blesses them?

Coming from a social context where hopes for any sort of future would typically evaporate into the darkest places of poverty and crime, Berkoff inhabited the sort of exotic but threadbare life of a continental artisan in the late 1950s. While juggling short-term contract jobs, he became a student once more, firstly at London's City Lit Institute, subsequently studying acting at the Webber Douglas Academy (1958), and then mime at L'Ecole Internationale de Théâtre Jacques Lecoq in Paris (1965).

Following several years as an actor in the British repertory system, and acutely aware of the emerging international cultural scene, Berkoff dared to become an exile once more and step away from a professional life of never-ending bit-part seasons in Agatha Christie adaptations and plays by J.B. Priestley. An essential lever for Berkoff at this critical moment was the Arts Lab in Drury Lane. Founded in 1967 and curated by the maverick Jim Haynes, in its two short years of life the Arts Lab was a free-spirited sanctuary and haven for avant-garde London, where those who served coffee or drinks at the bar would then go into rehearsal or on to the stage to do their thing. Haynes nurtured Berkoff and many other cultural exiles, with Drury Lane becoming a sort of lyrical refugee camp for those who had chosen to leave or been critically hounded out of the mainstream. With Berkoff at this time surrounded by such luminaries as Pip Simmons, Lindsay Kemp, Ken Campbell, Nancy Meckler and, on one unique occasion, Jean-Louis Barrault, the experience would later inscribe now-established principles in his works.

Berkoff's London Theatre Group (1968) used little or no set and very few costumes, being described as 'total theatre' – for his actors were the sole means of communication. The company's first production was Kafka's *In the Penal Colony*, which – unaided by the costly fog-machine technical kit of the 1970s pop-concert aesthetic that pervaded most West End theatre at the time – introduced a new form of actorly democracy to the stage. The use of stage space as a place for the imagination, so very much part of even main-house consideration today, was seen as an essentially fringe activity, conducted by those with little money and even less talent. The staging of this Kafka adaptation was undoubtedly inspired by international companies visiting London. Berkoff openly acknowledges that works by companies such as Café La Mama at the Mercury Theatre, the Open Theatre at the Royal Court and, in particular, the Living Theatre at the Roundhouse all gave him a new decidedly post-rep-theatre courage. Crucially, he inspired his actors with what he would later describe as a sort of Artaudian permission to take the stage space and use it with the imagined intensity of flames burning brightly – as opposed to the more typical 'no actual body required, but stand straight and speak the lines nicely' British style of theatre found in London and the provinces at the time.

Having written extensively on his process and experience of making theatre and performance, Berkoff is unusual in that these melancholic and insightful theatre discourses, including those explored in *I am Hamlet*, *Coriolanus in Deutschland*, *Meditations on Metamorphosis* and in the brutally observed *Shopping in the Santa Monica Mall*, feature some of the most revealing personal outpourings ever written about what it actually means to be an actor – not the depiction of some near-useless drama-school acting technique learnt years previously, but rather the recognition of the vast psychological and emotional resource that is required to live in the elusive 'moment' of performance and the no less extraordinary and utterly devastating, chasm of post-show loneliness often experienced by even the greatest actors. The bedsit and film set are alike haunted by the lonely.

Berkoff's original and sensational full-length plays, including *East*, *Greek*, *Decadence*, *West*, *Sink the Belgrano*, *Kvetch*, *Sturm und Drang* and *The Secret Love Life of Ophelia*, are widely considered as a roll call of classics in both form and content. His ghoulish art-house literary stage adaptations of Edgar Allan Poe and Franz Kafka, notably *Metamorphosis*, *The Trial*, *The Fall of the House of Usher* and *The Tell-Tale Heart*, have been performed throughout the world and in many different languages. Such works blend a predestined, dark-skied purgatorial landscape, full of yearning voices, with the unnoticed, simple, poetic brushstrokes of the real. What is fictional and actual within the Berkoffian frame becomes stylistically fused as though part of some overarching, predestined ordinance.

It is the one-act play, however, that most profoundly and immediately amplifies Berkoff's extraordinary literary and theatrical voice. His early one-act works, including the achingly poignant *Harry's Christmas*, alongside *Acapulco*, *Massage*, *Brighton Beach Scumbags* and *Dog* and *Actor*, are as exocet as any of the MM38 bombs at which he so chillingly screamed his utter despair in the full-length and controversial *Sink the Belgrano*. They, too, explode in one's mind and leave images painfully embedded.

This volume of one-act works disallows us to pin Berkoff's previously published plays to a board with the dates of his 'great' works fixed and labelled like butterflies to be later catalogued and displayed in a glass cabinet. In discussion, his eyes quite literally light up at the mere mention of the one-act construct. With relish, he outlines the bare-knuckled immediacy of its form and fatal but inevitable blow. Perhaps the very real pleasure in reading these nineteen one-act plays by Berkoff should not be about comparing them to his other plays at all, but imagining them newly and in performance. Berkoff's theatre continues to refuse smallness of theme and narrative, and defies those who wish to collapse the place of theatre into reality-inspired 'true'. A reading of these pieces will require the need for a performance alertness, 'real' at its very threshold. Berkoff's disdain for the naturalist agenda has not diminished, nor has his anger become less focused on social and political complacency, as he suggests in his preface to these plays:

> There are certain stories that need to be told and do not have to be told over an entire evening and in fact would lose their power if they were deliberately over-extended.

Like an exiled head of state, Berkoff has returned. The earlier themes are there, of course, and no less extraordinary, but new work always leaves the artist exposed. In the writing of these plays, there are moments of near-stylistic genius and a vivid formal economy – some plays are literally only a few pages long (*Gas*) while others occupy well over an hour's stage time (*Six Actors in Search of a Director*). Here, nineteen plays are offered as if the theatre were some kind of recurring dream where all the necessary archaeology of a life is investigated – a continuum visited by different characters with the same omnipresent father: Berkoff himself.

The plays in this volume colonise four thematic areas which dramatically freefall through some of the mythical pins that hold Berkoff's identity together; ACTORS (seven plays), BIBLICAL (four plays), PERSECUTION (five plays) and REJECTION (three plays). All are intertwined with a multitude of voices speaking in verse, slang or in recollection of the past. Some even stare at a loveless future. This volume is not a retrospective of previously acclaimed writing, but a tantalising little window into Berkoff's current and future preoccupations. His author's notes to some, but not all, of the plays further amplify this. He is certainly not coy in the process of self-revelation and I think that any reader, potential actor or director will quickly perceive his intentions.

The titles of the plays do not actually betray any real or fixed categorical placement of theme or intended style, and remain curiously ambiguous in what and how they label. In the 'Actors' grouping, for example, one play is called *Purgatory*, which one might more usefully employ as a title for the 'Biblical' cluster. In the 'Persecution' grouping one play is called *Line-Up*, something that all actors have to do at some point in their career, but equally something that prisoners and those to be executed are forced to do by order and command. Likewise, a character named Jesus, perhaps more suited to the 'Biblical' plays sequence, in name at least, actually visits our contemporary world in the 'Rejection' sequence. It is clear, then, that these thematic areas, and indeed the very titles of the works themselves, should remain porous in our consideration. They are fluid and can be combined and positioned in any number of permutations while still remaining vibrant and powerful. Each possible bespoke coupling of these works will speak very differently and directly to actors and audiences alike. It will be fascinating to experience the nuanced shifts of meaning and emphasis that will occur with such changes.

The seven thematically linked plays in the 'Actors' grouping are ostensibly familiar in territory. But with masterful and typical deceit, Berkoff leads us invisibly to the unfamiliar, rather like watching a once-loved movie that for some inexplicable reason feels unknown.

> **John** Saw me in a play, was bloody good, one of my best, he called, am I represented, he asked, no, not really, so I joined . . . a big office . . . you can't believe, huge! A large reception area . . . corridors going on for ever . . . offices every few feet, an agent in each office with a phone stuck up his arse, movie scripts to the ceiling . . . photos of the stars plastered the walls, contracts piled high. So he invited me to his office . . .

From the fake conversational bonhomie of *I Wanna Agent*, where the deluded and agent-less John desperately tries to convince himself and others of his bright future, to the much more audacious verse play *The Actor's Lament*, in which an established actor seemingly bemoans everything and everybody connected to the theatre industry, the theatre and the theatrical are common motifs in these one-act plays that have been in Berkoff's work for many years. Fellow actors, directors, theatre buildings and theatrical digs, playwrights and – above all – theatre critics, are sacrificed and judged with the vicious clarity of the insider. Often puffed up and egotistical, this is a world that both repulses and delights at a safe distance, affording a clear sense of the antique majesty and honour of being an actor and, simultaneously, the harsh but grubby reality of it.

Purgatory is technically more ambitious. Berkoff delightfully employs a poignant intertextual splicing of Shakespeare with the character John's very own yearning psychology. His language quite literally takes off into verse when he considers true companionship and love. John's life has been spent learning such lines, but not living them. This is touching and, in performance terms, highly effective. Such technical economy develops both the overarching narrative of the play and the sense of the character's own futility within it. The aching physical nearness of the two would-be lovers, divided by a guest-house wall, is perhaps a comically reminiscent echo of Pyramus and Thisbe in *A Midsummer Night's Dream*. As John's failed and misheard courtship progresses, the comic interlude transforms into something utterly felt and real. These are exquisite transitional moments that take both the actor playing them and the audience witnessing them from initial laughter and joyful expectation to a state of almost held anticipation – shallow breathing in wonder before the smiles and tears of love. This gentlest of technical touches is rarely acknowledged in Berkoff's writing for the theatre. The character Sarah understands, or at least tries to understand, what the theatre and actors are about. We are all, in some way, so desperately looking for someone like her to understand, to accept, to encourage. Though an outsider, she cries as if in ecstasy, 'Yes the world needs you, you actors are the messengers of the Gods . . . '

These often bleak and difficult stories require us to judge our own lives whether we are involved in the theatre or not. Berkoff's ability as a writer is distinguished by the fact that he provokes our senses, emotions and intellect all at once. Such technical mastery is notoriously difficult to appreciate fully on the page and, when such work is presented on stage we are often left without reasoning or analysis. These are plays that, for all their sometime coarseness, insist on real moments of respect, love and tenderness.

In *Mediocrity*, we see two actors chatting about their lives, but this quickly spirals into a lethal game of career comparison and, following this, both men unleash a reductive and ultimately disastrous pact with mediocrity itself. *Howl* presents a further two actors, Pat and Paul, who, like stones gradually sinking into ever-deep water, lose all definition, shape and form as they become enveloped by the most beautiful but disturbing reverie. Again, Berkoff demonstrates that he is not merely a loud-mouthed provocateur, but a writer of notable and delicate touch. The play's near ghost-like evocation of a single past moment of love – the result of a distant holiday romance and the piece's harsh, searing conclusion – is as painful as King Lear's breakdown: 'Howl your head off . . . for it cannot begin to match the storm inside my soul.'

This is an Emergency starts with faint echoes of Berkoff's memorable *Harry's Christmas* in that the character Brian (like Harry) is waiting for the phone to ring, waiting for something to happen in his life. The play's momentary sepulchral collapse into that of a psychological thriller is remarkable, as is its most erotically charged dénouement. The first group of plays concludes with the longest – *Six Actors in Search of a Director*. We are taken to a film set where actors wait, as if for Godot: ever-waiting for their call, ever-waiting for affirmation, ever-waiting for an absent but very busy director. Banter, momentarily playful and collegiate, slips imperceptibly into the realm of the toxic, rendering any shred of future companionship void. All is unified by the vapid concerns of the petty and broken. *Six Actors* is essentially a sophisticated morality tale set within the amoral chamber of the film-making industry. Its mercurial shifts and moral unease are hard to encounter.

The second brief grouping, 'Biblical', comprises a sequence of four plays, based on stories from the Old Testament – material that Berkoff was keen to turn into theatre 'as the myths are so pungent, so powerful in the stories they tell, with the strong underlying moral code that they just cry out for reinterpretation'. *Adam and Eve* and *David and Goliath* are strangely more reminiscent of the more loud-mouthed exchanges found in *East* as opposed to the sacred chanted words of a hushed synagogue or Anglican pulpit. It seems that, for Adam and Eve, the Garden of Eden is being overtaken by market forces and that the apple is certainly something worth investing in. In *David and Goliath*, to be strong is to be a boss who governs with gangland terms and conditions. *Samson's Hair* is exotic in tone and reminiscent of Oscar Wilde's *Salome* in its telling, rhythmic, pulsating style. The one-act immediacy of form and content described earlier is most certainly challenged here in that such ornate, poetic remove requires the words to be spoken free of naturalistic tempo. To be camera-real would be reductive. Berkoff's own incredible realisation of *Salome* might indeed offer a clue to the physical realisation of *Samson's Hair*. The play's rich, sensual language combines with a taut urgent narrative, a tragic eternal framework that initiates a fatal climactic end which is both florid and erotic:

> **Delilah**   Oh my darling, you poor simple man, to trust a woman who you crave so much, how simple you are, my darling warrior, to fall like all simple men to the wiles of women . . . But I do have love, I have love for my own people whom you have slaughtered with wild abandon.

Moses is suitably monolithic in tone and has a language as formal and solid as the commandment stones itself. Arguably the closest of the 'Biblical' group to one's imagined sense of the Old Testament, this piece features the plague upon plague destruction of those who question a 'Lord for ever and all time'. There is no onstage 'wink' to such gravity, no cut into the pantomimic or grotesque. Rather, this is Berkoff at his most respectful of an ancient sacred story.

Throughout so many of the plays in this collection, Berkoff appears to be grappling with his own Jewish working-class identity. Of course, this has been present in much of his earlier work, but its alignment here in such powerful one-act plays somehow sharpens this impression. The physical geography may vary from a Hollywood film set to the deserts of the Old Testament, but the actual emotional geography remains the same. Often nostalgic, but never aching for the past, the Old Testament plays merely use the remove of the mythical and ancient as a frame within which our current lives can be discussed and explored.

The third grouping, 'Persecution', is an emotionally complex and extreme set of plays. *How to Train an Anti-Semite*, *Roast*, *Line-Up*, *Pound of Flesh* and *Gas* are so extraordinarily diverse, haunting and difficult of subject matter that one wonders why this voice has taken so long to emerge. The bold and courageous handling of tough themes could be seen as the most revealing of Berkoff's lifelong political and cultural preoccupations.

In conversation, Berkoff shares that he is well aware that Jewish themes are difficult to set down without falling into a trap – that of making all Jews good and holy, and all gentiles villains and cold-blooded tyrants. In his preface he suggests that: 'I was provoked into examining them by a rather unwholesome flurry of anti-Israel sentiment that surfaces from time to time. Of course one must not equate just criticism with anti-Semitism but there can be no doubt that those with a certain "bias" will always seek an opportunity to condemn Israel.'

The plays in the 'Persecution' sequence have the removed authority of poetry, being more like fragments or woodcuts with all detail captured. We encounter middle-aged racists in *How to Train an Anti-Semite*, with well-rehearsed justifications for their hate. An 'appalling tale', so described by Berkoff in his author's note for *Roast*, this play describes a horrific anti-Semitic story in such rich and exquisite language that it acts as a sort of morphine-like cloak, numbing our ability to resist such an utterly gruesome account of a mother telling a story to a child. The antique repetition of its language sets this play apart from our own age, feeling almost late nineteenth century in style, as Wilde or Maeterlinck might have described the atrocity of a twentieth-century world war.

In *Line-Up*, two nameless, exceptionally vulnerable men stand in a most terrifying queue – the sort of queue that stands on the nightmarish edges of war and darkness. We learn that 'some are going to the left and some are going to the right', but know not where either point is ultimately destined. As if in a ghastly dream, one direction leads to survival and one to extinction. The men have to contemplate which route they will take. In this devastating moment, the truest of vows of love are exchanged in simple, mesmeric writing:

A I love you . . . I love you with every fibre in me . . . I love you, so hold your head up . . .

B I will . . . Yes . . . I will . . . my honourable brother . . .

The lights slowly fade, as one goes to the left and one to the right. They cast one last glance at each other.

Blackout.

In *Pound of Flesh*, two 'average' young men discuss the 'Jewish thing' and are well informed on both current and ancient Jewish history. This is perhaps the most polemical of all the plays in this volume, but also deceptively slight, for these two 'regular guys' are so very regular indeed (the regular of the train journey across town, the regular of the coffee grabbed at lunchtime, the regular of a brother or boyfriend), yet their conversation cuts open the deepest of wounds and evidences centuries of suffering. The fact that they remain nameless is a provocation – maybe they have our names on them.

Gas, at three pages long, is arguably the most impacting and devastating of all the plays in this collection. Three prisoners await the gas that will finally extinguish them, appearing here simply as nameless figures at their mortal end. The cold, last moments of their being are laid out as though on an undertaker's slab, last desperate prayers are uttered, and exchanges so pitiful and grasping are made in a desperate attempt to mean something. At the end comes not a prayer or scream, but the simple protestation of five simple, gasping, repeated statements of love:

C Yes . . . It's growing dark . . . dark . . . growing dark . . .

A Good . . . Soon . . . soon peace . . .

B   Soon . . . soon happy . . . Don't struggle . . .

A   No, it's growing dark . . . Shema Yisrael, Adoni, Elahaynu . . .

They all start joining in.

C   Dark . . . dark . . . Hand . . . hold my hand . . .

A   I love you, brother . . .

B   I love you . . . Oh, how I love you . . .

C   I love you . . . love you . . .

They continue as the light fades.

The remaining devastating image is both traumatic and inspirational.

The fourth and final group of plays, 'Rejection', contains the three short pieces *Guilt*, *'Ere* and *Exit*.

Guilt displays Berkoff's extraordinary ear for the shifting and complex rhythms of speech, and usefully demonstrates how he has continued to expand his technical mastery of dramatic writing. It feels almost verbatim and may well be, as it seems that Berkoff is casting his mind back to long conversations heard over the family dinner table as a child. This is an unusual play in that it is built around extended conversations about food: fishcakes, potato latkes, everything eating, everything celebration. For all the preparing and eating of food, the guilt of the title is borne by Henry, who mourns the loss of his son – lost to the world after an argument many years before. Should he beg him to come home for a meal? Can he forgive him?

Polly   No, tell him you're lonely for him, for him, for your beautiful son you're lonely, that's all you have to tell him, that you miss your lovely boy, your handsome son, that he should be well and that we miss him and that his mother misses him from the bottom of her soul and what a mitzvah it would be to have him here, to see his lovely face, his handsome face again and to know that he's well and thriving and to hear his voice again since it's been too

long, oh God it's been far too long, and that we miss him
so much, he would really love that, for you to tell him that,
because I know he misses us, and how painful it is not to
hear from him . . .

In *'Ere*, Doreen and Bill are in economic and emotional debt
– nothing touches their vapid lives – that is, until they are
visited first by a debt collector and then by the most unlikely
of men: Jesus. This comic play is both bizarre and profane,
and concludes with an absurd macabre twist. Whether set in
ancient times or in the kitchen of a high-rise, Berkoff's plays
are always essentially about the need for love and intimacy,
however crudely grasped for. Moments of true connection
somehow break through.

Finally, in *Exit*, we encounter a young couple having a
domestic squabble, the sort of which we overhear or have
every day of our lives. Nothing extraordinary, no heroic
deeds or tragic acts of generosity, just a tiff – or so it would
seem. Berkoff's use of language is so closely observed that the
argument at first seems playful, but then a dramatic war of
language ensues, fuelled *in vino veritas*. Berkoff refuses a
simplistic portioning out of gender and delicately exposes that
the painful human impulse will always be to connect.

These nineteen one-act plays add to an already major body of
work by Berkoff, which has predominantly rejected the
naturalistic school. It is, therefore, notable that the immediacy
of this collection is more closely aligned to the naturalistic
dramaturgies of the representational. This should not be seen
as a loss of faith in the stage metaphor, for these plays are rich
in allegory and symbol, but as a relative scaling down of its
use for the service of the immediate and crushing agit-prop of
a dramatist at the top of his game. Berkoff's distinctive style
fuses character and actor into one moment.

In this dynamic volume, you will encounter a never-comfortable
patina of tender, hateful private and public issues. The plays
are exhilarating because they cut deep into the Berkoff vein
both professionally and personally: Steven Berkoff himself is

inexorably present within this selection. Equally, they betray the vision of a theatre-maker whose work is often more vivid than real, enclosing the extraordinary emotional architecture of actor and audience member alike, and possessing them with themes both grotesque and elegant.

The old themes are there, of course, for all exiles wish to return. Still present are the genius of Berkoff's distinctive linguistic aesthetic and his insatiable need to tell ever-politicised stories. Though moral in dimension, the characters in these plays lack obvious sentimentality – indeed, in most of Berkoff's stage performances, audiences are confronted with his own bull-like, unsentimental figure: a dinner-dressed alien without friend or companion, searching through the chaos of a difficult life lived. In performance, the extraordinary physical energy that takes the stage space is like an impatient royal clown, ready to laugh or cry at any moment. This marks a terrifying transformation that can enter the nightmare spectrum. Berkoff evokes a past age of theatrical glory, an Irving-like actor-manager heroically leading from the front. It is intriguing to imagine what characters in this volume Berkoff would best realise in performance, for to see him act in one of his own plays is to experience sensual as opposed to intellectual passion.

Steven Berkoff has spun yarns for over fifty years. He is a great poet, dramatist and storyteller. His works for the theatre are heartfelt and indelibly loaded with portraits both ancient and modern. I was in the room when Harry cried out for loneliness, I shuddered in disgust at the man who became Gregor the beetle, I watched with guilt and pleasure as Salome slowly removed all. The characters in this volume, too, will one day become as recognisable as the fearful, beautiful creatures that have walked across his stages for over half a century. If you look closely, you will see the struggles of their lives etched in some way across the iconic face of Steven Berkoff as it stares at you from the the front cover of this volume.

GEOFFREY COLMAN
2012

ACTORS

I Wanna Agent

Author's Note

All actors need an agent. It is a perennial refrain. An agent often becomes more than a person who scours the market for good and well-paid jobs. They frequently become good friends – allies in times of need, a confidante, psychiatrist, mother. Moreover, a well-known and respected agent raises an actor's sense of worth, for an actor will tolerate a second-rate agent in the hope that eventually they will secure an upgrade, better than nothing.

Characters

John, *actor between thirty and forty. Desperate for an agent*
Bruce, *actor, his friend and sympathiser, aged thirty to forty*

John   So, I finished my performance last night and the agent didn't come, didn't turn up . . . She said she was coming . . . so I made a bit of an effort . . . pulled out a few stops . . . but when I went to the bar she wasn't there . . .

Bruce   That's a bitch . . .

John   Wasn't there. I came out like full of enthusiasm, 'cause I thought I'd done well, and she wasn't there . . . Bloody hell, what do you have to do to get an agent nowadays?

Bruce   I know what you mean.

John   A decent agent.

Bruce   Yeah.

John   I mean I was wired up last night, yeah, and a tad nervous, like knowing she was in, but it was a good night, could have been a dodgy one, but it was a good one, got some good laughs, smallish house but enthusiastic, so I came out, you know, a bit expectant, and she wasn't there . . .

Bruce   That's a choker . . .

John   Ain't it just! Used to have a good agent . . . was really good . . . chased down work for you . . . hustled, networked . . . didn't just wait for the phone to ring, he went out . . . he was a hunter.

Bruce   That's what you need . . .

John   A hunter . . . wined and dined them, first-name terms with all the casting agents . . . turned up at my first nights, even in some back-street dump . . . he was there!

Bruce   So what happened to him?

John   Yeah, well, he let me go . . . yeah!

Bruce   And he was so good for you?

John   He was, he loved me . . . but he had to let me go.

Bruce   What a choker . . .

John   Was going through a bit of a quiet period . . . you know . . . 's natural . . . from time to time . . . so you keep your head down . . . you know . . . go to the gym, bit of teaching, catch a mate's show . . . but you're just a bit edgy . . . so sometimes the odd call helps . . . Right? Sweetens the bitterness.

Bruce   Know what you mean.

John   Course you do!

Bruce   Yeah, I've been there . . .

John   Course you have, we all have.

Bruce   Tell me about it!

John   For sure! So I hadn't heard for a while . . . bit longer than usual, and like, once or twice a week I'd check in . . . you know, not nag, not one of those nagging actors who drive agents crazy.

Bruce   Yeah, I know a few!

John   Just a quick chat, check in, how's it going, you know and he says, 'Hang in there, kid, you're up for this and that, that and this, they're hot for you on that, we should hear soon, shortlisted for a TV series,' you know, agent waffle, but it calms you.

Bruce   Sure, some human contact.

John   Yeah, but not just that, I mean not just offering you the tit of human kindness, but filling you in . . .

Bruce   Course! You need that, gotta know what's going on, how it's shaping up . . . not kept in the dark . . . right.

John   'Xactly! So I rang . . . just my usual bi-weekly call . . . the secretary, his secretary, says, 'He's in Cannes.' He's in Cannes, like he's gone to the moon, like there's no phones in France, like you can't phone from France.

Bruce   She means he's busy, busy hustling, too busy to talk to you!

John I know that! Course I know that! I'm no fool, I know he's busy, he's hustling, but it was the tone of the bitch . . . That bitch had a 'tone', you know, that sound of smirk that runs through the bitch, like my knees should buckle when she says 'Cannes' . . . and like you're at the bottom of the pile . . .

Bruce Fucking secretaries, tell me about it!

John Course, you've been there, you know . . .

Bruce Oh, don't I!

John Like they're protecting the Crown Jewels, yeah, like they never sweated over anything in their lives, never broke their balls over any fucking thing, don't have the faintest idea of what makes an actor tick . . .

Bruce Course they don't, that's why they're secretaries . . .

John Too stupid to know that a gentle word can change your whole day, how a decent sound, a friendly sound can touch you, lighten you up.

Bruce Hey! That's for sure.

John So she said, 'He's in Cannes.'

Bruce Yeah, like you said, he's on the moon.

John 'Okay,' I said. 'Okay. You know the telephone's come a long way since it was invented, yeah, no disrespect,' I said, 'but one can fucking call, even from Cannes!'

Bruce You said 'fucking', you said that?

John Yeah, I fucking said that, like I couldn't care less that he was in Cannes, I know he's got to hustle, what pulled my chain was that fucking supercilious tone, that's what fucked me over, that slimy tone, that upper-class sneer from that parasitic bitch!

Bruce Yeah, so what did she say?

John She said, wait for it . . . 'John, would you please not be so rude to me. I can't help it if he's in Cannes and p-lease don't raise your voice!'

Bruce   OH! Oh!

John   I said, 'Listen you vacuous bitch, you calling me rude? Your whole being is rude . . . If you communicated one ounce of warmth, if you demonstrated just one ounce of care . . . you're a bridge between an actor and his agent . . . not a fucking jail door!'

Bruce   That's good, you're right . . . a bridge.

John   Not a fucking minefield, you have to crawl through on hands and knees!

Bruce   Ha ha! So what did the bitch say to that?

John   Nothing . . . she hung up! Yeah, she hung up!

Bruce   Course! You rattled her cage . . . so what happened?

John   What happened? The bum dropped me!

Bruce   What, your agent dropped you over his bloody secretary?!

John   Yea! Amazing isn't it . . . the bitch did me in . . . and he dropped me over a bitch! Secretary!

Bruce   Shit, that's not only bad, it's stupid.

John   Yeah, best agent I ever had.

Bruce   Shit, that's terrible, what he say?

John   He actually rang back! Yeah, within ten minutes . . . she must have blurted out all the venom in the bitch's soul . . . made me out to be Hannibal Lecter!

Bruce   Of course! Laid it on with a trowel, no doubt!

John   So he said . . . 'John, I love you but I've got to let you go!' That's what he said. 'You can't keep abusing my staff . . . It's true, I'm not getting you as much work for you like in the old days . . . so maybe you're under a bit of stress . . . changing agents might change your luck . . .' That's what he said . . . I could never forget it . . . Never! At least he was real . . . was human.

Bruce   At least he got right back to you.

John   Yeah, well, that's the least he could do . . . but what a bitch, eh?

Bruce   Yeah, well, the master's slave is known to be zealous.

John   They can poison the atmosphere . . .

Bruce   Only if the boss allows it, if he allows his slaves to treat his clients like toe-rags . . . Doesn't say much for him.

John   Yeah, you could be right there.

Bruce   So what happened?

John   Well, I rang a few agents and it's like . . . oh yes, we'd love to, love your work darling, but we wouldn't have time to look after you properly, we're rather full.

Bruce   In other words, fuck off!

John   So I slipped down a couple of rungs of the ladder and touted the smaller agents, you know, the second division . . . if not the third.

Bruce   Maybe best to be a big fish in a small pond.

John   Sure, except the big boys have got the stars, and what's left on the table after the stars have wolfed their share can still be quite tasty.

Bruce   For sure.

John   Yeah.

Bruce   So you found someone?

John   I did, yeah, some idiot who was once an actor, but he was ambitious as an agent.

Bruce   The small ones might hustle more than the big ones.

John   That's what I thought and he put me up for a few things, not so much movies as more theatre . . .

Bruce   Soul food, ha ha ha ha!

John   Oh yeah, so I got a six-month contract with some Shakespeare tossers! No money but, as you say, good for the fucking soul! Nearly went bloody mad.

Bruce   I believe you . . .

John   Out of my mind . . . you turn up ready, bursting to get out there and act, yeah! But do they use this? Do they fuck! Some wanker from Oxbridge has us sitting round a table for weeks, discussing the verse and the bloody subtext! I wanted to clout the prat, but after that stuff with my ex-agent's pissy secretary I learned to stuff my anger down in my pants . . . Ten weeks rehearsal! I nearly did my bloody brain in.

Bruce   But it worked out in the end?

John   It was a pile of poo! Critics shat on it, ten weeks to make a pile of shit, but believe it or not I got a good review! Yeah! Can you believe it . . . But then I'd had enough, so I split, couldn't stand any more!

Bruce   'T's no good if it does your head in, even if it is graft, John.

John   Course not! But the agent was pissed off, oh was he pissed off . . . said I had a chance to 'rise in the company', but I couldn't stand it . . . I couldn't . . . so I split . . .

Bruce   You have to follow your instincts.

John   Course you do! But the fucking agent whined about how he put a lot of work into getting me in and bang goes his ten per cent for six months. Couldn't give a fuck about whether it was doing my head in and turning me into a nervous wreck . . . no! Just his miserable sodding ten per cent.

Bruce   You don't need that . . .

John   Course I don't . . . that's the last thing I need, but he said I'd better find someone else.

Bruce   NO!

John   Yes! I swear . . . like I can't do what I want to do, what I'd like to do, what I *need* to do. *So* this agent, this third-division bum lets me go!

Bruce   Like you can't, you daren't turn down work?!

John   Can you believe it, lets me go!

Bruce   I can't believe it, I can't.

John   Just lets me go 'cause I won't be a fucking slave and take on everything just to give him his thirty pieces of silver! I fucking won't!

Bruce   Course you won't.

John   Sodding right I won't!

Bruce   Neither should you!

John   Fucking right I won't . . . An actor's got a soul, a soul that wants to leap.

Bruce   I'm with you . . .

John   Not to be led with a chain round your fucking neck! (*Pause.*) So, yeah, so there you fucking are.

Bruce (*pause, uncertain*)   So! You found another agent?

John   NO. No . . . don't have an agent.

Bruce   You don't have an agent?

John   No. I do not have a fucking agent..

Bruce   What a pisser!

John   Yep! For the first time in my life I do not have a fucking agent . . .

Bruce   But, how can you work . . . without an agent?

John   You don't . . . you don't work . . . So I still do my bit of teaching, that's all . . . I do that . . . It tides me over . . . some fringe shit, that's it . . . that's fucking it . . .

Bruce (*pause*)   Got to find you a fucking agent, John!

John   Yeah, sure, if you could . . .

Bruce   I mean, you're doing this play now, right? I mean it's a small theatre but it's a good part . . . and you can be *seen*!

John   Yeah, it's not a bad part . . .

Bruce   No, it's a bloody good part, a good showcase for you.

John   You think?

Bruce   Definitely . . . it's a great part.

John   I rang a lot of them . . . 'Yeah, we'll try and get there, okay, we'll call you when we know,' all that bollocks, but no one's come, Bruce, no one's come.

Bruce   No one's come?

John   No one, not one solitary agent. That bitch who didn't turn up last night was supposed to come, I put my guts into last night and she didn't turn up, didn't fucking turn up.

Bruce   That's a real pisser. Why do they do that, build your expectations up, don't they know what it does to an actor?

John   Do they fuck . . . they haven't a clue.

Bruce   We've got to find you an agent.

John   Yeah! I need an agent.

Bruce   You do. You need an agent, someone to hustle for you, take the pressure off!

John   Oh please. I mean, even with a good agent, you may not always work, don't matter, we actors handle dark days, but at least there's someone you can talk to, someone you can call, express yourself, sometimes.

Bruce   Course! You need to have a natter sometimes . . . know you're being put forward to casting agents.

John   Right!

Bruce   Know there's someone thinking about you! Rooting for you!

John   Yes!

Bruce   Knowing that when the right part, the right age, the right type turns up – *you* are being *considered*!

John   Yes!

Bruce   Know that when a TV or a movie is being cast and they're looking for someone, a bit funky, a bit edgy, a bit off the wall, they will think of *you*!

John   YES! YES! YES!

Bruce (*pause*)   I'll ask around, I will John, I'll ask around.

John   Will you, will you, Bruce?

Bruce   Course, I said I would and I will, yeah, I promise . . . I'll ask around.

John   Bless you, mate.

Bruce   I'll put the word about.

John   God bless you.

Bruce   Sure, no problem.

John   Yeah, you're a star, Bruce, you're a star!

Bruce   Nah!

John   You're a fucking mate, you fucking are . . .

Bruce   Hey, I can only try, ain't *guaranteeing* . . . just chat up some actors that's all. Let them know you're a free agent! Ha ha ha ha! That you're looking for representation.

John   Fucking aces and maybe they'll put the word to their agents.

Bruce   And if they don't, then no big deal . . .

John   It's terrible really.

Bruce   What?

John   This need we have for an agent.

Bruce   They need us, they also need us . . . without us they don't exist, they don't even live, not without us.

John   You'd never think so, you'd think they don't even need us, like we're a fucking nuisance.

Bruce   'Cause it's a buyers' market, they're buying and we're selling, we're just cattle, the city's full of actors, and each one needs an agent. Everyone wants to be an actor, every slag model wants to be in the movies.

John   Every idiot thinks they can act.

Bruce   Doesn't matter, most TV is crap anyway, so they just want young pretty wankers, don't need actors, not real actors, not so much.

John   I can't believe that.

Bruce   You don't have to . . . it's true.

John   'T's not true in the theatre, there you have to act, there you have to cut it.

Bruce   You're right, of course you do, but then you've gotta deal with Oxbridge wanker directors! And you've had a taste of that, right?!

John   For sure and more than a taste, a big rancid swallow.

Bruce   So there we are!

John   There we are . . .

Bruce   Yep. (*Pause.*)

John   Wish Joan Littlewood was still alive . . . she loved actors!

Bruce   Yeah, but she's not.

John   Wish old Olivier was alive . . . he gave one a chance, 'cause he was one of us.

Bruce   Yeah, he was one of us . . . but he's not here either.

John   So what we left with?

Bruce   You may well ask, but it's no good calling them tosspots, maybe they are, but you have to deal with them. They're trying, they may not be geniuses but if you piss all over them they're not going to like you, so you don't work. What good's that? Eh?

John   I read you. I hear what you're saying.

Bruce   Course you do. I know you do.

John   I just need an agent.

Bruce   I know.

John   Feel lost without an agent.

Bruce   That's natural.

John   'T's like being an orphan, sometimes. Being without an agent.

Bruce   Course, some get really close . . . buddies.

John   Fight your corner

Bruce   That's right. They do.

John   Then a stinking secretary can sour the whole thing up.

Bruce   Okay, forget about that. We'll find you a decent agent.

John   But I don't want a pisspot agent.

Bruce   Nobody does.

John   Some agents can be real pisspots!

Bruce   Don't I know it!

John   I was once with a big agent, one of those super agents.

Bruce   Oh, yeah?

John   Yeah! Real bigsy.

Bruce   What happened?

John   Saw me in a play, was bloody good, one of my best, he called, am I represented, he asked, no, not really, so I joined . . . a big office . . . you can't believe, huge! A large reception area . . . corridors going on for ever . . . offices every few feet, an agent in each office with a phone stuck up his arse, movie scripts to the ceiling . . . photos of the stars plastered the walls, contracts piled high. So he invited me to his office . . . then he calls in some colleagues to meet me, one deals with theatre and one in the movies. They offer me a drink . . . I say no thanks although I was parched. They all stare . . . smiling, trying to make me feel welcome. 'This,' he said, 'is the young man who made such an impression, and I'm sure we're going to see a lot more of him.' They all smile . . . I grin back like an idiot and can't think of anything to say. My lips are glued together. I don't know what I am doing there and want to escape. Get back to my crummy agent in his one-room slum in Soho, where I'm safe. I try to grin. They stare, still smiling benignly, above their heads sit the photos of real major actors, stars staring back at me, as if to say WHAT ARE YOU DOING HERE? You bum, you don't belong here with us, get out! Go on, get out!

Bruce   Nah! You're too sensitive.

John   OUT, YOU BUM! Then they asked how I see my career progressing? I smile . . . couldn't speak.

Bruce   You mean, you said nothing . . . ?

John   No, I, er, coughed, like to clear my throat, like you do before you go on the stage, get rid of that tight fucking ball of fear that's lodged inside . . . and I said that as long as I worked I didn't care . . . didn't matter, as long as the roles were good, that's all. Theatre, TV, movies, it's all the same and then I stopped, they just stared and then a light blinded me, Bruce.

Bruce   A light blinded you!

John   Yeah, for a moment I saw a blinding light.

Bruce   Woah!

John   Yes, this blinding light . . . it pierced my eye, like it was a sign, a revelation.

Bruce   Hey! Wow!

John   I shifted back in my seat, just to avoid that yellow spear in my eye, and then I saw what it was, I saw it!

Bruce   Yeah? What was it?

John   The sun! The sun was shining through the window and landed on the gold Rolex on the agent's wrist.

Bruce   What d'y'know!

John   Yeah, that was the piercing light, the sun's reflection on the gold strap of his Rolex.

Bruce   Ah, so what happened?

John   I walked out. I walked, I got on to the street, oh the fresh air!

Bruce   So what happened? They find some work for you?

John (*pause*)   Nothing . . . not a bean, not even a call . . . nothing.

Bruce   Nothing! That's unbelievable.

John   Nothing, that's right, nothing.

Bruce   Weird . . .

John   I swear, nothing. I mean, I rang, just once, got the secretary, 'Oh, he'll call you back, when he's got a moment.'

Bruce   You never heard . . .

John   NEVER! Not once.

Bruce   Scumbags!

John   Yeah, well . . . (*Pause.*)

Bruce   'T's a funny old life.

John   Isn't it just.

Bruce   Hey, John?

John   What?

Bruce   We gotta find you a fucking agent, mate!

John (*low*)   . . . Yeah.

Bruce   And we will . . . we'll put the word out.

John   Hmnn.

Bruce   'T's not the end of the world, kid! You're alive . . . you're here . . . you're strong . . . You can still kick arse on stage, right?

John   S'pose.

Bruce   Course! Come on, you can . . . You're the last of the breed of scene-chewers! You are! When you're out there you light up the stage! You're an entity!

John   Yeah?

Bruce   Fuckin' right, 'Yeah!' Now actors just dribble on the stage, you can hardly fuckin' hear the bastards . . . There's no guts anymore. Just directors' toys to be pushed around. The old scene-chewers are gone . . . Larry!

John   Oh yeah . . . Larry!

Bruce   O'Toole, Finney, McCowen, Robby Stephens . . .

John   Yeah, Robby Stephens . . . Great.

Bruce   Remember him as the great Aztec god?

John   Unbelievable, magic.

Bruce   Larry's Othello!

John   That was really something!

Bruce   What a blinding performance. Before those cunts got all PC about it.

John   For sure.

Bruce   Ooh, it's not polite to play Othello any more . . . piece of shit!

John   Actors never say that.

Bruce   Course not!

John   Actors play anything.

Bruce   And everything.

John   Course, that's what they do, they swallow the world and spit it out again.

Bruce   That's right, that's right . . . eat it up!

John   'I eat the air, promise-crammed'!

Bruce   There you go!

John   You know, I was good as Hamlet.

Bruce   Bet you were, bet you were, mate!

John   I was, I got some good reviews then.

Bruce   I believe you.

John   Except for one, there's always one cunt who's got it in for you, no matter what you do, how hard you work, how inventive you are.

Bruce   I know . . .

John   Always one self-satisfied smug cunt who wants to stick his knife into you.

Bruce   Don't they ever.

John   A real sadistic bastard, a real evil swine!

Bruce   Some are, some are, but some are good . . .

John   Some are, yeah!

Bruce   Forget the evil one.

John   Yeah, but it's hard, they seem to want to hunt you down . . . Bastards!

Bruce   Rise above it . . . They're just doing a job, like you, there's always one cunt in every barrel of apples!

John   Yeah, rise above it.

Bruce   'Cause, you have to, rise above it.

John   Yeah.

Bruce   That's what you have to do, John.

John   Rise above it.

Bruce   You must, or you'll alienate people.

John   Gotta, gotta, rise above it.

Bruce   Course you do and you will, 'cause you're the boss, you're out there . . . They come to see you right?

John   Right.

Bruce   That's right! And we'll find you an agent.

John   You think so?

Bruce   Of course we will.

He smiles at **John**. *Silence. They both look out, lost in their own thoughts. Lights slowly fade.*

Actor's Lament

Author's Note

John, an established actor, laments the critics' lack of appreciation for his first attempt at playwriting. David, his good friend and respected playwright, comforts him, and this leads to a debate, a familiar one, on what is perceived to be the 'iniquity' of the industry, especially the difference between stage actors and film actors . . .

Characters

John, *clever, cynical, witty, bitter, forty to fifty*
David, *urbane, sophisticated, successful, forty to fifty*
Sarah, *attractive, strong-willed, realistic, forty to fifty*

David

So! Tell me, please tell me, how was your play?
Go on John, I'm so eager to know . . .
The first play you've penned . . . My God what a task
To dip your toe into that seething morass
Of scribbling playwrights, each eager to win,
A secure place in the public's fickle heart
To be feted and worshipped by the adoring crits . . .
Who all say yes! Yes! A meteor has arrived
You've raised the game . . . You'll keep the theatre alive
You'll stand on the stage at the critics' awards . . .
That magical moment when your name is called . . .
Best drama . . . best drama of the year they'll shout
Step up to the platform, the spotlight hits your face,
You accept the trophy with all good grace,
That only a leading actor like yourself can command
An actor, now, stroke playwright, the world's in your hands.
So, tell me, how did it go?

John

Oh what a sordid bunch of bilious scum,
Strutting toe-rags, wallowing in the swamp,
Of self-importance bred from ignorance,
Tone deaf, half-blind rejected hacks,
Who, failing at all other worthy crafts,
Their talents barely scrape the bottom rung,
Too feeble then to climb to higher arts,
End up as critics in the daily trash!
So these, these meddling grubbies, half-baked slobs,
Who never made the grade, nor made their mark,
These half-wit tossers, Oxbridge dropouts, louts,
Submit their slobbering prejudices, their muddled views,
On works so far beyond their feeble wits,
That all they can achieve is seething rage,
And spit their venom at plays they'd love to write,
Had they a modicum of brain cells left,
Inside their skulls, that garbage pit,

The toilet walls more appropriate for their wits,
Where happily they can scrawl their puerile shit!

David

So, I take it, it's *not* a favourable review.
But John, don't let your mind get so unhinged,
It's only just a handful of poor dogs,
Who love so much to lift their legs and piss,
It's second nature to them, just pure bliss,
To leave their smelly mark upon the world!
They represent the rags for whom they write,
Mass opinion, halfway house, man in the street,
Their editors are not some wise and knowing men,
But simple, decent people of low taste,
Who hoover up some low neurotic scum,
Who can swiftly pen a review, throw in a pun.
To employ men of genius would be a waste,
They'd much prefer to thrive in higher arts,
And not by analysing others' farts.
Your play is but the first, the first you've penned,
But what a bold and brave auspicious start,
One day, I prophesy, the audience for whom you write,
Will crawl through broken glass to hear your words,
They'll scale great mountains, plough through treacherous
    seas,
If that was the only way of seeing thee.
They'll feast upon your words, your blistering imagery,
Those succinct syllables, blasting metaphors,
Alliterations, ricocheting across the darkened stalls,
Lightning strikes of language lit by wit,
And you, yes only you, will accomplish it!

John

Oh thanks, that makes me feel a tad relieved,
If only our enlightened friends were critics,
Minds alert, cognisant of the world,
Enriched with culture, esoteric, fresh,
Antennae always straining to detect
The subtlest motions of tectonic plates.

Such minds demand the complex twists and turns,
That only an original can create.
Not, please the banal and simplistic tripe,
That helps the punters through a turgid night,
Those 'heavy' worthy plays, self-serving chaff,
That demonstrate the writer's moral heart . . .
While it is possible to take a nap!
How decently they solve the world's demise
With crapitudes that tumble from their pen,
And make those punters feel oh! so satisfied,
Those that are still awake, I mean.

David

Of course, of course, and now you're making sense,
Don't give the lice free range to scratch and bite,
The more you're spat upon, provoked and hurt,
The more you scratch those fleabites on your flesh,
The more your pains broadcast to one and all,
The more you threaten, howl and vainly scream,
The more they gurgle in their stinking nests,
Delighted to have drawn a piece of flesh,
And if not quite a pound, an ounce will do,
But add ounce upon ounce and soon you'll shrink,
To quivering bones and rather scraggy meat!

John

Or pandering to the mob and writing 'kitchen sink'!

David

Oh God forbid! That dreary time I thought had gone,
Right down the plug-hole of some backstreet slum,
But now our dear John Osborne's reappeared,
Good luck to him, I say, he shook the lintels,
Broke a pane or two in Tunbridge Wells,
Let out some rancid stink of merry England,
Symbolised by music halls and ironing boards,
Oh! How so thrilling to the bourgeois mass
Who sat wide-eyed and trembling in their seats,
Lest Nicol Williamson would leap headlong,
And tear their bourgeois heads off in one swift beat!

John

But now the dead are back *again* to haunt,
The theatres where once they tasted fame,
Like crabby oldies sniffing for some minge.
Let's dig up some old classics!
The desperate producers vainly cry.
Drag them out their coffins, clean 'em up,
Find a star, kick start it into life,
And put some fresh paint on the well-worn tart,
And maybe, yes, just maybe, it will float,
Not sink down deep just like a lead balloon.
So now the West End's like a stinking morgue,
Revival after revival of the dead,
And poor old Chekhov once again exhumed.
Oh give the poor old sod a bloody rest,
And not the *Importance*, no, not again,
Can't hear '*a handbag*' one more time
And even living writers whose works once belly-flopped,
Parade them *yet* again in the vain hope
They will be viewed with sepia-tinged nostalgia,
Of course for *my* dynamic works, no bloody room!

David

Don't worry, Sarah's, lovely Sarah's on her way . . .
She'll heal your wounds, she'll know what to say,
Oh she's a saint, a darling and oh so brave . . .
And then, the way, the way she lights up a stage,
The special magic . . . well you know what I mean.
And when you two are on those precious boards
The sparks you both set off . . . One nearly gets scorched.

John

Oh, shut up, David please . . . I know you're trying to be kind
Massaging some balsam where the critics' vicious lash
Have left raw red stripes, but I wear them with pride . . .
So please put a sock in that loquacious gob,
My God, you never stop, the words just fly out . . .
An unremitting spew from your golden spout . . .
A festering tsunami of verbal bilge

David *is about to contradict him.*

John

No don't . . . not another word to ease my wounded soul

Sarah (*who has just arrived*)

Darling! (*Kisses.*)
I could hear you half way down the street,
What force, what power, such majestic tones!
A shame that actors now cannot project
Like you, my dearest one, your great deep sound,
That vibrates through your trunk and head,
That spews out in one glorious howl,
But do be careful or you'll wake the dead.
Some actors can't be heard beyond Row 3,
Except us oldies, who cut our teeth,
By leaping across the nation's hallowed boards,
In that great training ground, the Repertory!
So don't be sad my love, I read the reviews,
Written by a bunch of sallow drips,
And stick to acting, in which you shine,
For as a writer, they're just not . . . ready . . . for your
    dazzling wit!

David

Sarah, darling! I think you have a point,
They love you as an actor, think you're swell,
You've invested many years to hone your craft,
And worked your way into their simple hearts,
They love the roar, the panache, that mighty bell,
You carry in your throat, that pungent sound,
That suddenly you release, like strokes from hell.
You never croak on hitting the high notes . . .
Like so many lesser actors straining as they try
To score the knockout punch, oh some fat hope,
Their under-trained vocal chords are thin and light,
And so they heave, they push, they sweat, they shout,
Hoping to fire an arrow in our heart,
But then it comes out like a dismal fart.

They've lost the grand passion, the fiery sound,
The thunderclap, the lightning strokes of Edmund Kean,
That dazzling moment when Olivier,
As Oedipus, let out that awesome scream . . .
The rafter in that theatre is trembling still,
The sorely missed Ken Tynan eulogised,
Perceptive critic, what a light was shone,
Upon our stages, and now we're left with those
Whose words just crawl across the page like ants,
Clever and cunning and so quick to bite,
When genius dares to raise its glorious head,
And then they howl, they scream, they rage,
In future times they'll only be a footnote,
But you my friend will be a glorious page!

Sarah

Oh David you took the words right out my mouth,
I don't think I could have said it better,
But then you are the country's finest poet,
Playwright, novelist and wit, and actor too,
So who in their right minds could ever compete,
With such a mind as yours when it gets on heat . . .

John

Who says 'compete'? When words are just and true.
Who says they need be anything but honest,
Coming from the heart, untainted, lacking guile,
Not unctuous flattering and honey'd lies . . .
They come from you dear friend, whom I respect.
John Osborne, bless his heart, did once declaim
An actress, successful, on the brink of fame,
Was once a candidate for the loony bin,
But you, dear darling, lend honour to our art,
Your acting engraves itself upon our minds,
Unlike some self-seeking and shallow tart!
So tell us, Eleonora Duse, and Bernhardt too,
When next will our stages be graced once more by you?

Sarah

Alas not yet, I fear, but soon I hope.

David

Ah Sarah, is there something in the wind?
Something you're reluctant to give breath,
Since actors do not like to tempt the fates,
Until the contract signed, the ink still wet . . .
But give me the smallest hint, don't let us fret!

John

Do tell us darling, if you dare to speak,
Awake those roles that slumber in dusty books,
That need your brilliant spark to make them leap,
From out those ancient tomes in which they languish,
Cold, neglected, waiting for the art,
Of one great soul, an actress, born to play
The role, restore those *femmes fatales* to life.
So few could do it, few would ever dare.
Alas, where are the actresses today
Who can compete with those of yesteryear?
And so those mighty roles lay quiet and still,
Covered with the sad dust of neglect . . .
So darling, blow away the dust with one big blast,
And let us hear again Camille, and Clytemnestra,
Cleopatra too . . . let her be played by someone
Young and vital, still beautiful like you,
And not some worthy ancient crone, some hag,
Whose sap has long ago been drained.
Oh how this nation loves her character bags.
With you we'd understand in a lightning flash,
Those carnal, *bestial* drives in some poor men,
That makes them sacrifice their home and sanity,
Loving children, lifelong dearest friends,
All crushed upon the rancid bed of lust,
And yes, one day we'll do *Macbeth* together,
You'll be a fine and sensuous Lady **M**.
And then we'll see how easy to stir a man,
To do your every will, even to kill.
For men, when they're inspired by their lady,
Will stop at nothing, just to prove their worth,

So get up on that stage, my lady, thrive!
Fill the theatre with sound and female fury,
Let us shout, it's good to be alive!

Sarah

Dear John, you run before your horse to market,
For what I hope for is really rather slight,
Quite modest compared to all the dreams we share,
Of glory, danger, taking stunning risks,
Being immortalised and bringing back to life,
The great, the tragic, the heroines of our past,
That we may understand just who we are,
Since they, perhaps, in some much larger way,
Are mirror images of our own poor souls.
Like Madame Ranevsky and Antigone,
Nobility of motive, mixed with pride,
St Joan in all her glory, Blanche DuBois,
These women yearned for something dignified,
Something that gave meaning to their lives,
Something that you glory in, for which you'd die,
Words so absent in our trash-filled town,
Where superstars are junkies, TV clowns,
Gutter-mouthed entertainers, sleazy tarts,
The cesspits full to bursting, the landfills choked,
With fat-lipped, glazed-eyed sirens, skewed with rot,
And yet the slimy press can't get enough,
Their cameras trailing them like hungry rats,
So eager to put their dumb grins on the page,
As they slide out of yet another club,
So yes, we need Antigone, Rosalind and Roxanne,
To cleanse this putrid and germ-laden air,
But alas, it will not be myself this time.

David

It will be soon, believe me that's for sure!
I see in you such honour and such grace,
A mind well honed to capture every note,
Each nuance of a playwright's crafted text,
You would not miss a beat or genuflect,

To gain an easy belly laugh or two,
To cater to an audience that's crude,
Conditioned by directors so untrained,
In the precise skills of an actor's art.
They wear the audience down with cheap stage tricks,
Video screens in case we're getting bored,
As if we're bloody morons, can't make the leap
From Shakespeare's drama to the present time,
'On your imaginary forces work,'
The poet says, immortal lines so clear,
So leave your TV cameras, dry ice and sound effects,
And leave us with our undefiled Shakespeare,
Yes, let the bloody actors do the work,
So take your toys and play with them at home!
But Sarah, give me time to catch my breath,
To hear what shadows, waiting in the wings,
You will revive with your sweet, living flesh!

Sarah

Alas, it's hardly even just a wisp . . .
Nothing to shout about, even reveal,
The circumstances an actor finds sometimes,
When unemployment, bastard offspring of bad luck,
Will have you thrust your hands into the muck.
Auditions that just simply fail to hit
The kind part of a director's beady eye,
And no matter just how hard you strive,
To give your all, your best, your heart,
No matter how you work and slave to be
The character . . . you cannot seem to catch the part.
'We're thinking of you, dear . . . You came so close,
And what are you doing next? . . . We'd love to know,
And we will come and see you,' oh yes, fat chance,
So now to lighten up my empty days,
I took an understudy job, to earn some pay!

John

Nothing to be ashamed of, darling, never fear,
An understudy has been known to save the day!

Sarah

And now the opportunity has arrived,
The role, though sordid, cheap and somewhat light,
A lesser work from one now famous scribe,
Severely overwhelmed this actor's skills
In fact she rarely had set foot upon a stage
And going from A to B was about her range.
Her fame was gleaned from some dull TV soap,
The rancid junk food upon which the mob do feast,
And so producers, slobbering for a hit,
Saw pots of gold and not some gilded shit!
But when the poor bitch saw the yawning stage,
That darkened chasm that she one night must face,
That open jaw beneath a thousand eyes,
That every actor has to face or die,
She crawled away just like a frightened pup,
And so they thrust me on to save the night!

John

Con-bloody-gratulations, you saved the day!
Next time do please inform us when you're on.
But what a tragic, sordid little tale,
And so familiar to our profession's shame,
When lesser mortals dressed in the shabby fame,
That film and TV have on them bestowed,
Believe that now it's time to dip their toe,
On to the hallowed West End stage, no less,
But what a shock these creatures have to face,
No longer a mere two-minute take, 'Oh lovely, dear,
Now go to your trailer darling and have a break,
We'll try a few more takes until it's right.'
On stage you have one take that takes all night!
Can't do it in dribbles, nibble little chunks,
On stage you need some courage and good lungs!
On stage you run a marathon, on film they're little sprints.
On film the soundman makes your thin voice loud,
On stage your tiny shrieks will rouse the anger of the crowd,
On film you trail garlands of fame you seldom earned,

The camera made you beautiful, the sound man strong,
You did a multitude of endless takes,
So the public believe you can do no wrong,
On film the background music falls and swells,
It's brilliant at covering up a rancid smell,
On film, if you forget you lines, just do it . . . ten more
    bloody times,
On stage if you forget them, ow! you die!
On film your work is fixed for ever more,
On stage you change, develop, grow through sweat
    and tears,
On film you do *one* leading role, you're famous and adored!
On stage you do it every night . . . even for years!

David

Yes! But then one day, it's time to say farewell . . .
Your voice . . . the most dazzling instrument grows harsh,
The eyes grow slowly dim, the parts grow small,
The words are not quite clinging to the brain,
As when you were so young and sprightly fresh,
You end up playing servants waiting for madam's call,
The play is over, thank God, the curtain falls,
You stiffly bow and climb the well-worn stairs,
You wash your make-up off, but no friend calls,
But the stars are quaffing champagne down with theirs,
Goodnight you say, the doorman briefly nods,
You catch a train that leaves from Leicester Square,
That takes you to your tiny flat in . . . anywhere.
Meanwhile the Ivy's filling up, the stars welcomed with glee,
You put the kettle on and heat some beans,
They order champagne, tuna seared and wildly chat,
You turn the telly on and stroke the cat.

John

No! No! No! No! Stop! It's not so grim . . .
Dear God, you make it sound a living death.
An actor ages, who can turn back time?
The autumn curls our leaves and winter chops us down,
And no one can escape death's filthy leer . . .

The grim reaper beckons for your crown,
But not before you've left your searing mark,
Upon the citizens of this once so glorious town.
You leave your reputation, your enduring myth,
Forged from so many thousand gut-wrenched nights.
The curtain rises like a serpent's hiss,
Your heart is pounding and your tongue is dry,
The Tannoy calls . . . 'Beginners, places please . . . '
Your feet are turned into lead, your stomach mud,
Your hands are shaking and your sweat is cold,
The audience, that great and unknown mob,
Is calmly waiting for it to unfold,
Unaware that standing in the wings,
Is an actor, a trembling mass of fear,
You're waiting, waiting, several minutes more,
For late arrivals threading through the door,
The other actors smile as if they felt so fine,
Meanwhile their bladder's working overtime,
You run the first lines in your head to reassure
Yourself that they are safely bedded there.
Be careful, don't anticipate, take care!
Lest when you get right to that scene,
You'll find the lines have vanished in the air!
They're stored in your unconscious ready to explode,
But not if you keep testing them, they won't . . .
So hold back, just relax, although you want to bolt!
This is the time, the dreaded time, the living hell,
When actors wish they could just bloody walk,
Escape into the street where other feet
Are calmly strolling, or drinking café latte,
If only you could join them, oh what bliss,
But if you fled the stage, what bloody shame!
How could you even live another day?
Yet why, what shame, when others have trod that path,
Have bolted from the stage in fear . . . Dismay?
And lived and even thrived
But this is not the road for you . . . oh no!
You are a warrior, so this petty angst,

You'll turn to raw fuel, to living fire,
Flowing freely, pounding through your veins!
Oh yes! You feel it, mouth no longer dry,
Your pulse has calmed, a leopard walks in your stride,
The curtain, like a giant eyelid rises,
You face a thousand pairs of watching eyes,
Staring, cynical, ready to eat you alive,
Wanting to tear you limb from bloody limb,
With curses, depredations and foul slurs,
If you do not fulfil their raging thirst,
For passion, drama, fury, *Sturm und Drang*,
Excitement, brilliance, genius, yes, most of all
Their wish to be transported, carried away.
Oh how apt these words are, for they say . . .
That you, dear punters, sitting in cramped seats,
Ripped off by fat producers, overcharged for drinks,
Bitterly disappointed in the past,
By underwhelming actors, tedious plays,
That preach and seldom entertain,
But now you'll be taken from your mortal clay.

So much the actor carries on his back.
The playwright sitting in the stalls just quakes,
Oh will you serve his rather modest play?
Serve it! You make it sound a lot less fake!
The director, standing, too nervous by far to sit,
His sphincter winking faster than a Soho whore,
Prays that his thousand light-cues will impress the crits
And that they won't call his direction shit!
So all this baggage riding on your back,
Before you've drawn a breath you're on the rack,
Your words, like greyhounds waiting in the slips,
But then! But *then* . . .
Othello slowly stirs within your guts,
Iago wakes from out his hate-filled dreams,
And then Prince Hamlet casts his piercing stare,
O'er Elsinore's foul unwholesome air,
Macbeth is in your voice and hand and brain,

You feel a murderer striding through your veins,
Or else you're Romeo, sweet and light and pure,
With lust that flows through you like molten ore,
Now Oberon will soar through moonlit skies,
Casting his spell o'er Titania's sleeping eyes,
And Cyrano de Bergerac will fight
A hundred foul assassins in one night,
And yes, poor Oedipus tears out his eyes,
While sad Jocasta hangs herself and dies.
Mercutio, Coriolanus and King Lear,
In you they are reborn, in you they reappear.
You are no longer there, you are the medium
That brings to life these ghosts, you are the meat,
The flesh and blood upon which they must feast,
Or like a God who breathes into dead clay,
Your soul, so they may live another day!

David

Bravo! . . . Well, I am chastised, I really am.
Oh what a sacrifice you actors make,
You mortgage your poor tortured soul each night
To live a little in some hero's clothes.
They may be a little stale, a touch BO
From so many thespians' dried-up sweat,
Pounding out the same old weary text,
But at least for them the lines are new.
But, what a payment, what a great reward,
To climb Parnassus, feast with gods,
You must feel truly great, immortal even,
A payment for some bravery . . . no doubt,
And courage, I do not underestimate.
And so bravo, yes, bravo to you all . . .
But when you've fed so many hungry ghosts,
Turned their grey faces pink with your own blood,
Pumped your emotions nightly in their hearts,
Just tell me, really, what is left of you?
When you have wiped the make-up off, who's there?
What do you see, and who stares back at you?

Don't think me callous, I do respect your craft,
I'm just so curious to know what's left of you.
I've heard so many actors say, I don't know,
Really, who I am, when I'm not in a play.
Is that why so many love to drink,
Perhaps to fill that empty gaping hole you think,
Some stoutly spout, they're servants of the stage,
But a servant serves and has no mind
But to be another's pair of limbs, another's soul.
Is that why unemployment is so cruel,
Since all the actor's toys are locked away,
You're once again in limbo, one might say.
I think, *you* are the ghost without a soul,
A living ghost and while you always say
You bring the ancient dead to life once more,
Is it not true that it is they who are reviving *you*.
Oh do not think me cruel, my dearest friend,
For you give joy, excitement and so many thrills,
But it is I, the playwright who gives you life,
Our words will last, long after you are dead!

Sarah

Now that's a rather sour thing to say,
As if we actors were just bits of dough,
Ready to be shaped by the master chef,
Pasty, insensate, without free will.
You're talking crap, forgive me, but it's true,
You need the actor, just as he needs you!
It's not a banal question of who's best,
My God, you men, like children must compete,
Unhappy till you give yourselves a test,
Mocking each other's contributions, gifts.
Oh yes, maybe it is true, I have to say,
That to the writer we are merely slaves,
But then the playwright is a slave to us,
We bring the words to life, we give them wings,
We give them flesh and blood, we fill the gaps,
We work on it, refine it till it sings.

Take care, an actor has a nose for crap . . .
We take it on the road for endless weeks,
Trailing through the grimmest English towns,
That's hell on Earth to make your play more sleek.
While you get pissed in Groucho's, acting the clown,
Smirking on chat shows and pontificate,
Grinning through your teeth and feeling smart,
We pack our heavy suitcases, depart
For yet another dreary, gormless date,
Eating a greasy breakfast with a heavy heart,
While in the Ivy you wolf down your steak.
Your agent has her tongue right up your arse,
'You happy with ten per cent, should we ask for more?
Perhaps we'll wait until six months have passed.'
The first night comes, we're thinking on our feet,
We strive so hard to make your thin play strong,
Put muscles where there was no bloody meat,
And try and cover up the stinking pong,
Of dead ideas, regurgitated shit,
We do our best to cut the rot away,
And in the end, your crusty, flaccid play,
Is one ginormous hit! Okay!

David

That's *very* wicked darling, so unkind.
Do you insinuate that what I write,
Is drivel, specious, just some vacuous pulp?
That you, dear genius, with such clear insight,
Reshape, reform, and even, yes, resculpt,
Like Michelangelo from cold stone blocks,
When really the reverse is mostly true,
That what I labour on with loving care,
Burning the midnight oil through sleepless nights,
Might just as well be tossed into the loo!
For when I witness just how bloody trite,
My work appears when you have stamped your feet,
All over what was once my glorious face,
(My play) . . . I want to run to London Bridge and leap!

(*To* **John**.) You want to be a playwright, then good luck,
But you should better stick to what you know.
You're a successful actor, best to suck
The tit of fame, turn out familiar tricks,
The audience love your old familiar 'shtick',
But, once you dare to try to raise the stakes,
To actually create the words and characters,
When what your forte is to *imitate* . . .
Be careful less you stretch yourself too far!
You may provoke once more the critic's hate,
And while we say we do not give a toss,
No producer loves to make a loss.
Please tell me, since I really long to know,
What plots, what themes, what dramas stir inside
The seething cauldron of an actor's brain?
I dread to think my friend what we would find,
Once we stepped inside an actor's mind!
What a fascinating journey that must be,
Treading, oh so careful, through the wrecks
Of past ambition, cadavers of ancient roles,
Egos squawling in their filthy beds.
Oh God! An endless line of broken hearts,
Discarded brats, you actors have a tendency,
To change your partners quicker than you change
    your parts . . .
Long lists of names of friends you've long discarded,
Friends you made when acting on the stage,
All brought together nightly by my play,
But once the curtain's down, the memory fades,
And then a trunk of half-digested texts,
That pop up to the surface now and then,
Like when you're in a pub and in your cups,
A little quote from Hamlet might erupt,
Or even Oscar Wilde, that makes you seem,
That even when you're pissed you still have sheen,
And from this bubbling stew, this witch's broth,
You wish to write a bold inspiring play!
You will excite again the critic's wrath!

John

> Oh, what fine antennae you are gifted with,
> To accurately survey the complex world
> That constitutes my inner universe,
> And reach the sad conclusion that it's junk,
> Or like a stinking slum backyard.
> I readily concede that there are some actors,
> Whose skulls it would be folly to unscrew,
> Lest you succumb to some almighty stench,
> From some poor brain that's turning into glue . . .
> BUT
> Molière was an actor, Shakespeare too,
> The greatest dramas of the age they penned,
> Because they learned their craft as actors, knew,
> How much an actor thrives on dazzling plots,
> On conflicts 'tween the heart and mind and words
> To set the soul on fire, so don't talk rot!
> So, tell me, maestro, who sets *your* heart aflame?
> Go on, tell me please, I'd love to know
> Who touches the deepest chords inside your soul,
> Has you biting your knuckles, crying on your sleeve,
> Opening up emotions that were dead to thee,
> Even making you a better person
> Than you were before you stepped inside the theatre's door,
> So, go on, tell me, who does it for you?
> I'd say they're mostly rotting in their graves . . . !

Sarah

> Darlings! Shut the fuck up, both of you,
> You can't possibly imagine how it feels,
> To hear each one of you proclaim, the other's
> Just a pile of well-laid stinking poo!
> Forgive me if I've come all over crude.
> Didn't mean to swear, it's just too crazy
> To compare, eviscerate or disembowel,
> Just like two gladiators in the ring,
> Eager to stick their point in, hurt or maim,
> To entertain the muck of Rome, plebeian scum.

We've come a little further, haven't we?
Or have we, when we flock to see a naked cock,
Just dimly lit, but how the audience flit,
To see his pale protuberance from Row C.
And how the tabloid press focus on nothing else,
And scumbag TV hosts moisten their lips,
Ready to expel their lurid jokes,
To tell the truth, I think theatre sucks!
When you pay fifty pounds to see some ancient ducks,
Waddling around, remembering their lines, with any luck.
The audience is of a *certain* age,
The young ones having fled so long ago,
The chaps resemble a tray of shiny eggs,
Happily smiling at the limpid text,
'It's fifty years since first I saw that Dame,
It's so grand to see her once again.'
At last the curtain lowers, the audience give a cheer,
Is it for the play, the actors, or the fact,
The actors are still alive by the second act?

David

Sarah, poor thing, you're becoming very shrewish,
Cos every night, you're waiting in the wings,
In case the star has gone AWOL again.
God what a dreadful job, with all respect,
Does it affect your spirit, turn your brain?
Waiting for the phone to say . . . 'You're on tonight,'
And no rehearsal time to hone your text.
How can you not be bitter after all,
Thrust on, until the bitch regains her nerve,
And then once again you're waiting in the wings,
And knowing you're the better one by far,
I'm sure if it was me, I'd be unhinged,
And John, just cos you earned the critics' scorn,
Just let that be a spur to you . . . Create!
You'll improve with time, so have another go,
Maybe the muse will visit you . . . Hope so!
One other thing and most importantly,

Choose a director very carefully,
He'll sort the wheat out from the chaff,
Know how to draw from actors their very best,
And tells the playwright when to bloody cut,
Spits out the pips and takes no shit
From temperamental tarts and swaggering jakes!
So if there is a next time, please refrain
From directing your own beloved play!
Another pair of eyes, another brain,
You'll see how very much you'll gain.
Remember how you felt when you were young,
And a director cast you . . . said you were the one!
Each day you read your performances in his face,
He also guides you from that dangerous swamp,
Which is . . .

John

I long to know, so please don't hesitate . . .

David

The actor's overweening self-embrace!

John

Thank you so much for your esteemed advice!
I'll take it seriously as from a friend.
The first time I was chosen for a play,
I gulped huge quaffs of undiluted joy,
Excitement, fantasies of being great . . .
Exceeding expectation, without compare.
You study hard before the actual read,
The first time all the cast assemble there,
Each flush with pride and chattering like birds,
Now you sit, the director welcomes all,
And so begins to make his solemn speech,
To establish his authority from the start,
And the weaker his authority is
The longer is his aria to the cast!
He outlines how he sees the theme, the shape,
Talks about its history and its roots,

What period he will set it in, and takes
His time, he's done his research, scrawled his notes.
He talks, we sit and listen dutifully,
He talks and smiles, sometimes gesticulates,
He talks, we nod and grin and try to show,
Oh just how much we do appreciate
The endless font of knowledge he has gleaned,
And, like the best anatomist, he cuts,
He slices, he renders the play in little chunks
Shows us the heart, the nerves, the muscle of the piece,
What this play is made of so we know.
And on and on he spouts, we're getting bored,
For fuck's sake, shut up will you, stop the flow,
Of junkyard scraps and pithy stale conceits.
We're actors first and do not need to know
What we will find out when we suck the teat,
Or when we bite into the playwright's text,
The flavour that we'll taste from eating lines.
The actor knows, is an instrument, if you like, a string,
That when it's plucked, will sure, emit the sound,
Convey the thought, sprung from the author's hand,
So shut it, shut that ever spouting hole!
Direct the traffic, do the lights, tell us fast or slow,
And please, don't make me take my knickers off,
The audience really don't crave nudity,
And do me one last favour if you will,
Just let the bloody actors do it, *please*!

David

Oh thank God for the director, oh thank God!
Can you just imagine what it was,
When actors did control, the business of the stage,
Does it bear thinking about? No disrespect,
But please, you do need someone wise, outside,
To guide you, yes, and to advise,
And yes, that's absolutely right, so don't resist.
The actor-manager, is that some oxymoron!
Some outsize ego, or anathema!

Holding forth, as if this work, this play,
Were solely just a vehicle, to display
His wondrous talents to the awestruck world,
To strut out centre stage and strike a pose,
The other actors in the play just slaves,
Ready to do their lines and then piss off!
Since no one dare upstage the sacred monster,
Since he casts the play with lesser lights,
So he should, by contrast, appear to shine, like gold,
And not the dull and cheap iron ore he is.
As for one's play, don't hope too much to see
The play you wrote, oh dear no, God forbid!
Your masterpiece you wove, so carefully, thread by thread,
So thoughtfully designed, just like tapestry,
Each theme, each colour balanced carefully.
But when you see it, feel your blood run cold,
Just like you witnessed some appalling accident,
A body, slaughtered, mangled, ripped apart,
Its entrails dripping on some dusty street,
No less, your precious play, with words torn out,
Speeches broken, disjointed, and worst of all
The actors' own banal additions!
Sneaky little bits he thinks add colour,
Gives some glitter to his dullard wit!
And when he's not on stage, the other actors,
Taking their cue from this self-centred twit,
Slip and slide, improvise, throw in a joke,
And then, if you survive this ghastly night,
If your heart has not quite burst or stopped,
You'll be invited for a first-night drink,
And say 'Well done' between your gritted teeth,
Because you don't like to offend the 'star',
Especially when he's torn apart your play,
Like some eccentric filthy beast!
(*Smiling, to* **Sarah**.)
Let's hope, my darling, that those days are past . . .

Sarah

Oh David, what a simply awful plight,
To see your work abused, made trite,
By some mad actor's ego running rampant,
But that can't be too often, can it, dear?
I mean, how many actors are in charge
Of theatres? Very very few I'd say.
I love to be directed, helped and shaped,
Guided by a knowing, feeling hand . . .
Who carefully assuages all my fears,
In fact a good director's like a dad,
And I can be his trusting, willing child,
Urging him to show me how to act,
Do what he implores and never whine,
If he shows me how best to do a line,
Because he's smart, he knows, he has *degrees*,
And we're just actors, one rung over swine.
Of course, occasionally they like to flirt,
And chat you up while dangling the hope,
That for a fuck – sorry! Lifting of a skirt,
You might be considered for juicy role.
There's one director, I really dare not name,
Who was the biggest slag I ever met,
But his reputation was so big in Brecht,
Few knew he was a dirty groping pest!
But those are the hazards of the game,
And if you're gay, I'm sure it's just the same.
But actually I don't really bloody care,
Cos in the end you need a clever dick, John,
Someone watching over you, someone out there!

John

Someone out there! Someone out there, you say,
Some pisspot, lecher, half-drunken ponce,
Who mostly lisps, when seeing you backstage,
'Darling, you were marvellous,' and you'll see him once!
Twice if you're lucky, and then he's off.
The play becomes worn out, overstretched,

But 'daddy' is no longer there, he's sick to death
Of all of you, can't see it one more time,
He sits on his fat arse and while you sweat,
He cops a juicy royalty cheque
That's why it's *musicals* that they adore,
They're like an ever-running tap of gold,
Not too demanding, flashy sets, an uninspiring score.
Some directors have a genius, I admit,
For putting their grubby fingers on the pulse,
Of mediocrity, a second sense!

Yes, actors once directed their own shows,
Instructed the cast, gave perceptive hints,
Filled them with courage, and a certain pride,
Who else could do it, tell me who has the skill
To show you how to project your voice,
To use your gestures, when to be still,
Is with you not just once, or maybe twice,
Or slips into the matinee to give
Some tired and listless notes to actors
Half dead with exhaustion doing eight shows
A bloody week, no wonder they go mad!
An actor-manager leads his stalwart team,
Is with them every night and matinees,
And they, his team know that he's there for them,
Will always be, the captain, on the deck!

David

Oh jolly good! What sentimental muck!
Thank God we've banished for all time the actor
Who stands centre stage and spits,
Who wears his luvviedom on his sleeve.
You must admit that theatre's come some way,
From Oscar Wilde and Beerbohm Tree,
We are a little more demanding now,
And whilst it must have been great fun
To see an ancient warhorse puff and strut,
The subtlety might get a little stretched,
And when there's two of them on stage beware,

Don't ever hope to see a fine duet,
More like a battle to the bloody death,
Fighting, clawing, just to see who's best,
Like your legendary Edmund Kean,
The actors 'God' enshrined in myth,
Playing Othello one night at Drury Lane,
Feared that his Iago, played by Junius Booth,
Was glittering far too brightly on that stage,
So, seizing an opportunity in the play,
Grabs his sprightly opposition by the throat,
And strangles the poor actor – hardly the way,
I think, that even *actors* should behave,
In later years he was a poor old soak,
No doubt he was a marvel in his prime,
But actors never seem to know when to call time!

But now it's time for me to say farewell my friends,
I had a ball and loved our little chat,
But now I need different nourishment,
(*Exiting.*) Do join me for dessert, the usual place,
The food's a little bland, but the clientele's first rate.
(*Exits.*)

John

Oh, God, How that man rambles on and on,
So no more questions, trite comparisons,
But we, dear heart, bring fire down from the Gods,
Just like Prometheus, to bring some light
And let the poets dance again for joy
Re-ignite their words, bring them to life,
Train ourselves to be the messengers,
Bring Caesar's Rome to vivid life again,
Come see Othello in his towering rage,
Spitting blood over a handkerchief,
Roll up folks and see the damned Macbeth,
Be swift decapitated by brave Macduff,
Tonight see Hamlet contemplating death,
Gently weep as he draws his final breath,
And dies again tomorrow, matinee at three.

Tomorrow night you'll wear a crumpled hat,
And feel for Willy Loman as he tries,
To sell his forlorn bric-a-brac.
And since the actor's end is drawing near,
For this I'll need no make-up and false beard,
For I've *become* the dotty old King Lear.
Hear me, howling, howling, howling in the storm,
That's if of course the 'director's' sound effects,
Do not conspire to drown out the text!

Sarah

Then I will be your own Cordelia,
I help you, you can rest on me awhile,
You'll not be alone, I'll be your comforter.
But now, my dearest sweet, it's time to go,
The understudy is waiting in the wings,
Just in case I'm called . . . You never know! (*Exits.*)

John

Oh well, I've got a voice-over next week.
Like Edmund Kean, I do not wish to die on stage,
Nor like Sir Henry Irving, the Lyceum King,
He gave his every breath to make that theatre sing,
Dying in some dull provincial town.
I'm now the voice of Huggies, baby's nappies,
Isn't that a treat! And if you're lucky
You can earn a fortune in repeats.
But never mind, for soon we'll be enshrined
In ancient yellowing reviews,
Meanwhile we will play our final part
A filthy rotting corpse and food for worms!

Blackout.

Purgatory

Characters

Betty, *landlady, a type found in most northern cities where actors are obliged to tour – ghastly, intolerant but practical*

John, *actor, middle-aged, genteel, unsuccessful, but still hopeful*

Sarah, *a romantic spinster who has ended up sadly in a lodging house but is still looking for better*

Ted, *offstage, one of the landlady's favourite tenants whose main virtue is his blunt stupidity*

A middle-aged grumpy woman who is the landlady of a run-down guest house is showing an elegant middle-aged man a room. He bears the hallmarks of run-down gentility.

Betty So you like the room? It's south facing and has a pleasant view over the central post office . . . Commodious . . . Roomy and pleasant.

John And the kitchen is . . . ? (*Offstage.*)

Betty Behind the screen.

John (*gently pulling the screen to one side*) Aah!

Betty Careful, don't drag it, just lift it gently . . . it's an old screen . . . I'm gonna change it one day.

John Hmm!

Betty It's nothing fancy, it's a no-frills guest house, but it's clean . . . if you want fancy you'd pay a lot more, that I can tell ya . . . and the bathroom's down the hall.

John I see . . . Share the bathroom . . .

Betty Just on your floor. Listen, all the tenants are clean, self-respecting and when they forget to be they're shown the door.

John Ah ha!

Betty Yep, that's the law, it's called Betty's Law 'cause I'm Betty; just leave things just as you found them . . .

John Sensible law I'd say, Betty! And, er, the heating's included?

Betty Ha ha! If you hadn't told me you're an actor I'd have you down as a comedian . . . Come on! Not at that rent, mister. There's a meter next to the stove . . . Takes only 50p coins so make sure you get a stack while you're out 'cause believe me I gotta stack of patience but there's nothing worse than being woken at midnight by a whining voice, 'Got some change for a pound, Betty?' . . .

John   I can quite imagine . . . It must be . . . jarring . . .

Betty   Yeah . . . jarring . . . Okay. 'T's up to you . . . You don't have to take it, ya know . . . 'T's up to you . . .

John   I know that . . . May I be permitted to meditate for a few moments . . . To take a pause . . .

Betty   Ha ha! Make as long a . . . pause . . . as you like . . . But I got another prospective tenant coming in half an hour . . .

John   So my pause will be a brief one . . . Not what is known as the 'Macready' pause . . .

Betty   What's that?

John   Well, Macready was a famous actor of the last century who apart from his striking qualities as an actor was famous for the pauses he would make . . . Like, to make a point . . . To emphasise a moment . . .

Betty   Don't everyone take pauses when they speak?

John   Of course, true, but his pauses were . . . elongated . . .

Betty   Well, don't take too long a pause, I got someone coming . . . I told ya . . .

John   Sometimes in rehearsal the stage manager, unsure as to whether the maestro had forgotten his lines, would give him a prompt – i.e. shout out the line for him – and Macready would roar back 'It's a PAUSE DAMN YOU!' Ha ha!

Betty (*looking at him like he's a bit cuckoo*)   I ain't had an actor here before . . . Watcha been in?

John   Oh, I was afraid you'd ask that . . . People always do . . . But nothing you may have seen . . . Not lately . . . Since I've been doing repertory . . . Guesting in rep . . . Ha ha ha! The backbone of the performing arts.

Betty   Oh yeah.

John   Indeed, yes, repertory is still the best training for the actor . . .

Betty   What? Ya still in training at your age . . . Ha ha! I thought you'd be retiring!

John   Oh no! Got to keep one's technique fresh, tuned up. Anyway, I gave my John of Gaunt recently . . . That's the last role . . . So to speak . . .

Betty   Wot, on the telly?

John   No, oh no, *that* was in rep, in a town called Buxton, in Derbyshire . . .

Betty   Buxton? Never heard of it . . .

John   Well, you can't hear of everything, can you? Your brain must be overwrought as it is running a guesthouse . . .

Betty   I know enough to keep my nose clean . . .

John   Well, allow me to say that it's a very charming nose . . . If you were a man you'd be a perfect Cyrano de Bergerac . . . ha ha ha!

Betty   You're not taking the piss outta my hooter are ya . . . 'cause if you are . . .

John (*quickly adjusting*)   Heaven forefend. No! Cyrano was a great poet, a hero . . . I actually played him once . . . Oh, do forgive me . . . I was being . . . flippant.

Betty   So watcha done on the telly? Eh? That I might have seen?

John   Ah yes, the dear old telly, well not for some time I'm afraid . . . Not for some time . . . No . . .

Betty   Aintcha been in *EastEnders* or nuffin?

John   Alas . . . No . . . Not that I wouldn't mind . . . Oh yes . . . You know it pays the rent . . . And we all need to do that . . . But I'm more of what you might call . . . a classical actor . . .

Betty   That mean you don't work too much?

John   Ooh ho! Ho! How very witty of you . . . Yes, indeed, but alas too true . . . Not so much but I do get by, and yes once I played Oberon in a schools' TV broadcast . . .

Betty   Wotsat?

John (*awkward*)   Well, Oberon is an ethereal creature . . . He's the king of the fairies . . . In *Midsummer Night's Dream* . . . You know . . . Shakespeare . . .

Betty (*smirk*)   Cor blimey, you're not one of them, are ya? Not that it matters . . . I ain't prejudiced and we get lots of weirdos round here.

John   No, he's really a king of the real fairy world, the world of night, of elves, imps and even ghosts . . .

Betty   So you play a lot of weirdos, do ya?

John   Play as cast, that's me . . .

Betty   'Cause I gotta tell ya now, I don't want any nutters or weirdos in this house . . . I tell you that straight from the off . . . The last geeza here was mad as a box of frogs and we 'ad to get the law in . . . So I'm ultra-wary as you might say . . .

John   Quite right too . . . Yes indeed, this is your home . . . Your domain, in fact, your castle and you can't be too careful in your choice of . . . casting! Ha ha!

Betty (*relaxing*)   Was that a . . . Macready pause? That wait, before you said the last word?

John   Excellent my dear! Yes, indeed, that could be called a . . . Macready pause.

Betty   So it's just you, eh?

John   Yes, alas, just me.

Betty   Like just you and no wives or girlfriends turning up . . .

John No, just me I'm afraid . . . Just me . . . Hee hee . . . All alone in the big world . . .

Betty Ya wife left ya, or passed away or something . . . ?

John Too true . . . I'm afraid . . . Yes, she's gone . . . Er, cancer . . . We shall not look upon her like again!

Betty So ya a bit of a loner, eh . . . We got a few here . . . But I don't like stray visitors coming an' goin' . . . Now and again I can understand . . . I'm human after all, and a man can't sweat it through his ribs . . . But I don't keep a knocking shop.

John My dear, actors are not what you charmingly call loners . . . Oh no, we have the theatre . . . The theatre's my family . . . My brothers and sisters, sons and daughters . . . they're all there . . . We hold on to each other . . . We actors . . . We join up . . . We bond . . . Even stronger, dare I say, than blood ties . . . Oh yes, when I played John of Gaunt, Bolingbroke my son was just as real to me as my own flesh and blood . . .

'The blessed plot, this Earth, this England.'

Betty Oh. you mean your son in the play . . . That's make-believe, that's not for real!

John Oh, no, madam, when you play it is for real . . . It has to be . . . Deep in the heart or the audience won't feel it in their heart, they won't believe you unless you feel it, the tears are real!

Betty Okay, actor! I can't gossip all day . . . So have you made up your mind?

John Oh yes, of course, certainly, it's, er, charming and will suit me well.

Betty Okay, a month's rent in advance and £500 deposit against breakages . . . But you can do that later . . . Okay . . . I'll leave you to unpack, Romeo. Romeo, ha! ha!

She exits and **John** *stares for a while at her departed back.*

John   'Thou lump of foul deformity that was from thy mother's womb untimely ripped.'

Pause. He unpacks. As he carefully empties his suitcase he recites Gaunt's speech to England, addressing it almost to the room. Ironically.

John
'This royal throne of kings, this sceptred isle,
This Earth of majesty, this seat of Mars,
This other Eden, demi-paradise,
This fortress built by nature for herself
Against infection and the hand of war,
This happy breed of men, this little world,
This precious stone set in the silver sea,
Which serves it in the office of a wall,
Or as a moat defensive to a house,
Against the envy of less happier lands;
This blessed plot, this Earth, this realm, this England,
This nurse, this teeming womb of royal kings,
Fear'd by their breed and famous by their birth,
Renowned for their deeds as far from home,
For Christian service and true chivalry,
As is the sepulchre in stubborn Jewry
This land of such dear souls, this dear dear land,
Dear for her reputation through the world,
Is now leas'd out (I die pronouncing it)
Like to a tenement or pelting farm.'

There is a light rap on the door. A moment's silence.

John   Knock, knock, knock, who's there in the name of Beelzebub?

He opens the door and a middle-aged, nearly attractive lady slides in.

Sarah   Oh, do excuse me for bothering you but I live, or shall we say, rent the next room and I heard you, not loud, but just clearly reciting so charmingly and I thought to myself, oh . . . Now that's strange, yes, that's really odd . . . To hear poetry, language, words, that keep you alive . . . 'Cause I just got used to the TV blaring day and night and so when the previous tenant left I thought . . . Oh thank God, thank God just for a few days off, a few precious days of peace until the next . . . creature comes and switches on that infernal machine for poor dead souls, dead solitary souls absorbing all the junk of the world and then, and then when I heard you coming up the stairs being shown the room, heard the landlady leave with you still inside . . . I waited . . . I just waited with pounding heart, waited, preparing myself for the sound of that infernal beast to start barking again . . . Was ready . . . yes, ready to cover my ears, plug in my ear plugs and turn on my radio . . . When . . . when I heard this voice . . . YOUR VOICE . . . This sublime tender voice . . . Reciting poetry . . . Or a play . . . A monologue perhaps . . . Yes . . . And oh God . . . It was beautiful . . . Yes, it was, and maybe, yes maybe that was the reason I had to . . . Forgive me, but I just had to . . . Oh please, don't say anything . . . Not just yet . . . Because I want to say that this time (I was so moved you see) that this time I had to *say* something . . . I couldn't hold it back . . . Something in the way you speak . . . made me, gave me . . . No, *permitted* me to come to you . . . No please . . . And now I have to say thank you, oh yes, thank you, sir, oh God yes, to hear *words* again!

No, don't worry, the walls are a little thin, but in this case . . . Oh God, what a pleasure, yes, what a divine pleasure . . . Sorry, no sorry, I made a fool of myself . . . No matter, no matter, that's me . . . In a good cause and to say . . . Feel free . . . Don't stop reciting . . . And welcome . . . Be happy here . . . It's not such a bad house and now there's a poet in our midst or an actor . . . Yes . . . ? Reciting . . . Ah Shakespeare . . . ? No, don't speak, I won't, I promise you, I won't bother you again . . .

John   Oh you can . . . You must . . . You . . .

Sarah   No, no, farewell and take care . . . Feel free . . . Please . . . And oh . . . THANK YOU!

She exits.

John *sits on the bed completely stunned and contemplates. Is almost nervous to attempt anything. Keeps unpacking and then whispers so as not to be heard at first or knowing that he now has an audience. He starts quietly and then goes to the wall.*

John (*gently at first*)
'Shall I compare thee to a summer's day?
Thou art more lovely and more temperate.
Rough winds to bend the darling buds of May,
And summer's lease hath all too short a date.'

He stops and puts his ear to the wall imagining that she is listening.

'But thy eternal summer shall not fade,
Nor lose possession of that fair thou ow'st . . .
So long as men can read [breathe] or eyes can see,
So long lives this, and this brings [gives] life to thee.'

Goes to the bed and sits as if waiting for a knock. Is uncertain. Puts away a few more things, then goes back to the wall. Stares at it, puts his ear to it trying to determine what she is doing.

John (*as Romeo*)
'See how she leans her cheek upon her hand!
O that I were a glove upon that hand,
That I might touch that cheek!'

Silence. Listens. Wonders whether to knock on the wall. Paces the room. Tries again and now his voice is rising.

'It is the East, and Juliet is the sun!
Arise, fair sun, and kill the envious moon,
Who is already sick and pale with grief
That thou . . . '

Ted (*other side of the wall*) SHUT THE FUCK UP WILL YA . . . YA NOISY CUNT!

John *backs away in horror.*

Ted (*off*) I'M TRYING TO GET SOME FUCKING SLEEP YA CUNT! I WORK NIGHTS SO SHUT THE FUCK UP OR I'LL KICK YA FUCKIN' HEAD IN. OK! CUNT!

John *sits on the bed, utterly perplexed, slowly continues unpacking but in a kind of daze, stares at wall then slowly goes back to it, wonders whether to knock but instead just whispers . . .*

John *(in a whisper)*   Sorry . . . So sorry . . .

He takes a drink from a bottle of sherry from his case. Voices outside. **Betty** *and noisy tenant,* **Ted***.*

Betty *(off)*   Watsup, Ted? . . . What's all the rumpus, mate . . . Eh? Oo's pulled ya tail . . . ?

Ted *(off)*   'S awright now! 'E's shut up . . . Sounds like a flaming nutter you got there, Betty . . .

Betty *(off)*   Nah, 'e's an actor . . . Doin his fuckin' lines in't 'e!

Ted *(off)*   Oooh fuck . . . An actor . . . Ope e's not a bum bandit 'n all . . . Better lock me door, eh!

Betty *(off)* Nah, don't throw ya toys . . . 'E's an old cunt . . . 'E's harmless . . . A bit pathetic, if ya ask me . . . Sa get your 'ead down, Ted.

They continue to talk offstage.

Ted   Yeah, fuck that . . . Bit 'ard now . . . Was in a luvly kip an' all.

Betty   Go on, you'll drop off soon . . .

Ted   Yeah, better 'ave . . . tada.

Betty   Tada, Ted luv . . .

Silence. **John** *just sits contemplating. Then whispers.*

John
'Oh what a rogue and peasant slave am I?
Is it not monstrous that this player here –

Indicates neighbour.

But in a fiction, in a dream of passion
Could force his soul so to his own conceit . . .
And all for nothing! For Hecuba! . . . '

Trails off. Quiet tapping on the door.

John Knock, knock, knock! (*Opens the door.*)

Sarah . . . Shh, shhhh! Oh dear! Oh dear! I'm so sorry, so sorry . . . I heard it all. (*Tuts.*) Oh oh! I feel so responsible. Yes . . . I do . . . No! No! Don't, don't speak . . . Let me explain . . . Er . . .

John John . . .

Sarah Oh, er, John. I realise now what happened . . . My fault . . . My stupid fault . . . No, listen . . . Please . . . Listen, or I won't have the courage to get it out . . . I'll collapse in a quivering heap of embarrassment . . . I said I live next door but on the other side . . . You thought on your left facing the door, but no . . . on the right . . . You saw me going left as I left your room but I was just popping out to buy something . . . When I came back I heard the noise . . . I even heard it from the street! The shouting . . . That man's a lunatic, a madman . . . He should have bravo'd you, but sadly these people can't hear, can't see they're troglodytes . . . They're Neanderthals, their knuckles still scraping the ground, and so poor, poor man, so gracious, so encouraged. I flatter myself that, yes, I encouraged you and so you sweetly opened that divine heart of yours, to make your song, but that awoke the wrath of the beast, and you gave some such beauty, such elegance, yes, you did, believe me I do not flatter, you put some soul back into this house . . . But poor thing you faced the wrong way . . . What a shock, oh what a dreadful shock for you . . . An artist, a poet and, yes, even an actor . . . No, no not just an actor . . . Forgive me, for you breathe life into words, you give them life . . . Noble messenger of the gods, more like . . . And I blame myself . . . Oh yes, of course I do . . . I provoked you and now I even hate myself . . . Yes . . . For my audacity . . . So please forgive . . . Find it in your heart to forgive me . . . No, don't say 'yes' now . . . Wait . . . Wait . . . Let it sink in . . . And if you can find just a little ember of forgiveness in you . . . then recite another sonnet or speech to me . . . through the wall . . . Better at night when the beast has gone to his evil labours . . . And then, yes, I'll take it as a sign . . . Thank you . . . Oh thank you again . . . Shhh! No need, no need!

She exits. **John** *sits on his bed again, perplexed to the limit. Hangs up his clothes. Goes to the wall, this time on her side and gently strokes it. Checks the time. Looks at the other wall and grimaces, pulls a face. Back to bed. Sits. Takes out a cigarette. Goes to the fridge and finds a can of beer the prior tenant has left.*

John That's a bit of luck, I must say . . . (*Pours drink. Smiles, contented.*) Amazing, wonderful, I mean who would believe it!? She's so . . . Nice . . . Ah yes . . . Mature but nice . . . Aah yes . . . Like a fine wine . . . That feminine edge . . . Yes, she has that tang, that bittersweet taste that suffering gives a woman . . . Let's say a tad bohemian . . . Yes, rather poetic, sensitive, and who would have thought that in a place like this . . . Which goes to show that you can never know just what might be round the corner . . . Or in the next room . . . Hmm. And there's a pleasant fragrance . . . Hmm, that she's left behind . . . Sandalwood perhaps.

A knocking on the door. **John** *smiles and takes a breath.*

John Knock, knock, who's there?

Opens the door and it's **Betty**.

John Oh it's you . . .

Betty And who did you expect it to be, fast worker! Listen, mister, I took you in, right, and as soon as my back's turned you're makin a nuisance of yourself! Shoutin' and ravin' . . . What's goin' on . . . ? Woke up my best lodger . . . 'E's been here for years and I don't wan' 'im upset by ya nutty talking ta yaself and shoutin . . . Watsamata with ya, eh?! Ya don't know how to behave, do ya? There's others here ya know . . . Workers, people who graft, 'ope you appreciate that . . .

John Not only appreciate but even envy . . .

Betty Yeah, well, they keep the country goin', and turn the wheels and pay the rent and wad ju do . . . Just entertain a few faces . . . That's when you get a job . . .

John   We're mere frivolity . . .

Betty   And he's as good as gold . . . So I don't need outa work actors . . . Ya got me . . . eh? Now, mister, I took a bit of a risk wiv ya . . . Right . . . But any more complaints and it's a fast exit for ya!

John   A heap of apologies, I do apologise . . . I never realised the walls were that thin . . .

Betty   Nah, not *that* thin, just normal, mate, and you were ravin' and rantin' weren't cha . . . Wos all that abaht . . . Why ya gotta do that, eh . . . ? Eh? Oh, ya quiet now aintcha . . . If ya gotta practice do ya lines quiet like . . . Then 't's okay innit . . . We're normal people, we ain't monsters is we . . . We live and let live . . . (*Pause.*) So wadja do wiv yaself when ya not workin' . . . Eh, hang abaht . . . 'Restin', ha ha . . . Work on ya lines that you might do some day . . . Is that watya do? Eh? Ha! . . . Poor thing . . . I don't tell ya what to do . . . If it makes you 'appy then keep on doin' it but keep ya voice down . . . okay? So you got anyfing coming up . . . ? Like any prospects, eh? Watcha got in the pipeline so to speak?

John   You know and I am sure you appreciate that as an actor one must keep one's instrument tuned . . . You can't let it get neglected, rusting away, since an audition may come up at any moment. So at every moment one has to be ready . . . But quite right, in future I shall keep my bellows low . . . I understand . . .

Betty   Then there's no problem . . .

John   No, no problem at all . . . But of course one must keep one's soul alive, alert. Language is like music or painting . . . It has colour and range . . . It awakes the spirit . . . It is a call to the heart, it frees the emotion to read a poem or sing or act a play . . . It touches the area where our soul lives. It has to be allowed out or it may die . . . But I didn't realise how my voice penetrates and I shall be quiet; I shall roar as quiet as any turtle dove . . . Until the Duke says 'Let him roar again, let him roar again.'

Betty   Oh yeah . . . Ya not takin the piss, are ya?

John   Good God no! It was a line from a play . . . I would never . . . as you say . . . take the piss . . .

Betty   Okay, so, ya got nuffin comin up? Eh?

John   Don't worry, you shall not wait for the rent . . .

Betty   Too right I won't, and don't forget, one month in advance and deposit against breakages . . .

John   I shall not forget and shall put a cheque in an envelope before the night's out.

Betty   Yeah . . . Better had done . . . 'Ere, get ya agent to get ya on *EastEnders* . . . Plenty of old buggers in that . . . !

John   Indeed . . . I shall remind them and thanks for the suggestion . . .

Betty   Ya welcome, I'm sure.

She exits.

John (*quiet*)   'Bloody bawdy villain, remorseless, leacherous, treacherous, kindless woman!'

He sits on the bed wearily. Light tap on the door.

John   'What angel wakes me from my flowery bed?'

Opens door and **Sarah** *slips swiftly in.*

Sarah   Oh! Oh! Shh! Poor you! Yes . . . ! Poor, poor you! How the poet is persecuted . . .

John   Thank you but merely . . . An actor who 'frets his hour upon . . . '

Sarah (*cuts him off*)   Shh! It's the same . . . You speak, others write, you live the words, yes, poor you . . . On your first day they can't wait to throw stones, barbarians! How unjust are the Pharisees of the world . . . The artist is always persecuted . . . Why?

John   I'm afraid I was to blame . . . I was too loud.

Sarah   No! No! Art hurts them . . . Makes them feel uncomfortable, shabby, its light exposes their sad, miserable lives and so they wish to shut it out . . .

John   'Put out the light and then put out the light!'

Sarah   Yes, put out the light, and so they mock you, YOU! How ironic, those crude plebeians!

John   A 'common cry of curs'!

Sarah   So true . . . But shh . . . shh! Don't let it get you down, you mustn't, and you know why? 'Cause we need you . . . Yes the world needs you, you actors are the messengers of the gods, like Prometheus bringing the fire from heaven . . . For without you the world is a colder place.

John   Ha! I don't think that the world shares your enlightened view . . . And I was a bit loud, a bit carried away . . .

Sarah   Shh! Don't! Don't say that the singing birds are too loud when their shrill music wakes us . . . Is the thunder too loud? For lowlife bats in their murky cave, anything is too loud, only the shrill sounds of each other's brutish squeaks do they understand, with their nasty little voices . . . no! Never too loud.

John (*somewhat moved by this strange lady*)   Thank you . . . Thank you . . . Sarah . . .

Sarah   Aah, how you speak my name, how you express it . . . With such . . . Oh I don't know but dare I say . . . tenderness. Dare I . . . I dare . . . Yes . . .

They are both silent for a while as if unable to say more to each other lest they both expose more than they wish at this time.

John   Sarah.

Sarah   Yes . . .

John   SARAAH, Sarah . . .

Sarah   Oh yes . . . Yes . . .

John
'Shall I compare thee to a summer's day?
Thou art more lovely and more temperate.
Rough winds to bend the darling buds of May,
And summer's lease hath all too short a date . . . '

Betty (*off*)   DON'T FORGET I'M WAITING FOR
YOUR BLOODY DEPOSIT . . .

John (*pauses momentarily*)
'Sometime too hot the eye of heaven . . . '

Betty (*off*)   I'LL GIVE YA ANOTHER HOUR . . . OK?
THEN YOU'RE OUT OF IT, MATE!

John (*responding, then continues his poem*)   OK! . . .

'And often is his gold complexion dimm'd . . . '

Ted (*next door*)   FOR FUCK'S SAKE, BETTY, WATCHA
SHOUTIN FOR . . . YA FUCKIN' WOKE ME UP
AGAIN! SODDIN' 'ELL!

Betty (*off*)   SORRY, LUV, GET BACK TA SLEEP!

John
'But thy eternal summer shall not fade . . . '

Ted (*off*)   BIT FUCKIN' DIFFICULT NOW INNIT.
FIRST THAT CUNT NEXT DOOR AND NOW YOU.
WASUPWIVYA!

John (*repeats*)
'But thy eternal summer shall not fade . . . '

Betty (*off, overlapping*)   SORRY, DARLIN! I'LL MAKE IT
UP TO YA! RIGHT, TED!

Ted (*off*)   FUCK ME!

John

'Nor lose possession of that fair thou ow'st . . . '

Betty   'CAUSE THE ACTOR AIN'T PAID ME
DEPOSIT YET, TED . . . GETS ME AGITATED!

John

'As long as men can breathe or eyes can see . . . '

Ted (*off*)   THEN FUCKIN' GO IN AND TELL HIM . . .
DON'T SWALLOW IT!

Betty   CAN'T, 'E'S WITH THAT MAD TART FROM
NEXT DOOR, PROBABLY GIVING HER ONE.

John

'So long lives this, and this gives life to thee . . . '

Lights slowly fade as voices increase in volume and venom.

Ted (*off*)   AH SHIT . . . I'LL NEVER GET BACK TO
FUCKIN' SLEEP NOW . . . I MEAN I GOTTA FUCKIN'
WORK!

Lights fade.

Betty (*off*)   OK . . . SHUT IT NAH, TED . . . IT'S GORN
QUIET . . . JUST FUCKIN' SHUT IT!

The lights fade to black as **John** *and* **Sarah** *gently hold each other.*

Mediocrity

Characters

Steve, *actor, thirty to thirty-five – he's not found the success he had hoped for, either through bad luck or perhaps a negative attitude*

Barry, *actor, thirty to thirty-five – an old friend of Steve's since drama school, who has found steady work either through good luck or perhaps a more adaptable if not compromising attitude*

Steve   So how long since you left drama school?

Barry   Oh about six years . . . Yeah, six years now . . .

Steve   And how's it been . . . I mean, has it been tough?

Barry   No, good! Yeah . . . It's been good, you know . . . A little stiff at first . . . Right . . . You expect that . . . But I got lucky, yeah . . . With a TV series . . . Just lucky . . . You know . . . I just happened to fill the role . . .

Steve   Yes . . . That was lucky, but I'm sure your talent had something to do with it . . .

Barry   Ha ha! No great talent needed really, but just happened to fit into the scheme of things . . . And you?

Steve   Well, me . . . I had to . . . you know, hit all the auditions . . . But, er . . . Was a difficult period and the reps were closing down, the grants were drying up . . . So actors hung on to their jobs . . . Yeah . . . So I did odd jobs.

Barry   Good for you! Good for the soul! Lots of research . . . Ha ha! Gene Hackman was a barman in New York for years, you know . . .

Steve   That right?

Barry   Oh yes . . . So was Dustin Hoffman, I'm pretty sure . . .

Steve   So I'm in good company . . .

Barry   Oh yeah . . . Ha ha! You're in the best company . . . Definitely! . . .

Steve   Yeah . . . So what then? After the TV series . . . You didn't stay with it?

Barry   Tell you the truth, I got bored with it . . . The same formula each week . . . I wasn't stretching myself as an actor . . . I wasn't using that expensive training . . .

Steve   You mean you paid . . . You didn't get a grant?

Barry   Hey, the grants just dried up . . . You were lucky . . . You got in just before the big freeze, so Dad helped out, bless him . . .

Steve   That was fortunate for you . . . That your folks had the money . . .

Barry   Hey listen, that was the best thing they could have done for me . . . And their investment paid . . . paid them back with knobs on.

Steve   Really? You paid them back . . . ?

Barry   No! No! Not in money, they didn't expect that . . . In fact they didn't need that . . . But paid back in pride . . . Pride in my humble efforts. Didn't let them down . . . Didn't drop out . . . Fold up . . . Spend months out of work . . . Or hassle them for more dosh . . . That must be horrible to spend months out of work . . . Hustling for a job like a beggar . . . Horrible . . . I've been lucky . . . I suppose, although I won't be so modest as to deny that a modicum of talent may have helped . . .

Steve   Of course.

Barry   I mean, it's not all luck . . .

Steve   Course not!

Barry   I mean, some poor actors, out of work . . . months on end . . . How can they call themselves actors? You know what I mean . . . A writer can still write, a painter can still paint . . . Has to . . . But what can an actor do? He needs other actors to work with . . . He needs a stage . . . An audience . . .

Steve   You can . . . study texts, learn roles . . . prepare yourself . . . do voice classes.

Barry   Oh sure, some actors do nothing but . . . But in the end you need to act, to PERFORM!

Steve   Of course . . . You do . . . Yes . . . You're right . . .

Barry I mean you really do . . . So, you spent much time out of work, Steve . . . ? I mean a sizeable time . . . ?

Steve Oh yeah, I've had my share of . . . grey periods, oh yes.

Barry Like what . . . What was the longest time?

Steve Oh . . . Nearly a year . . .

Barry CHRIST! Oh my God . . . Christ . . . Poor you . . . How did you cope?

Steve Time passes . . . I did classes, worked nights as a waiter . . . three . . . four nights a week . . . Sometimes worked in a pub, long hours and horrible, dull work . . . And the stench of beer in your clothes and on your skin, went on the dole, great British institution . . . Was a part-time salesman . . . I got by . . .

Barry Bully for you and well done . . . Yeah, well done . . . Don't know if I could do that . . . Thank God I haven't needed to . . . Yet . . .

Steve Let's hope you never do . . .

Barry Amen to that quothe I, ha ha! But did it depress you . . . Get you down . . . Make you want to give up?

Steve No, why should I want to give up . . . ?

Barry Like people turning you down . . . All the time . . . Not wanting to employ you . . . Like being *rejected* . . . so much . . .

Steve Funnily enough it didn't even occur to me . . . Never, not for an instance . . . Since there was nothing else I wanted to do . . . Or could do . . . Or would do . . . This was my last chance . . . Had no choice . . . And one day it happened. One day I got a job . . . I broke the spell . . . The long drought . . . But I do admit . . . at times I thought I'd never work again . . . All actors feel that sometimes.

Barry   Worse, even, and I've not been out of work that much. So well done, Steve . . . You broke it . . . That's determination for you . . . Good . . . You got guts . . . Others might have thrown in the towel, and believe me I'm not crowing since God forbid it might happen to me . . . Might happen that my luck runs out.

Steve   So would you give up . . . If it did . . . if you found the months crawling past . . . ?

Barry   Well . . . Yeah . . . Well . . . Difficult decision . . . Like if you're not wanted, why flog a dead horse . . .

Steve   So you'd give up?

Barry   No, no, not saying that, not saying I would. But, it would make me think, but thank God I've never been out of work for more than . . . say . . . three or four weeks . . . So I've been lucky . . .

Steve   Good for you . . .

Barry   Sure, touch wood . . . Been lucky . . . Yeah, been really lucky . . . but with I hope a modicum of talent . . . Right . . . You need that!

Steve   Of course!

Barry   To give me a lift-off.

Steve   Course!

Barry   I mean, you can be lucky . . . Get loads of auditions . . . the right agent . . . the right meeting . . . But without the talent . . . won't last . . .

Steve   Course . . . But talent is often not recognised . . . Sometimes I think that the most unique talents are passed over for the more obvious . . . dross . . . That's possible . . . That some rare talents, some unique or original are passed over . . . for that very reason . . . For being unique . . .

Barry   Sure, oh, I'm sure you're right . . . Hmm!

Steve   And that very uniqueness, the originality, that difference might, or could possibly intimidate a lesser light . . .

Barry   Oh sure, sometimes, that's possible, but I never, like in my case felt . . .

Steve   I mean it is possible, just possible, that directors, some directors, might possibly feel 'threatened' or at least intimidated by an unusual talent since they are more at ease with the 'safe', 'dependable', reasonably skilful . . . not an oaf, but not too gifted, not so gifted as to create further problems . . . A difference of opinion, for example, an innovative idea, since directors love to be needed, to be asked how to do it, to be mummy or daddy . . . Directors love to feel important, looked up to, *listened* to . . . Some directors can't even stop talking . . . You know, the ones who come in on the first day with a bellyful of theories and puke them all over you . . . They just sit there and spray you with their research . . .

Barry   Ha ha! Sure, well, they've got to show you where they're coming from, what their ideas are . . . Right? As long as they don't go on all day, ha ha! . . . I know what you mean . . .

Steve   An unusual, a confident talent just might cause a bit of uneasiness in a director that's a tad insecure . . . A little wobbly maybe . . . Don't you think?

Barry   That's possible . . . I'm sure it's possible and why not . . . Can't a director be a bit insecure . . . ? That's normal . . . at the beginning . . . Then you grow together . . .

Steve   Course!

Barry   But I have to say . . . and not just because I've been well employed . . . I have to say that the directors I've worked for have definitely not been wankers . . . They were gifted people . . . Very smart, knew what they wanted . . . what they were looking for . . . were particular . . . I got no impression that they were insecure twits who cast only safe, modest personalities, I mean I don't necessarily think that I'm a safe predictable, jobbing actor . . . 'Yes sir, three bags full, sir!'

Steve   Course not!

Barry   I mean, I was cast, chosen out of quite a few talented actors in my last series . . . That I know . . .

Steve   How do you know?

Barry   How do I know?

Steve   I mean how would you know that . . . ?

Barry   My agent . . . She told me, she always tells me . . . There were a few 'faces' going up for the job, you know, from top agencies, so I don't think he chose me because I was a little cuddly teddy bear . . .

Steve   Course not.

Barry   No, there were some big names up for the parts . . .

Steve   Your agent told you that?

Barry   I told you, yes, what are you making out of it . . . ?

Steve   How does she know?

Barry   Because the casting director told her . . . It's no big secret . . .

Steve   Isn't she betraying the trust the employer gave her . . .

Barry   Twaddle, course not, it's part of the business to know . . . Look, the casting directors called my agent . . . to make her feel proud . . . that I was competing with top talent and they chose me, that's all . . .

Steve   Course.

Barry   That's right, but I'm getting the drift . . .

Steve   What drift . . . ?

Barry   Your drift, Stevey baby . . . Your drift . . .

Steve   Didn't know I had a drift . . .

Barry   I think you know you have a drift . . .

Steve   Do I? I don't think I have, but you may think something . . . You may think I have a drift . . . So what's my drift?

Barry   What's your drift?

Steve   Hmm . . . What do you think is my 'drift'?

Barry   I could tell you what your drift is. I could . . .

Steve   So what's stopping you . . . ?

Barry   Don't want to make ripples . . .

Steve   Oh go on . . . Make a big splash . . . Drench me with your insights, Barry . . .

Barry   Hey, chill out, it's hardly worth the breath . . .

Steve   I'm chilled, so dive in . . .

Barry   Look, I get work . . . I get employed . . . Right, not because of my ability, skill, drive and, yes, dedication . . . No, I get work because you think . . . I'm safe, predictable, unthreatening and make directors feel . . . safe . . . secure . . .

Steve   And that's my drift?

Barry   Could be . . . Yep . . .

Steve   I wasn't implying you, Barry, I didn't say you, I just said that there was a possibility amongst some . . . a few directors . . .

Barry   And you, you have vast deserts of unemployment because you are unique, dazzling and therefore threatening for those lesser lights who quake, whose knees rattle under your great spotlight . . . Oh yes, you're too original and therefore are cast out into the great wilderness . . . John the Baptist raving . . .

Steve Hey, hey, I didn't say that . . . I didn't imply you!
Why would I . . . You're my friend . . . Aren't you?

Barry No, of course not . . . No . . . Not me . . . No . . . But
maybe, maybe, yes . . . maybe anyone who works, in your
mind, must therefore be a safe, dull, predictable actor . . . Not
going to *rock the boat*! And you know what . . . I also have a
theory . . .

Steve Of course.

Barry Yes, of course, and I'll tell you what that is . . .

Steve I'm throbbing to hear . . .

Barry Throb away . . . Well, my little theory is that there
are some actors, of course not necessarily you, whose biggest
get-out, whose biggest excuse for ending up on the dole queue
week after endless week is that they think they are too
'talented' . . . too 'unusual,' too 'working class' . . . Oh, the
great unwashed, unemployed, bless them, give themselves the
biggest excuse, the biggest justification in history . . . So this
gives a get-out for every bum, every lazy untalented scumbag
who couldn't be bothered to prepare, think, work out, every
lazy sod who never made it for the second audition or call-
back . . . Every pathetic untalented actor can whine, 'It's a
conspiracy' . . . Oh how many excuses do you need to make
the pain of rejection tolerable . . . 'It's the gay mafia' . . . 'It's
the Oxbridge set' . . . And do you know what? I understand it
now, after listening to you . . . Yes! You need these theories . . .
How you need them . . . because just to contemplate the
thought that maybe . . . just maybe . . .

Steve Yes. Go on . . .

Barry You weren't fucking talented enough . . . Ow! That's
too hard too take . . . That's a door few of us . . . dare open!

Steve I didn't say that . . .

Barry What did you say then? . . . Eh?

Steve It wasn't that important . . . But it obviously pressed some buttons . . . Touched a nerve . . .

Barry Oh, now it's a nerve . . . You said. Just listen to what you said, that if you're suffering from a lack or work . . . You can, with reasonable confidence, attribute that to your 'unusual gifts', and that's the biggest get-out of all time, don't you think?

Steve Of course . . . But whilst it's also true that there are paradoxically directors who are vulnerable, easily spooked, this doesn't mean to say that all directors are cowards who only employ the faces that fit, any more than all rejected actors are geniuses, but there may be some . . . And so the paradox is that the rejected can take comfort that genius is rejected too . . . That's all I was saying . . .

Barry Oh, okay, so, I get your drift. Now you, as an actor of some talent, believe that your uniqueness and individuality is the sole reason in this 'mediocre' world for not being fairly accepted, and you never think that part of the blame for your languishing in waste lands lays with you . . . That you just might have a bad attitude and that's a vibe that makes itself felt very swiftly like a bad smell and employers don't like to smell 'attitude', it makes for trouble, and a company is a vulnerable group of actors and they don't need a virus in their midst . . . Wow! What a massive amount of geniuses are being overlooked . . . The streets are seething with them . . . They, these geniuses, are serving you drinks and waiting for your tips! Ha ha ha ha!

Steve Of course they are, and that's the crime . . . The sad but unfortunate fact is that for every genius that manages to crawl through the mediocre minefield without getting blown up, ten die by the wayside . . . I don't think that any important artist or even scientist ever brought human consciousness to a higher level without incredible resistance from the mediocrity . . . But some do get through, and thank God for that . . . So there is, maybe, some justice in the world . . . But the mediocrity are powerful . . . Why? Because there are so many

of them, such massive support from the masses. So if you
really want success try a dash of mediocrity and it will catch
on . . . You'll fit in . . . fill the groove . . .

Barry   Oh good, how happy that makes me suspect that if I
get a job, if I work, if I get lucky it won't be because I worked
my arse off while you whined in the pub about your lot, but
because of my utter mediocrity . . . Only because I don't
aspire to those rarefied fields . . . Because I'm safe, fit the bill,
am docile, and do you know, if I were younger I might feel
hurt, distraught and even believe that crock pot of shit . . . I'd
listen to you . . . Develop a complex, an inferior one . . . But
in some way, yes, I do believe you . . . Yes, I do think most
directors are creeps, with a few great exceptions and most are
power-mad lunatics playing God, and maybe that's as it
should be, for the peak of the mountain is the smallest part . . .
So we all aspire to hit the peak, one day, we start small and
mediocre and crawl up, yes, crawl painfully up . . . And
maybe it's okay and the masses are there and I am speaking
to them. I communicate to them . . . On their wavelength and
they like that . . . Like to see themselves in me, those big red
ugly faces like it, that I relate to them! But you come along . . .
You can't . . . No you can't relate, can't communicate to
them because you're too good . . . TOO TOO FUCKING
CLEVER! TOO SMART . . . ON A HIGHER WAVELENGTH
. . . Hey, you know what you are . . . You're *symbolic*! Ha
ha ha!

Steve   Listen . . . You've got it worked out and that's good.
It means you don't cripple yourself with self-doubt . . . You've
made it work for you and there's nothing wrong in being a
mediocre jerk 'cause you'll relate, as you say, to the masses
and that's not bad, and one day . . . if you have it in you . . .
you'll crawl out of the slime and reach the high open air . . .
Why not . . . ? You're right . . . Sure, it's my attitude . . . How
come I didn't see it before?

Barry   And don't you think, just for a moment, that this
rather supercilious attitude might just be a cover for your

insecurity . . . yes, a cover . . . just in case they see through your 'act' . . . You come knowing, suspecting, that since there's a good chance of being rejected you'll slap on a veneer of sneer between you and them . . . Yeah? Stops the rejection chafing so much! GOTCHA!

Steve Maybe you're right . . . I come fully dressed in my attitude of sneering superiority and the maître d' says . . . NO NO! You can't come in here wearing that attitude . . . no, not those insupportable contemptible loafers, not those radical filthy jeans. No, not that anarchic sweater . . . No no, you can't come in . . . Here you wear the proper shoes of conformity, a decent jacket that holds your opinions in check, and a tie to choke off any howl of joy . . . We'll fucking well show you, you are one of us, oh and a tight collar to keep in the free flow of obstinate opinions . . . Yes, that's how they see me . . . You're right . . .

Barry In fact, I'm beginning to believe that you may in fact be more mediocre than me . . . But you cover it better . . . Yes . . . You spray your deodorant called 'superior' over yourself . . . to make yourself more sexy . . . I am . . . in your eyes . . . mediocre . . . But I handle it better . . . I accept it . . . But I shall grow . . . I shall . . . My mediocrity is my base from which I shall climb . . .

Steve Long live mediocrity!

Barry For we shall conquer the world . . .

Steve You have . . . Oh yes my friend . . . You already have!

Slow fade as they both smile at each other.

Howl

Author's Note

Two actors, in the autumn of their years, reflect on the past as all actors, especially older ones, are prone to do. In doing so they discover some less-than-palatable events.

Characters

Patrick, *elderly actor*
Paul, *elderly actor's friend*

Patrick (*to* **Paul**)   Have you done Leeds . . . ?

Paul   Leeds? . . . No . . . Missed out on that one, oddly enough it never came my way, no reason, some places you never get asked to . . . Leeds? Hmm. Any good?

Patrick   Avoid, avoid . . . It is the pits, no, it really is, drab! . . . Sure, a few boutiques now liven the scene, but something grim, yes, grim about the place.

Paul   Doesn't it depend on what you're playing?

Patrick   Sure, that keeps you going during the day, waiting for the night, that's what you wait for. To get into the theatre, see your mates . . . get ready . . . perform . . . That's your moment, your moment of bliss . . . The audience happy and expectant, then the curtain, cheers . . . Sometimes, if it's been really good. Then the pub, a race to the Chinese, then that's it until the next day.

Paul   That doesn't sound so bad, not so bad as you make out, no, that sounds, actually good, some actors might find that enviable!

Patrick   Yeah, like you adjust when you're out of work . . . You adjust to that . . . to your hunger, so even a crust tastes really delicious . . . when you're out of work . . . Sure. It tastes like the best gourmet on Earth, but when you get your crust your hunger abates and you're working and that feels great at first, but then . . .

Paul   You adjust . . .

Patrick   That's right you adjust, check out the towns you play in . . . And soon you're bored, you'd be surprised at their relentless monotony, you've seen what's on at the movies, you're sick of each other's company, but that's okay, that happens, you've got adjusted and then you can't wait for the end . . .

Paul   That doesn't sound too good!

Patrick   Well, it depends, like when you're a young buck, right, then there's adventure in the skin trade . . . You're a juv, a juvenile lead . . . Soon as you arrive at the theatre for the first time you make a bee-line for the nearest piece of female flesh, 'cause she may be your only sanctuary, your sex life, company . . . Oh, it can get so lonely, so very lonely . . .

Paul   So the women were the rafts to take you across the great lakes of loneliness?

Patrick   Oh, so nicely put, yes, exactly, and as you are for them – it's not a one-sided transaction . . . Oh yes, such vitality, adventures, little day trips to the surrounding countryside, quiet dinners together . . . That's good . . . So necessary . . .

Paul   And after?

Patrick   After . . . You get back to London . . . you're back and it falls apart . . . it crumbles . . . Slowly, bit at a time, like stale bread . . . Since the structure that held it together is gone . . . It might linger on for a while . . . You see each other for a while . . . then she gets a job . . . or you do, and the chemistry isn't there . . . It goes . . . It's a shame . . . And so you start all over again.

Paul   Why should it crumble? You have everything in common . . . You worked together, you're both actors . . . You have common interests, it should in fact grow . . . Should, I think . . . I mean what's more intimate than working together? . . . I used to love that . . . Acting together with someone I loved.

Patrick   Well, it was kept together in a way . . . artificially . . . You really believe you both love each other but that's because you really both need each other, need each other to survive, 'cause you're both strangers in the town and to the company . . . You know no one else . . . You both grab on to each other . . . Need the comfort . . . desperately . . . Look forward to the end of each performance . . . to hold each other . . . It's an adventure, and the play binds you even more tightly together,

so somehow all the elements hold you in a special place . . .
The outer world disappears.

Paul   So when you both return . . . Now that you know and
love each other why can't you evolve your own structure . . .
You've gone through something together that gave you both
sustenance, nourishment . . . love. Otherwise . . . otherwise
you're saying that without the job . . . without being employed,
your life has no meaning, no shape? That would be terrible . . .
To be so vulnerable . . . That's sad.

Patrick   Yes, that is terrible, pathetic, but somehow that's
how it is . . . Terrible . . . When you're working, no matter
where, for a while you're a king, a king of your little fantasy
kingdom and then you're dethroned and so you search for
another kingdom . . . What do you do, you wait . . . You hang
around, see each other but listlessly, not so many friends since
your mates are the company, your actors, and you're a subject,
you might even see another woman that you hadn't quite
finished with . . . The city's vast and you get swallowed back
into your little groove . . . she in hers . . . Somehow when you're
back she looks a little plainer then you thought she was . . .
and maybe she is plainer since it was the work that watered
her and made her flush with excitement, it was the town, it
was us, in that town, in that work, in our little world, so how
could we now, both of us, not be plainer, drier . . . Dull.

Paul   Oh dear . . . Oh dear . . .

Patrick   Yeah, but that's the good side . . . If you manage to
find someone suitable . . . That's good, but if you don't . . . Ow!

Paul   Yes . . . ow!

Patrick   Then on a tour . . . Oh my God, those endless
weeks in those drab, grim British towns, the days weigh like
lead on you, like some huge burden you're carrying around
and that's . . . you! Your terrible loneliness . . . That's terrible
. . . But you try . . . make an effort . . . join a gym, discount
for the touring actors, see all the films, read a bit . . . But if

you're lucky and a young buck you might score with a local bitch . . . That's quite romantic . . .

Paul   Why, why more than the actress you work with?

Patrick   Because she's there, all the time, lives there, and you are just passing through, she's maybe a shop assistant or something and she looks up to you as something rather exotic and even mysterious. You're from London, you're an actor . . . And how do you learn all those lines? Then in a week you're gone, like it was all a dream . . .

Paul   In my early days in the theatre there used to be a summer season, each summer the theatre would re-open since the theatre died in the winter just like the flowers and trees, just curled up until the spring . . . And sometimes even the same actors would return . . . And be looked forward to . . . Usually in seaside or pretty tourists towns . . . from May to September . . . The summer season.

Patrick   Yeah, the summer season . . . I did that . . .

Paul   In the summer season you don't have the time to get bored, not like touring with one show only and when it's on waiting for the long days to pass . . . Oh, that can be terrible, oh yes, but in the summer season you rehearse each and every day . . . Oh, you've no time to get bored, or lonely, and once the play opens, once the first night is over, you all meet the next morning and begin blocking the next one . . . Ha ha, oh my God, it was never-ending, and you craved a day off! Yes, the very next day you're in the theatre blocking the next play, and then you have lunch and spend the afternoon learning the first act! And of course at nights you do the play you just opened, and it's good, 'cause you're into it now, the first scary night being over . . . The next morning you actually run the whole first act . . . have lunch and go home and learn the second act, and repeat the performances at night. Well into it now, the third night . . . And after the show a drink in the local, but not too much since you need to run the lines before you go to bed, the lines for the next morning's rehearsal! Ha ha. So just one drink . . . In the local, where the actors go . . . And that's where I met her, yes there in the pub, and she smiled as if to acknowledge that she knew I was one of the actors, and had maybe enjoyed the show . . . Then we ran the second act in the morning and if there was a third as there usually was in those days we learned that in the afternoon and then it was the fourth performance or the Friday and this time I went to the pub I looked for her. Yes, I was in a state of anticipation . . . of seeing her . . . I was hopeful . . . Had built that smile the night before in my mind, imbued it with fantasy.

Patrick   Or of worse. I know.

Paul   Of meeting her and, yes, she was there but I had just bought a drink and sat with the actors and she smiles and I smile across the room, but I couldn't get up and speak to her since I was talking to the actors about the show and didn't want to break it . . . Didn't want to leave them . . . so visibly . . . But I sensed we would be lovers, knew something was special between us . . .

Patrick   So? You did eventually talk to her. You chatted her up and made a date?

Paul   Not quite, but just as we were leaving, the pub was closing, I said 'hello' and she 'hello'd back . . . Her voice was all gurgling, a little shyly excited, like a gurgling brook, a slender brook that winds it's way through the Peak District since that's where the theatre was situated, amongst the hills in the Peak District . . . within a valley, and her voice was of the valley, was of that area, and such a smile, such a radiance.

Patrick   Ha ha!

Paul   It was dazzling . . . unreal . . . And she said she had liked the show, since the night before she went to see it . . . Her hair was rich chestnut brown and her eyes were as shining agates.

Patrick   Oh! Sounds like you fell! A bit heavy I should say . . . Oh yes, one of those.

Paul   Oh yes, it was one of those, summer seasons, since it could only happen in the summer, only then, since in the winter we didn't exist . . . And on the Saturday we ran the next week's play in the morning and at night did the final performance of the week since we ran a play for only a week!

Patrick   I know, best training in the world, your brain's on full alert!

Paul   Then the play was done, over, and I rushed, yes rushed, into the pub, and yes, she was there, she was, yes, yes, I remember it so clearly, her being there . . . Like a reward for my efforts . . .

Patrick   Oh God, how we need that for sure, a reward . . .

Paul   So she was there . . . Like, as if, she knew, she sensed . . . My yearning . . . My longing, for her, sensed it . . . Was drawn to it . . . Somehow . . .

Patrick   Hey! I suppose it was chemistry, that's all, a big hungry lust . . . That's good, that's beautiful, but it's amazing what a little fantasy does for you in a lonely town . . .

Paul   So, on Sunday, we arranged to meet . . . to go for a walk, 'cause that's what you do on a Sunday in the country, walk . . . And so we did, the day was perfect, sunny, windy, typical moors day, and so we walked across the moor, or rather we leapt, from rock to rock, had to, would be tiring to just walk, and then we lay on the bracken on the summit, lay there with the wind in our ears, and then we kissed, our first, sealed it with a kiss.

Patrick   Ha ha!

Paul   But what I didn't know, what I failed to see . . . was that this was magic, unreal, the circumstances, me being there, in that small town, in that summer season, and the moors, that were there for ever and for so many feet of young men and women . . . walking, climbing up the moors, and we needed nothing else . . . Only each other and we loved each other . . . Even then . . . even at the beginning . . . Such a smile, perfect love, such a warm soothing sweet love . . . In love . . . Sweet, gently warm . . .

Patrick   Yes, it was magic . . . It always is . . . For that time . . . In that place . . . And then? She kicked you out . . . It came to an end . . .

Paul   No not really . . . But it's like . . . what you said . . . a fantasy . . . Perhaps . . . The place, my work as a low-paid actor in a little repertory theatre, a strange little town, but my youth flourished there, came alive there, but she was born there, born of who knows how many generations and so we were destined to meet there, to come together, to be lovers there in that summer season . . .

Patrick   A holiday romance! I told you. But you get back to your own environment, your city and your star has dimmed, no longer on that stage, a nightly deity, to be admired, envied, smiled at, to be waited for, to look for, to be excited by the thought of the end of the evening. When you have her . . . to see . . . waiting for you, and then? I know . . . The dinner together in the Chinese restaurant at the top of the hill, and laughing, giggling, gushing . . . Looking at, feeling, smelling, holding hands . . .

Paul   That's right!

Patrick   Can you eat, can you barely eat your chicken chop suey, then strolling home, under the stars, oh the wonders of love . . . And then it goes, like a play you're in, it has to end, slowly it goes, you get home and there's a letter each week, an occasional phone call, but her letters are soft and just a tad, maybe sloshy, aren't they . . .

Paul   Ha ha! Of course, what else?

Patrick   And she quotes poetry in them, she writes about the past, your past and yet it was only weeks ago . . . One day she comes to London and meets your two and a half friends and maybe your mum. But you're no longer up there on the stage each night . . . In her small town, you're now an exiled king, a fallen star, you're unemployed, your light's gone out . . .

for a while . . . But she stills loves you, you are a city boy . . .
She comes to London . . . She has pinned a lot of unexpressed
hopes on you . . . hopes she dare not express, give words to . . .
But secretly hopes . . . oh, so much hope you carry in your
heart . . . A hope, for her . . . For a life with her . . . But you
don't like being exposed as an unemployed actor . . .

Paul   True!

Patrick   A low thing because without your role . . . your
character . . . you are partially without a personality, you are
a no . . . thing. But she doesn't care . . . She doesn't care . . .
She's almost relieved in some way to see you brought back to
Earth . . . as you . . . But you can take it . . . Can you . . .
Silent, a being without a function? You could take it . . . Not
give a damn . . . Work at anything, just so you could keep the
bright beautiful love alive and, yes, maybe she'd love you
more . . . by admiring you less . . . But where are you? Yes,
where are you . . . You threw away a pearl did you . . . in
your summer season.

Paul   Maybe, maybe, maybe it was only meant to last for
that summer season . . . maybe it was . . .

Patrick   But you're not a season are you? You are for life!
Not a fruit or a flower that lasts a season?

Paul   No. True, it's true what you say. We know we last a
lifetime, but at that particular time, at that moment in time . . .
everything seemed to fit into that time, like she belonged to
that time . . . And that town and the hills and moors and
pretending to be Heathcliff and Cathy and I belonged to that
time . . . And when it was over something seemed to go . . . to
slowly dissolve . . . The love was there, the feeling was there,
but what supported, what nourished it . . . was gone . . . like
props in a mineshaft . . . Then it collapsed . . . although I did
see her . . . She came to London and we saw each other . . .
Sometimes . . . She took a bedsit in Belsize Park . . . She found a
job . . . in an office . . . But I saw her less. I should have seized
her and shown her my life!

Patrick   Should! Should have! What a filthy word is should, what a vile terrible word . . .

Paul   Yes . . . A terrible word . . .

Patrick   Shown her life, your life, no matter how frail, how poor, your life . . . But you were young, vital, ambitious . . . There's more fish in the sea . . . But you had no life to show, did you . . . You existed like a dummy in a shop window waiting to be dressed . . . Afraid to show your nakedness . . . But we're all naked . . .

Paul   So true!

Patrick   Underneath we're all naked! And does it matter . . . ? Let her see you naked . . . not just in bed but in life . . . Naked. Stark bollock naked . . . In bed we are so naked, so purely naked, but then you have so much to give . . . Then you give your body, your love, your desire, you're so rich in giving, so so abundant in the riches of youth, which makes you richer than the richest millionaire . . . makes you the richest man in the world and her the richest woman . . . Oh, how lucky you were to meet . . . to ignite those fires in both of you . . . The background was nothing . . . that's all it was, background, but you . . . you, she can change your background a hundred times . . . You live . . . you live now . . . a spark ignited after a billon years of space!

Paul   Yeah maybe. Should have . . . ugh!

Patrick   Yes . . . ugh!

Paul   But maybe it was not meant to be . . .

Patrick   Oh howl! Howl! Howl! Is that what King Lear says to the storm? . . . Howl your head off . . . for it cannot begin to match the storm inside my soul . . .

Paul   Why so emphatic, when you were just saying that you . . . You experienced that . . . Those fleeting adventures . . . And then the downward slope . . . the return to normality . . .

Patrick   Yes . . . yes, I did . . . 'Cause I did experience just that exactly that so I know, yes, and condemn it in myself just as I see it in you . . . So what happens . . . ? You don't commit . . . You start again and where do you end up? A series of broken affairs . . . Broken like shattered pottery . . . You start again and yet again and then one day . . . you look in the mirror and guess what you see? A lonely old wreck of a human being . . . a wreck that shat on every opportunity.

Paul   Maybe . . . Maybe . . . Yes . . .

Patrick   Aah . . . The memories, she still keeps you alive, doesn't she?

Paul   She does . . . Her memory does . . . Keeps me alive . . . I see her as she was, eternally young.

Patrick   Of course, they always remain young . . . How crazy . . . We grieve scores of years later . . . For something we might so easily have had . . . A road we were too timid to go down . . .

Paul   We nearly did . . .

Patrick   Another terrible word nearly. You nearly did . . . But . . . ?

Paul   She didn't make anything of it . . . She didn't make a fuss . . . She had an abortion, but she didn't want to involve me . . .

Pause.

Patrick   Oh, perfect . . . So you not only lose your love, this beautiful love of your youth . . . You help to kill its fruit . . . Oh . . . Howl!

Paul   Yes . . . Howl! Howl! Howl! Indeed . . .

Slow fade as the two just stare at each other with the pain etched across their faces as is for ever.

This is an Emergency

Characters

Brian, *actor, unemployed, in his mid-sixties but still optimistic and wishing to work, intelligent and sensitive*

Barbra, *his wife, mid-fifties, attractive, even voluptuous, who loves and supports him but is getting increasingly frustrated with her husband's lack of drive*

Joe, *a large, loutish but strangely attractive minicab driver who invades their lives one evening*

Voices, *offstage*

Brian   So anything on the telly?

Barbra   Dunno, haven't looked . . . Why don't you check the papers.

Brian (*does so*)   It's Clint Eastwood in *Pale Rider* . . . That's good . . .

Barbra   Seen it dozen times . . .

Brian   *The Ring*?

Barbra   Oh God, no!

Brian   *Casablanca*?

Barbra   Help!

Brian   *Willy Wonka and the Chocolate Factory*?

Barbra   I wanna gag!

Brian   Well, that's all, until nine p.m. . . .

Barbra   Don't wanna stay up till nine p.m. then . . .

Brian   Let's check what's on the documentary channel . . . Wanna see wild life in Kenya?

Barbra   You see one lion, you've seen them all . . . Anyway, I can't bear to watch them catching some poor beast and tearing it to pieces. It's like a porn show!

Brian   Oh! There's a play or docu about the Moors Murders, but it's not on till nine p.m.

Barbra   Quite like to see that . . . Yeah. I would . . .

Brian   So we'll try to stay up . . . OK?

Barbra   OK, whatever you like . . . But I must have an early night . . .

Brian   Yeah, you always say that . . . Must have an early night . . . But what do you do all day that makes you so tired . . . ?

Barbra   What do I do?

Brian   Yeah, I mean you don't go to work . . . You don't have to get up and jump on the tube, and then pack a hard day's work in . . . Do you, eh? I mean. let's be fair . . .

Barbra   I do plenty . . . Looking after you's a full-time job . . .

Brian   Yeah sure!

Barbra   . . . Going to the supermarket, buying the food, cleaning the house, washing your stinking knickers, dealing with the bills, cooking your food, making sure you got variety, entertaining the cat, then listening to your problems . . . Which are endless . . . You've got a full-time shrink in me . . . Plenty to do . . . 'What do you do?' . . . Don't make me laugh!

Brian   Oh thanks . . . Whenever I come in the door all I see you do is reading magazines . . .

Barbra   Oh sure, that's all I do, sit around reading glossy mags! And the food gets on the table by magic. Believe me, I do plenty but I don't see you doing much . . .

Brian   Believe me, I also do plenty . . . I go out and earn the wages . . .

Barbra   What you talking about . . . You haven't worked in months, you chump!

Brian   Oh thanks, rub it in . . . As if I didn't know it . . . It's quiet at the moment . . . A lot of actors are out of work . . . Running up to Christmas . . . It's tough. I'd love to be out working every day . . . But it's quiet.

Barbra   So you should change your agent . . . He doesn't seem to get you very much.

Brian   He does his best . . . There's not so much about.

Barbra   Obviously not . . . You've been saying that for a few years . . .

Brian   That's an actor's life . . . It's up and down, you can take it or leave it . . .

Barbra Oh yeah. I think then that you should leave it . . .

Brian You really believe that . . . That I should give up what's been my life?

Barbra It seems, my old darling, to have given you up . . . Sorry.

Brian One has to accept it . . . It'll change . . .

Barbra So, and don't get your knickers in a twist, so why not get another job . . . Just something to fill in, part-time, a lot of actors do that. It also gives them some pride . . . Some independence . . .

Brian Yeah, sure . . .

Barbra Yeah, that's right, so they're not just waiting for the phone to ring . . . Like some poor dumb tart waiting for a bloke that couldn't care less . . . Work makes you into a man . . . Unemployment feminisies you . . . Turns you into a drip . . . Hanging about the house . . . Always whining . . . That's the worst . . . The bloody whining . . .

Brian OK, don't make my life more of a misery than you have to . . .

Barbra I'm just trying to give you a little push . . . Get the motor running . . . That's all . . . That's all . . .

Brian I know.

Barbra I mean, I don't like to see you . . . getting depressed, hanging about, tormenting yourself . . .

Brian Like I said, it's part and parcel of being . . . an actor . . .

Barbra Yeah, I know, you keep saying that . . . But darling, it's a game for wankers . . . Yeah, I mean, think of all those actors hanging about . . . Drifting, begging for a bit of work, phoning their agents for a bit of reassurance . . . What a wanky way to live . . . Always waiting . . . Waiting for some ponce to give you a little job . . . A little playtime . . . Then you're back on the slagheap again . . . Get a life!

Brian   Yeah, well . . .

Barbra   Yeah! So get a fucking job and get your self-esteem back again.

Brian   Yeah . . . You're right . . .

Barbra   Yeah, you will, believe me you will . . .

Brian   Yeah, yeah, I know you're right . . . I'll think of something . . . Something part-time . . . Till something better turns up.

Barbra   There you see, you'll feel better, a lot better . . . You'll . . . you'll be alive, using yourself . . . Otherwise you've no life . . . Like you're dead . . . Yeah . . . I mean a man without a purpose to get up in the morning is a dead thing . . . I'm sorry . . . I have to tell you . . .

Brian   Yeah, you're right, I feel dead at times . . . I do . . .

Barbra   Course you do . . . It's natural . . . You've a good brain and it's going to waste, and you're a good actor . . . But if it's not used . . . Then you become just another hopeless bum . . . That's terrible . . . It is . . . Sometimes I think acting is such a wanker's life . . .

Brian   I used to work all the time, at one time I was hardly out of work . . .

Barbra   Yeah . . . 'at one time'. Now it's *this* time . . . Maybe you're past it, maybe now you're getting older, they don't need you so much . . . So why wait for them to throw you on the junk heap? . . . Get weaving!

Brian   OK, OK yeah . . . So what do you think I should do? Eh? I mean I hear what you're saying but what else can I do?

Barbra   Brian! Cor, there's a million things you can do . . . Once you get going you'll find a million things . . . Once you get over this waiting for the bloody phone to ring like some old tart . . . You block out life, block out the possibility of communicating, bonding, working with millions of others . . . 'Cause you're trapped in the thinking of a wanker . . . ! You don't see the life, I mean there's a life out there, mister!

Brian Yeah, you're making sense.

Barbra Course . . . Once you start, you'll amaze yourself at all the possibilities . . . You will . . . And you might . . . yes, yes even might . . . get happy again! Oh, that would be something, wouldn't it, to see a happy expression on your face again? . . . That really would be something.

Brian Ha ha! For sure, ha ha, that certainly would be something . . . !

Barbra Ya see, you're laughing again . . . You're getting into it . . . like even the thought of leaving a prison . . .

Brian So, what do you think I should do?

Barbra You know what?

Brian What . . . ?

Barbra I tell you what . . . It doesn't matter a monkey's toss what you do . . . As long as you're out . . . I tell you something . . . If you got a job washing dishes in some big hotel you'd be more alive than you are now! It doesn't matter. It really doesn't matter . . . You've got to do something . . . So anything will do . . . Whatcha think you could do?

Brian Washing dishes?

Barbra I just used that as an example. In my mind, work, even any work, gives you more dignity than hanging around like a dead soul.

Brian Thank God you don't use that word 'wanker' again . . .

Barbra   Just used that as an example, to jolt you a bit . . .
But in my mind any work is better than drifting round the
streets. That's all I'm saying . . .

Brian   Yeah, thanks, I'm sixty-four, that's a good way to
end up, washing dishes . . .

Barbra   Still better than drifting, anything's better than
that . . . Just using it as an example . . . And I'm thinking of
you . . . I'm thinking of your welfare . . . and your mental
state.

Brian   Thanks.

Long silence.

No, but you're right . . . You are . . . I know . . . It's not a
life . . .

Barbra   That's all I'm saying . . . That's what I'm trying to
tell you.

Brian   Yeah, I know.

Barbra   Not trying to upset you . . . Not having a go at
you . . . You know that, don't you?

Brian   Course.

Barbra   Course you do . . . So what do you think?

Brian   What do I think?

Barbra   Yeah . . . what do you think?

Brian   What do I think?

Barbra   Yeah . . . what do you think?

Brian   I'll look for something to do . . . Doesn't matter
what . . .

Barbra   Course it doesn't matter . . . Just until something
turns up . . . But in the meantime you'll step into life again.

Brian   Yeah, don't want to be a wanker!

Barbra   Course you don't. It's terrible, for a grown man, for an intelligent man, and you're not a wanker . . . I just said that, didn't mean that you are . . . No, just that you'll turn into one.

Brian   So, I'll try to think of what I can do . . .

Barbra   That's the first step.

Brian   I could teach, teach kids acting . . .

Barbra   You'd be good, you'd be very good at that . . .

Brian   But that takes time . . . Sending in applications and waiting and then you're booked for a term so you can rarely take off when an acting job comes up . . .

Barbra   You need something you can just dive into . . .

Brian   I could . . . I could drive a minicab . . .

Barbra   Well, that's a start . . . Yeah, that's a start . . . You'd meet lots of people. And you could pick it up or drop it as it suits you, meet lots of people . . . have responsibilities.

Brian   Yeah . . . Makes sense . . .

Barbra   What else . . . Catering . . . Catering's OK . . . I used to do that. There's an agency that finds you work . . . Lot of actors go there . . . Like waiting tables, pub work, that's easy, working behind the bar in a pub . . . I did that, it's not difficult . . . Meet lots of people . . . Easy work, the hours can be a mite long but when you're busy they fly . . . But you get used to it . . . And it's easy to learn, just pulling pumps and opening bottles . . . It's not hard . . .

Brian   Yeah, maybe I could do that . . . I'll make some enquiries, but maybe I'm too old . . . Don't they want young people?

Barbra   Maybe, but you never know until you ask . . . They might like someone a bit more mature . . . a bit more responsible . . .

Brian   Hmm. I could try that.

Barbra   Yeah, then you're out . . . you're in the flow

Brian   Yeah . . .

Barbra   Or . . . you could go into retail . . . They always need salesmen, like in one of those big stores . . . Not a boutique, maybe they wouldn't have you there, it's all tarts and teeny boppers . . . But a big store . . .

Brian   But you can't take time off . . . not easily.

Barbra   Yeah, suppose . . . It's worth a try . . . You could ask, just ask . . . See, got you thinking . . . That's a start . . . That's . . . See what they say . . .

Brian   OK, lots to think about . . .

Barbra   Course . . . At least it's got you thinking . . . That's a start . . . That's a step forward . . .

Brian   But I'm thinking.

Barbra   OK, what you thinking?

Brian   I'm thinking . . . Suppose . . . I mean just suppose I'm working in a pub, OK?

Barbra   Yeah?

Brian   Serving drinks, wiping down tables, all that stuff . . .

Barbra   Yeah . . . OK.

Brian   Then in walks a casting director, or maybe some actors . . . whom I know . . . whom I've worked with . . . right? They're working and have just popped in the pub and there I am like a skivvy pulling pints . . . And they see me . . . see me wiping tables . . . How do you think I'd feel? I, an actor, who may have worked with these same actors in the West End . . . On the telly . . . Seeing me work in a pub?

Barbra   . . . So what? . . . So fucking what? What, you'd feel ashamed?

Brian   Even now . . . at the thought of it . . . feel the blood rising . . . my gorge rising in shame . . .

Barbra   I understand that, but it's bollocks . . . But I do understand that . . . And it takes a bit of guts. I know, but remember, they don't *keep you*! They don't pay the rent.

Brian   I know that but . . . I mean . . . Let's face it . . . Wouldn't feel good . . .

Barbra   Yeah, I can see that . . . *But*, if you say to yourself . . . I DON'T GIVE A MONKEYS FUCK! Then there's no shame . . . None, they might even admire you . . .

Brian   Ha! Sure, admire me!

Barbra   They'd admire you . . . that you don't care . . . Just takes a little guts . . . and I'm not sure you got the guts . . . Have you?

Brian   What, you think I've got no guts? That's what you think isn't it . . . ?

Barbra   Course you got guts, just winding you up, any idiot can work in a pub . . . Doesn't take guts . . . But for you it would, 'cause for you it's different . . .

Brian   When it's *needed* I got guts.

Barbra   Course you have . . . So we'll forget the pub . . .

Brian   Yeah, I think so.

Long silence. He smokes.

Barbra   But the minicab, what about the minicab?

Brian   Hmm . . .

Barbra   That's better . . . That maybe better . . . I mean you might pick up someone you know . . . but it's much less likely, and if you do, so what, you can handle that . . .

Brian   Yeah, I can sure . . . I think I could handle that . . . At least I would be a driver . . . not a skivvy in stinking pub . . .

Barbra   But that may never happen, an outside chance
that you'd pick up someone who knows you. and if you did,
so what? . . . Eh? So effin' what . . . You're grafting . . . Lots
of actors drive minicabs between jobs.

Brian   Yeah, they do . . .

Barbra   Then you're out, you're out, you're in the world,
you're in the swim . . . You're *functioning*.

Brian   Functioning . . . yeah . . .

Barbra   So give them a ring . . .

Brian   What, now?

Barbra   Why not, whilst your spirits up . . . Whilst you're
in the mood . . . I'll get the Yellow Pages. (*She gets the book.*) I
mean, make the first step, a small step for an actor but a great
leap for mankind! Ha ha ha!

Brian   Yeah, a huge leap!

Barbra   Look, you can only ask . . . See, there's loads of
numbers . . . Just pick one.

Brian   Christ, there's so many . . .

Barbra   So start at the top . . .

Brian (*dials*)   Hello, Dalston minicab service?

Voice   Yeah . . . Ya need a cab?

Brian   Er, no, actually I'm ringing to see if you're taking on
any drivers . . .

Voice   'Old on . . . Joe!

Silence and then another equally gruff voice.

Joe's Voice   'Allo, can I help you?

Brian   Yes, I'm wondering if you need, er, drivers?

Joe's Voice   Yeah, we always need good drivers . . .

Barbra (*whispering*)   You see!

Joe's Voice   'Ad any experience driving minicabs . . . ?

Brian   Not not really . . . but I'm a good driver, clean licence
. . . Oh and I know London well.

Joe's Voice   So what's your regular job, then?

Brian   Well, I'm an actor . . . or used to be . . . Ha ha!

Joe's Voice (*to someone*)   Got an actor on the phone, wants a
job . . . ! Well, don't think I can help you, mate!

Brian   But, why is that?

Voice (*coughing, smoker's cough*)   Insurance! Insurance too high
mate . . . for actors . . .

Brian   . . . Oh, I see . . .

Joe's Voice   Unless you drive your own car you're
responsible for all insurance.

Brian   Of course . . .

Joe's Voice (*hang on*)   Yeah . . . 'E's got 'is own motor, yeah,
yeah . . . Awright . . . (*Back to* **Brian**.) Wot car ya got?

Brian   Hmm it's a Merc . . .

Joe's Voice   . . . Yeah, OK, what year?

Brian   It's about ten years old . . .

Joe's Voice   What registration?

Brian   It's a Y registration . . .

Joe's Voice   Might get away wiv it . . . 'Ow old are you,
mister?

Brian   Er . . . Coming up to sixty-four . . .

Joe's Voice   Ow! Sorry, mate. Sixty's the limit here. Nah,
sorry, mate . . . Too old for us, some other firms might take
you on . . .

Brian   Bloody hell. I'm fit, I see well and I'm a good driver . . .

Joe's Voice   That's the rules . . .

Brian   Stupid rules . . .

Joe's Voice   Look, don't get all stroppy, I tried to 'elp ya, I don't make the rules, right!

Brian (*sarcastic*)   Oh yeah, I'm sure you don't . . .

Joe's Voice   . . . 'Scuse me . . . But you takin' the piss?!

Brian   I just said I'm sure you don't . . . You don't sound like you could make up your mind . . .

Joe's Voice (*loud*)   Listen, you tosspot, don't get lippy when I tried to fuckin' 'elp you out . . .

Brian   Stupid moron!

Joe's Voice   Listen, cunt . . . You want some of it . . . eh? – I'll be round your gaff quicker then you can wank . . . You fuckin' pooftah . . . I got your number . . . WANKAAAA!

Brian *hangs up, visibly shaken.*

Barbra   You shouldn't have insulted him . . . Shouldn't have done that, Brian . . .

Brian   Bastard!

Barbra   Shouldn't have . . . It's your fault . . . You were sarcastic . . . You OK?

Brian   Dirty yob!

Barbra   Course he was . . . So you should have just hung up!

Brian   Do you . . . do you think he'll come round?

Barbra   Course not . . . He's just a yob . . . Having a vent . . . Anyway . . . hasn't got our address, only the number.

Brian   He can find the address from that?

Barbra   Nooo! He was only letting off steam 'cause you called him a moron . . . Silly boy you are!

Brian   Well, he was . . .

Barbra   For sure, but you can't start insulting people 'cause they're morons, just be polite and get off the phone . . .

He (*still shaking*)   Yeah . . .

Barbra   You wanna try another number?

Brian   I think I need a drink . . .

Barbra   Silly boy, ha ha! I'll get you a nice drink

She gets drink and gives it to him. He takes it . . . Silence for a while.

Brian   So you don't think . . .

Barbra   No! He's not coming round . . . It's more than his job's worth . . . But it's a lesson . . . Just keep cool in future . . . You never know who you're dealing with . . . I mean, these are not actors . . . They are real people . . .

Brian   What a dodgy lot . . . eh? These bloody minicab drivers . . .

Barbra   Yeah, well . . . I'm sure they're not all like that . . . But for some it's a last resort . . . Some are ex-jailbirds . . . Can't get any other work . . . Not like the black cabs . . .

Brian   I'll try something else . . .

Barbra   Course you will . . . There's a thousand things for an intelligent, healthy man to do . . . You know . . . I think that's why he got so upset . . . He could hear you were an intelligent bloke . . . And he's just a yob . . . Felt humiliated . . .

Phone rings. They're startled. Suddenly all normal things are filled with terror.

Barbra   . . . You wanna answer it?

Brian   Let it go on the answerphone . . .

Joe's Voice (*slight chuckle as if he indicates he knows they're there*)
Hallo! . . . The cab you ordered is outside . . . Waitin' . . . It's
a pale blue car . . . OK! (*Hangs up.*)

Brian (*in shock*)   He's come! The bastard found our address .
. . How did he do that!?

Barbra   Dunno, I dunno, maybe our number's on the
computer . . . I mean, we called lots of minicabs over the
years . . . maybe this one . . . How should I know?

Brian   I'll call the police . . .

Barbra   What will you say?

Brian   I'll say we're being threatened.

Barbra   Wait! Maybe they made a mistake . . . 'Cause you
rang . . . Maybe the switchboard made a mistake . . .

Brian   No, it was the same bloke, the loony that threatened
me . . .

Barbra   Dunno, all those working-class yobs sound alike to
me . . .

Brian   I'll call the police . . . At least they'll get it sorted . . .

*Phone rings. Louder. They watch frozen, waiting for the answerphone
to come on.*

Joe's Voice   'Allo, I'm waiting for ya . . . Blue car . . . just
outside . . . I know you're there . . . The meter's tickin', the
longer I wait the more it's gonna cost ya . . .

She (*suddenly grabs the phone*)   I'm sorry but there's been a
mistake, we didn't order a cab . . . So please go away!

Slams phone down. Both are shaken. **Brian** *pours another drink.*

Brian   He's a fuckin' madman, he's mad . . .

Barbra   Yeah, maybe . . . Call the law.

Brian   Yeah, I bloody will, I can't believe it! (*He dials.*)

Voice   Fire, police or ambulance?

Brian   Er, police please . . . It's an emergency . . .

Voice   What area are you in . . . ?

Brian   Hackney, E8.

Voice   One moment . . .

Phone rings several times.

Police Voice   Hallo, Dalston Police Station, how can I help you?

Brian   Er, I'm being threatened . . . with violence.

Police Voice   Threatened by who sir?

Brian   By a minicab driver . . . There was a bit of an argument and he verbally threatened me . . . and now he's come over to our house . . . He's waiting just outside the door!

Police Voice   OK. sir, just calm down and give me your address . . .

Brian   20 Dalston Lane, Flat 1B.

Police Voice   And your name is . . . ?

Brian   Brian Phillips

Police Voice   You the owner of the flat?

Brian   Yes! And he's outside now . . . He threatened me and now he's come.

Police Voice   He's outside, you say?

Brian   Yes, yes, do you think you could send someone?

Police Voice   How did he threaten you? Verbally or physically?

Brian   No, no just on the phone . . .

Police Voice   So you had a row on the phone and it got a bit . . . out of hand.

Brian   Yes! Yes!

Police Voice   What exactly did he say . . .

Brian   Oh, blimey, er, 'I'll be round your gaff . . .' Er, 'Quicker than you can wank!' Something like that and other insults.

Police Voice   Hmm. And now you say, this same man has turned up . . .

Brian   Yes, yes, he's outside . . . waiting . . .

Police Voice   What's the number of the minicab service . . . ?

Brian   Just a minute please . . . (*To her.*) Get the number of the cab . . . The NUMBER OF THE MINICAB!

Barbra   OK, OK . . .

She finds it and hands it over.

Brian   Oh, here y'are . . . 88410072. Smartcabs.

Police Voice   OK, we're a bit busy tonight, being a Friday, but we'll look into it . . . And call you back . . .

Brian   So, you're not coming round?

Police Voice   We'll look into it, we'll contact your driver, so stay by your phone . . .

Brian   OK, thanks . . . Thanks very much . . . (*Hangs up.*) So they are on the case!

Barbra   What a bloody business . . .

Brian   God! I love the police . . . Sometimes when you need them . . . they're like . . . God

Barbra   Yeah, but they're not coming round, are they?

Brian   No . . . But they'll sort it . . . He said he would . . . Hope he nabs the bastard . . .

Silence for several seconds.

Think he's still there . . .

Barbra   Don't really like to look . . .

Brian   Peek out . . .

She (*she does so, very carefully*)   Yeah, I think . . . I see something
. . . a car with its lights on . . . Yeah, maybe it's him . . .

Brian   So the police haven't contacted him yet . . .

Barbra   Don't worry, they will . . .

Phone blasts into sound.

Police Voice   Hallo, Mr Phillips?

Brian   Yes, yes!

Police Voice   We just rang the taxi firm, Smartcabs . . .

Brian   Yes?

Police Voice   They claim there's been a mistake . . .

Brian   Mistake?

Police Voice   They thought you needed a cab.

Brian   But the man threatened me!

Police Voice   Well, they've given me their side of the
story . . . which is that you were rude to one of their drivers . . .
Called him a moron. Did you do that?

Brian   Only after he insulted me, was abusive to me . . .

Police Voice   Yeah, well, every side has their own story,
but you can't go round insulting people. However, the callout
was a mistake . . . So no problem . . . OK . . .

Brian   But he's still there . . . Still outside my house.

Police Voice   Don't worry, just spoken to him . . . He'll be
on his way . . .

Brian   OK, OK, well, thank you . . . Oh wait . . . Do you mind if we check . . .

Police Voice   Go on . . .

Brian   Barb, is he still there?

She goes to window.

Barbra   Wait . . . Oh, he's going . . . he's driving off.

Brian   Yeah, he's just going, thank you so much!

Police Voice   OK, no problem . . . G'night. (*Hangs up.*)

Brian   Ahhhh! Thank God. Thank God for that. A real nice bloke. What would we do without a copper? . . . Worth their weight in gold . . .

Barbra   For sure.

Sound of car pulling up. Silence. They both stare at phone. Then phone burts into life. Goes to answerphone.

Joe's Voice   Just spoke to the Bill, nice geezer, all sorted . . . So I'm still waiting for ya . . . Are you coming out . . . ? It's gonna cost a lot of waiting time. I know ya there.

Breathing sounds, getting louder, sounds of cigarette being lit, smoke exhaling.

Brian   He's raving mad . . . Call the police!

Barbra   I can't! He's still on! He's blocking the line. He won't hang up!

Brian   Lift the phone off and then put it straight down. It'll cut him off.

Barbra *lifts phone off cradle and puts it down, waits, picks it up again.*

Joe's Voice (*still there*)   'Allo! 'Allo!

Barbra (*slams it down*)   Bastard's still there!

Brian   You have to give it a bit longer . . . It'll clear . . .

Barbra   What a fuckin' nightmare . . .

Brian   Use the bloody mobile!

Barbra   Forgot to recharge it!

Brian   Bloody hell . . . OK, try again.

Barbra (*slowly picks up phone*)   Oh thank God, he's hung up!

Brian   Thank fuck . . . So dial . . .

She does.

Voice   Fire, police or ambulance?

Barbra   Police please, it's an emergency . . .

Voice   What's your address, please?

Barbra   20 Dalston Lane, E8.

Voice   Name?

Barbra   Barbra Phillips . . .

Voice   One moment, we're experiencing a lot of calls tonight . . . I'll put you through as soon as possible.

We hear ringing tone.

Brian   Well?

Barbra   . . . It's ringing . . . Said they're busy . . .

Brian   Fucking hell. (*He grabs another drink.*)

Barbra   Still ringing . . .

Brian   You didn't say it was an emergency . . . You should have said that!

Barbra   Didn't I say that?

Brian   I said that before.

Barbra   Yeah, but only after they put you through.

Brian   Hang up and try again, tell them it's an emergency. Our lives are in danger . . .

Barbra   Go on, you do it . . . You're a bloke . . . Maybe they'll take more notice.

Brian *takes phone, puts it down, waits a moment, picks it up. Suddenly it bursts into life!*

Barbra *(snatches phone in fury)*   Why don't you go away! Just fuck off. Leave us alone. Leave us bloody well alone! You . . . sick pervert. *(She's just about to hang up.)*

Police Voice   This is the police, Dalston Station, we're responding to a call from Miss Barbra Philllips . . .

Barbra   Oooh! Sorry, so sorry . . . Please don't go, don't go! I thought it was him. He's back!

Police Voice   OK, calm down please . . . You're referring to the minicab nuisance call . . . Half hour or so ago?

Barbra   Yes! Yes!

Police Voice   We contacted the firm . . . Smartcabs . . . That right?

Barbra   Yes! Yes!

Police Voice   They claimed you called them for a cab at 8.09 p.m., they got your number on their callsheet, but then you cancelled, right?

Barbra   No, no! My husband called for a job . . . driving job . . .

Police Voice   You called for a job at eight o'clock at night?

Barbra   Yes, yes, it was the spur of the moment . . . You see my husband's an out-of-work actor . . . He was just looking for a part-time job . . .

Police Voice   Well, I had a word with him and it's sorted, they shouldn't be bothering you again but don't give people lip . . . No one likes that.

Barbra   We didn't, he threatened us . . .

Police Voice   Look at the lip you just gave me!

Barbra   Oh sorry, we thought it was him!

Police Voice   Why do you want to insult him?

Barbra   'Cause he's persecuting us . . . He's outside our house now . . . waiting for us . . .

Police Voice   He's outside now, you say?

Barbra   After we spoke to you before and you said then it was sorted he came back . . .

Brian (*looks through curtains*)   Hey, he's driving off . . .

Barbra   My husband says he's just driven off . . .

Police Voice   Look, sounds as if he's got something up his nose . . . But if he threatens you, don't exchange words, just call us. We'll check him out.

Barbra   Thank you, oh, thank you, sorry for all the trouble. (*Hangs up.*) Well, I think that's got to be the end of it.

Brian   Bloody hope so . . .

Barbra   The cop was nice . . . At least the bastard knows we're on his case . . .

Brian   Oh yes! OK, let's have a cuppa . . .

Barbra   Yeah, right.

Brian   Phew, what a bloody night!

Barbra   Yeah, it is . . .

Brian   Bloody police, useless, should just have come round . . . Should have come round and then they might have caught the bastard.

Barbra   But he had a word with him, scared him off, most of those drivers are ex-crims, it's the only work they can get.

Brian   Yeah, and that one sounded like fucking Jack the Ripper! Ha ha ha!

Barbra   'T's all we need . . . Ha ha ha ha!

Phone rings. They both look startled. They let it ring.

Brian   It's him!

Barbra   Yeah, 'spect it is!

Brian   What a bastard.

Barbra   Maybe it's the police again.

Brian   Don't think so.

Answerphone snaps on.

Joe's Voice (*thicker, angrier*)   Your cab's outside . . . I'm waitin', OK? I'm waitin' for ya . . .

Barbra   I've called the police . . . Go away!

Joe's Voice   It's sorted. The copper's OK . . . I told 'em . . . been a cock-up . . . but now it's sorted.

Barbra (*tearful*)   What do you want? . . . Why don't you leave us alone?

Joe's Voice   What do I want . . . What do you think a moron like me could want?

Barbra   Alright . . . We're sorry, OK, he's sorry he called you a moron . . .

Joe's Voice   He has to come outside and tell me, tell me face to face . . . that he's sorry.

She (*hands over phone*)   He wants you to go outside and apologise . . . Go on, won't take a minute, then it's all over . . .

Brian   . . . No, I'm not going outside . . . He's a madman . . . He could stick a knife into me . . . I'm not going outside!

Barbra   Look, he won't go outside . . . He'll apologise to you on the phone. (*Signals her husband to come over.*)

Joe's Voice   OK, I'll come inside. (*Hangs up.*)

Barbra   He said . . . he said . . . he's coming inside . . .

Brian   Call the police . . . Call the fucking police!

Barbra   It'll take too fucking long!

Brian   Call them, call them!

Barbra   You fucking call them . . . You got us into this!

Brian *fumbles with phone, eventually dials . . . Suddenly there is a knock . . . They freeze.*

Barbra   He's there.

Voice (*recorded voice comes on*)   We're receiving a high volume of calls so please hold on and an operator will be with you as soon as possible . . . If it's an emergency, please call 999.

Brian   Fucking hell, well, it's an emergency innit?!

Barbra   The police don't seem to think so or they would have come round.

Brian   Fucking hell!

Barbra (*goes to door*)   Please go away . . . The police are on the way!

Joe's Voice   Oh yeah . . .

Barbra   They'll take you away!

Voice   Told ya, it's sorted, he won't come . . . They think you're a nuisance call.

Barbra   So what do you bloody want? Who are you?

Joe's Voice   I'm Mr Moron . . . got it? OK.

Barbra   . . . Apologise . . . Go on and fucking apologise to him and then he'll go away.

Brian (*holding on to phone which is still just ringing*)   Oh, bloody hell . . .

Barbra   Go on!

Brian   Hold on to the phone (*She takes it.*) Look mate . . . I'm sorry . . . Yeah, didn't mean to call you a moron . . . Got a bit upset . . . OK?

Joe's Voice   To my face, pal, don't be a fuckin' coward. To my face!

Brian   . . . Can't do that . . . No. No . . . Can't trust you . . . You're violent.

Joe's Voice   I can bust this door down in two minutes.

Brian *looks at her, re phone – any answer?* **Barbra** *shakes her head.*

Barbra   Nothing . . . not answering . . .

Brian   Police will be here any minute . . .

Joe's Voice   I wouldn't be too sure about that . . . But I'll be there first!

Brian   If, if I open it . . . apologise . . . you'll go away? . . .

Joe's Voice   Course! Just want an apology, face to face, be a man about it . . . Not through a door . . .

Brian   Then you'll go away . . . ?

Joe's Voice   Listen, I said I would . . . Won't 'urtcha . . . I got a living to make, ain't I . . . ?

She (*still holding phone, shakes her head*)   NO! NO! NO!

Brian   I don't know if I can . . .

Suddenly there's a huge slam at the door.

Brian   Hey, stop that . . . Stop that!

Joe's Voice   Then open the door . . . Apologise . . . I'll go and you'll never see me again.

Brian   OK! OK!

He looks at **Barbra** *who grasps her head in torment.*

Brian OK . . .

He opens the door slowly . . . In walks a hard, huge working-class thug, **Joe**. *He looks around.*

They freeze. **Barbra** *puts phone down . . . It's all up. They expect the worst. Silence. They are all breathing hard.*

Joe What a fuckin' dump! . . . What a poxy shit-hole! So you're the fuckin' out-of-work ponce, actor?

Brian (*stammering*) I'm sorry, so sorry . . . I was out of . . . order . . . Yes! . . . I was . . .

Joe You was, weren'tcha?

Brian Yes . . . Er, yes, I was.

Joe (*silence for a while*) Your big bollocks on the phone aren'tcha? All mouth and fuckin' trousers . . . In the flesh . . . you're just a fuckin' tosser!

Brian Yeah . . . OK, you're right . . . I'm sorry . . . I really . . . am . . . I was stupid . . . Er, yeah . . .

Joe . . . What a pathetic heap of shit I'm looking at . . . What a fuckin' man! (*To* **Barbra**.) And you're married to this heap of shit . . . Poor you . . .

Barbra . . . Yeah . . . I am . . .

Joe You're not a bad-looking slag . . . You might have been a decent shag once. How come you ended up with that snivelling scumbag . . . ?

Barbra 'Cause I loved him. And er . . . I was pregnant . . .

Joe Fuck me . . . That's no reason for ya to tie yourself to a piece of shit for the rest of your fuckin' life . . .

Barbra Well, we all make mistakes . . . I s'pose . . .

Brian *looks at her in shock, but she slips him a look that she's just humouring* **Joe**.

Joe   Well, you certainly made one, poor cow . . . 'E's an actor is 'e, this last drop from his dad's balls?

Barbra   Hmm, yeah, sometimes . . .

Joe   Fuck me! Look at him . . . I mean, who'd want to pay to see that snivelly maggot?

Barbra   Well, he only does bits and pieces now . . .

Joe   Yeah, like what?

Barbra   Oh, dunno, postmen, clerks, vicars sometimes, you know, bit and pieces . . .

Joe   Yeah, like old slags . . . fill in . . . Yeah.

Barbra   Yeah . . . Like that . . .

Joe   Fuck me, what a pony fuckin' life . . .

Barbra   I s'pose . . .

Joe   And you have to live . . . live with that piece of garbage every fuckin' day?

Barbra   Yeah . . . I guess . . . I do . . .

Brian   Look! I apologised . . . I did . . . So please be fair and go!

Joe (*stares at him*)   Listen, you piece of rat shit. Shut up! Shut the fuck up! I'm chattin to your wife . . . OK! You're lucky! She may be the reason I haven't kicked your fuckin' head in! Right?

Brian (*small*)   Sure . . . Yeah . . .

Joe   So shut the fuck up! Got it!

Brian   Yeah, oh yeah.

Barbra   Leave him be . . . please . . .

Joe   Leave him be . . . Fuck me, look at it! I mean, how do you stomach it? I mean, either you're barmy or you've got some fuckin' guts.

Barbra   Yeah, well, thanks . . .

Joe   I mean you sleep with that ponce . . . ?

Barbra   Er . . . Yeah, well, I'm married to him . . .

Joe   Poor you . . . Yeah . . .

Barbra   Hmm . . .

Joe   Poor fuckin' you . . . That's all I can say . . . When did he last shag ya?

Brian   Hey! Please!

Joe   Told ya . . . Shut the fuck up!

Barbra   'T's OK, Brian . . . Just be quiet . . . I'm dealing with it . . .

Joe   There y'are . . . She's dealing with it, so shut it . . . Yeah!!

Brian *just nods.*

Joe   So, I was saying . . . When he last gave ya one . . .

Barbra   Dunno, can't remember . . .

Joe   'Can't remember'! That aint a life, is it!

Barbra   S'pose not . . .

Joe   Nah, it's not, and you look like you got some juice left in ya. You don't look like a worn-out dog-end like this ponce . . .

Barbra   Oh, thanks . . .

Joe   Nah, there's some gallup left in you, gal!

Barbra   Oh . . . er . . . thanks . . . (*Tight grin.*)

Joe (*sees teapot*)   Any more tea in the pot ya think?

Barbra   Yeah, I just made it . . . I'll pour you a cup.

Joe   Great, ta, my tongue's hanging out . . . for . . . a cuppa . . .

Barbra   You want a biscuit?

Joe   Whatcha got?

Barbra   Plain or chocolate . . .

Joe   Well, I won't say no to chocolate . . . Ta.

Sits in armchair, stirs his tea, feels satisfied, situation under control.

So, whatcha been in? I'll let you chat now . . .

Brian   Got nothing to say to you . . .

Joe   Ya got nuffin to say . . . Y' hear that . . . He's got the hump . . . Your old man's got the hump!

Barbra   Yeah, well it's natural, you've been bullying him . . .

*We must feel that the wife is being accommodating only because she believes **Joe** is a psychopath.*

Joe   Only told the truth, that's all, only the truth . . . Right! I mean!

Barbra   Yeah, I s'pose so . . .

Joe   So, what's the old poof been in?

Brian   I'm not a poof!

Joe   Hey! Shut it! Shut the fuck up. Not talking to you . . . You had your chance and ya blew it. Right! So shut it or . . . (*Threatening.*)

Barbra   He's quiet, leave him alone . . . He'll be quiet now . . .

Joe   Hey, nice tea . . . Ta!

Barbra   Not too sweet?

Joe   Nah, just right . . . Ta, and the bickies are going down a bomb.

Barbra   Oh, good, got some more . . .

Joe   Nah, but ta . . . Gotta watch me weight . . . Ha ha! Sitting all day in a cab . . . you get a bit lardy . . .

Barbra   You look alright . . . don't look overweight . . .

Joe   Oh ta, darlin, sweet of ya . . .

Barbra   'T's OK.

Joe *just stares at her.*

Barbra   The police will be here any second now . . .

Joe   You fink?

Barbra   They said . . . Yeah . . .

Joe   I got it sorted . . . Told ya . . . They called . . . Nice copper . . . Told 'em you called a cab . . . Got stroppy, abusive . . . It's sorted . . .

Barbra   'T's not what I heard . . .

Joe   Don't worry, gal, you'll be alright . . .

Barbra   I should hope so!

Joe   Course ya will . . . Never hurt a bird . . . never . . . never in my life . . . I like 'em far too much . . . Really I do, yeah . . . They'll be the death of me . . . Tarts! Ha ha!

Barbra   OK then . . .

Joe   But feel sorry for you with that streak of piss . . . I do, yeah, I do . . .

Barbra   Thanks . . .

Joe   I mean you're gonna go to your grave stuck to that piece of flypaper . . . are ya?!

Barbra   S'pose I am, yeah . . .

Joe   Never having your knickers steamed up . . . never having a nice stiffy in ya paws . . .

Barbra   . . . Don't think so . . . No . . .

Joe   But I got the feeling that you wouldn't mind a bit of nooky, now and then . . . Would ya?

Barbra *is silent . . . looks at husband.*

Joe   Don't fuckin' look at him . . . Tell me . . . ain't you bloody seen enough of him? . . . Tell me . . . ya fancy a bit of hot sausage now and then . . . don'tcha?!

Barbra   Well . . . er . . . (*Deep breath.*) Yeah, yeah, I suppose . . .

Joe   Course you do. Atta girl . . . Course you're alive . . . You're . . . a live tart still, anyone can see that . . .

Barbra   . . . Oh, thanks . . .

Joe   I can tell, 'cause a man can . . . can tell when a bird's battery needs recharging

Barbra   Hmm, you're clever . . .

Joe   Oh I am, I can even tell when you're covering it up with a touch of sarcasm . . . But I bet you could fuckin' give it some . . . when you get going . . . Bet you could make a bloke right chuffed!

Barbra   . . . Maybe . . . Yeah . . .

Joe   You naughty little wriggler you!

Barbra   Umm . . . Want some more tea?

Joe   Nah . . . I'm lovely, thanks . . .

Long silence.

Joe   What colour knickers you got on?

Barbra (*looks at husband*)   I . . . er, can't . . .

Joe   Don't look at him! He don't exist!

Barbra   It's not your business . . .

Joe   I can make it my business . . .

Brian *makes a move of exasperation.*

Joe   Don't fuckin' move . . . Don't you fuckin' move or you're dead meat!

Barbra   He's still . . . He's OK . . . Leave him . . . They are blue . . .

Joe   Blue knickers, eh . . . Nice . . . Panties or thongs?

Barbra   Just plain knickers . . . brief ones . . .

Joe   Ah, brief ones . . . Ain't that sweet . . . (*Silence.*) Let's see.

Barbra   What?

Joe   Your knickers, darling, give us a bit of a treat . . .

Barbra   Can't do that . . .

Joe   Can't ya?

Barbra   No, can't . . .

Joe   'Cause he's here, shit-face watching you . . . ?

Barbra   Hmm . . . maybe . . .

Joe   Well, I'm telling ya . . . so you don't have to feel guilty . . . pull your skirt up or I'll whack him . . .

Barbra   You would do that, wouldn't you?

Joe   Ya wanna see? (*Makes move to get up.*)

Barbra   No, don't . . . I'll do it . . .

Joe   SEE, NOW YA WON'T FEEL GUILTY.

Barbra *slowly lifts skirt. Has decent legs and blue knickers.*

Joe   Hey, that's sweet. That's really sweet, luv . . . Didn't hurt, did it?

Barbra   S'pose not . . .

Joe   When was the last time you flashed your knickers to a geezer?

Barbra   Well, er . . . He sees me every day . . .

Joe   Fat lot of good that is, eh . . . May as well flash to a lamp post . . . Nah . . . I mean to a man that fancies you rotten.

Barbra (*almost involuntarily giggles*)   Oh, ha ha! Far too long to remember . . . (*As if she suddenly forgets her husband is there.*)

Joe   That's fuckin' tragic . . . (*Silence.*) 'Ere . . . Come 'ere darling'.

Barbra   I don't think I . . .

Joe   I said . . . come 'ere!

Barbra *slowly comes over.*

Joe   Sit . . . Sit, darling . . . On my lap . . .

Barbra *does slowly and . . . reluctantly?*

Joe   Don't worry 'bout him . . . 'E's imprisoned you for years . . . I'm letting you out for a bit . . . Cor, you're making me feel right randy . . . Can you tell?

Barbra   Er, yeah, I s'pose I can

Joe   See, that's what you can still do to a man!

Barbra   Oh . . . really?

Joe   Really . . . (*Slow.*) Really . . . nice . . . luvly . . .

Barbra   Oh . . .

Joe (*squeezes her tits*)   How ya feelin . . . eh? Feelin' alright? Not so worried now?

Barbra   Hmm . . .

Joe   Hmm . . . Course you're not . . . Nice . . . to have a bloke . . . feelin' you up? Eh . . . darlin?

Barbra (*growing excited almost against her will*)   I dunno . . . S'pose . . . Maybe . . .

Joe   Bit shy, are ya? With ponce here?

Barbra   . . . Yeah, am a bit . . .

Joe (*continues squeezing*)   He's dead . . . Make out he's not here.

Barbra   That's hard . . .

Joe   . . . Hey doll . . . You feel nice . . . Getting a bit randy?

Barbra   Well . . . er . . . a bit, yeah . . .

Joe   Good girl . . . 'Ow long since you felt that . . . eh?

Barbra   I dunno . . . Too long . . . (*Giggles shyly.*)

Joe   Course it is . . . And you need stirring up . . . 'S natural . . . innit? Kiss me . . . Go on . . . 'E don't mind . . .

Barbra   He's staring . . .

Joe (*to him*)   Hey, fuck'ead . . . Stop staring or do you want me to get up and do something to ya?

Brian *turns slightly away.*

Joe   OK, 'e's OK. Awright . . . A nice wet kiss, lover . . .

Barbra *looks at* **Joe** *and turns back, then gives him a soft little kiss. He pulls her head on to his mouth to hold her there. She now relishes it.*

Joe   Oh, that's nice, sweetheart.

Now **Barbra** *starts to get enthusiastic and gives in to it.*

Joe   Hey! You're a hot little bitch, ain'tcha . . . Getting very horny, darling . . . Be a doll . . . open my flies will ya, luv?

Barbra *is almost hypnotised by him, turns again to her husband, who turns away. She slowly takes his zip and is about to pull it down an inch when* **Joe**'s *mobile goes.*

Joe   Fuck it! Hold on a bit love. (*On phone.*) Yeah, yeah, course it's me, ya cunt . . . Well you got me at a dicky moment . . . An airport job! What, now? Yeah . . . What, the copper rang back?

Brian *turns.*

Joe   But you got it sorted, yeah . . . Nice one! So it's the fuckin' airport . . . OK, gotcha.

Back to her.

Sorry, darling . . . Gotta work . . . That's a choker ain't it?!

But **Barbra** *holds on.*

Joe   We'll finish off another time . . .

Barbra   OK . . . yeah . . .

She's panting slightly.

Joe   Short of drivers . . . So always rely on me. Dependable Joe . . .

Barbra   OK . . . Joe.

Joe   Fuck! I'm as hard as rock!

She (*giggles*)   I know

Joe   Well . . . a bloke's gotta work before he can play . . . Not like some ponces I know . . . So tada.

He kisses her and **Barbra** *kisses freely back.*

Joe   I'll be in touch

Barbra   OK . . .

Joe   Hey! If maggot here gets stroppy wiv ya . . . or abuses ya . . . you call me . . . Right?

Barbra   . . . OK. Yeah, I will.

Joe   Tada, darling . . .

Barbra   Bye . . . Joe . . .

Joe *goes. The couple stand silent . . . Car goes off. They can't speak . . . She looks at him.*

Brian   Horrible . . .

Barbra   Yeah . . .

Brian   That was the worst night of my entire life . . . !

Barbra   Yeah . . . Me too . . .

Brian *turns to look at her.*

Brian   You too? You were enjoying it . . . You were kissing him . . . I couldn't believe my eyes . . . in front of me.

Barbra   Don't be a prat . . . He forced me . . . He forced me . . . I did it to save you.

Brian   Oh sure . . . I couldn't believe what you did . . . You were getting excited like some dirty old slag!

Barbra   Acting! I was acting . . . That's all, to calm him down.

Brian   Oh yeah, acting? You were getting the hots for the beast . . . I saw it . . . How could you? How could you?

Barbra   Just played the game . . . And it calmed him down . . . Stopped him from beating you up . . . You should be grateful for what I put myself through for you!

Brian   I know what's acting . . . I know . . . I should know . . . And that wasn't . . . You came apart at the seams . . . Fuckin' women . . . Easy, aren't you . . . Quick to betray us . . . Aren't you? . . . Couldn't believe what you did . . . Yeah 'save me from a beating', but you went beyond the call of duty, far beyond . . . I think you would have let him fuck you . . . in front of me . . . in my house! Wouldn't you . . . Eh, wouldn't you!

Barbra   No! Don't be so daft, that was it . . . Wouldn't have gone further . . .

Brian   Why are you smiling?

Barbra   I might . . . I might have gone further to save you . . . Save my husband . . . That would have been a heroic act on my part . . .

Brian   You're unbelievable . . .

Barbra   An act of heroism to save you! I would have felt nothing, nothing. But you would have felt a lot . . . if he hurt you!

Brian   What a fuckin' hypocrite . . . Now it's heroism.

Barbra   Yes . . . You don't think, you can't be sick enough to think I enjoyed all that, can you? I mean, would you rather have been beaten up . . . Eh – would you? Big tough bloke he was . . . Might have hurt you bad . . .

Brian   He wouldn't have done . . . It was a con . . . How could he? We'd have got the police on to him like a rash and evidence to boot . . . He'd have gone to jail . . . You'd be a witness . . . He threatened, but he wouldn't . . . But you believed him . . . You wanted to believe him . . .

Barbra   We can still call the police . . .

Brian   Oh sure, stopped by for a cuppa tea . . . and a nice chocolate bickie, my wife entertains him . . . Sure.

Barbra   Look . . . let's be a bit cool about this . . . Look at the worst-case scenario . . . I mean let's be quite frank . . .

Brian   Go on . . .

Barbra   He wanted something . . . you don't want . . . No, let me finish that – you don't want any more . . . And that's quite normal . . . nothing abnormal about it . . . We've been together a long time . . . So, he wanted something you don't want . . . not interested . . . couldn't care less about . . . like an old suit in the cupboard you never wear . . . Now . . . if you never wear it . . . does it really matter, does it . . . if some sod . . . borrows it . . . Eh? Does it? Come on?

Brian   It does matter, it should matter!

Barbra   Come on . . . You know it doesn't, not really, and that is important, I love you and you know that . . .

Brian   Do you? Do you still love me?

Barbra   Course, you silly bugger, you're all I got . . . You're my loving mate . . . And I'd bloody fall apart without you . . . You know that . . . Don'tcha?

Brian   . . . Yeah, s'pose so . . .

Barbra   Course you do . . . Now it's getting late . . . I'm going to make a nice cup of tea and then we'll hit bed . . . Ooh, bloody exhausted . . .

Brian   Yeah, me too.

Barbra   And tomorrow we'll look for a nice job for you . . . OK?

Brian   Yeah . . . We'll try something else . . . Tomorrow.

Phone goes. They both freeze.

Joe's Voice   'Allo, Sweetpants. It's Joe.

Brian *looks shocked.* **Barbra** *looks almost expectant and a small smile appears on her face.*

Joe's Voice   I'm missing ya darlin'!

Slow fade.

Six Actors in Search of a Director

Characters

Director, *thirties, suave, smart – the new brigade*

Alan, *cautious, brash at times, realistic but a no-hoper – takes the easy way out*

Brian, *young, smart, cynical and bold, couldn't care less, confident*

Frances, *attractive, courageous, self-motivated, still has hopes*

Charles, *older man, impeccable manners, dislikes the 'New Age', a father figure*

Eve, *attractive, experienced, smart and highly cynical*

Debra, *still young and idealistic, romantic, dreams of an ideal actor world*

Maid

A large lounge in a hotel where actors are waiting to be called. In the lounge is a large, long breakfast table and on the other side two sofas facing each other plus one or two chairs. Against the wall runs a long shelf with snacks and coffee pots which are refilled from time to time by a young **Maid** *who then disappears.*

Voices are heard offstage.

Director   OK! Alan, I want you to drive up . . . Pull up in front of the door . . . Just before . . . Keep close to the house . . . You get out first . . . But leave a beat . . .

Alan   OK, fine . . .

Director   Then she follows you in . . .

Alan   Got it!

Director   ACTION!

CUT!

That was fine but get there before her . . . Give a beat . . . Don't forget it's really cold . . . 40 degrees below! Shake yourself . . . it's biting cold . . .

Alan   OK, fine . . .

Director   ACTION!

CUT!

You're taking too long to get to the door . . . Too long . . . it's freezing. You're dying to get in the warm cosy house.

Alan   But I'm waiting for her . . .

Director   She'll speed up if you speed up!

Alan   OK, fine . . .

Director   ACTION!

CUT!

That's fine but when you get there, when you get to the step . . . stomp your feet . . . stamp your feet . . . Get the snow off, before you go in.

Alan   OK, fine . . .

Director   ACTION!

CUT!

Good, very good. Just take a beat before you get out of the car. Then you go in . . . This is nothing for you . . . You have been here a thousand times . . . For you it's nothing.

Alan   OK, fine . . .

Director   ACTION!

CUT!

Brian! When you open the door for him, to welcome him, it's your first time you laid eyes on him. Who is this dude? What's he like? Give him a bit of scrutiny . . .

Brian   Right . . . you've got it . . .

Director   ACTION!

CUT!

Brian, open the door . . . You see him . . . He's not such a dude as you thought he might be . . . He's no challenge . . . Just take him in . . . welcome him . . . warmly.

Brian   Right . . . you've got it . . .

Director   ACTION!

CUT!

Good, Brian, you open the door . . . take a beat . . . Like you're preparing yourself for the meeting . . . You take a beat . . . clench your jaw . . . as they get out of the car . . . Like a preparation . . .

Brian   Right, you got it!

Director   ACTION!

CUT!

Brian, just a tad late on cue . . . Soon as the car stops . . .
Soon as it stops, Brian, you must be out the door . . .

Brian   Didn't hear the bloody cue!

Director   OK, someone give him a verbal cue . . . Just
shout it through the door . . . OK, go again . . . Sound
running, pictures up . . . ACTION!

CUUUT!

Good, Brian, good! But sense the air . . . imagine it's 30
below . . . Clench your jaw . . . It's bitter but you're used to it.

Brian   Right, you've got it!

Director   You look at him . . . you're pleased . . . he's
no challenge . . . You can handle him . . . for you this is
nothing . . . just a visit . . .

Brian   Right, you got it.

Director   ACTION!

CUUUUT!

Alan, just get on the top step . . . Shake your leg . . . Get the
snow off your boots . . .

Alan   OK, fine . . .

Brian   Right, you got it . . .

Director   ACTION!

CUT!

Director   OK, that's dinner break everyone!

Alan *and* **Brian** *burst into the room with keenness, glad to be out of
the cold.*

Alan   He's really covering himself.

Brian   He is, but I like that. You have to find something different to do each take.

Alan   Oh, for sure . . .

Brian   Some actors might tire of so many takes but it only means they've run out. The cupboard is bare . . . There's nothing more to say . . .

Alan   Oh, I know . . . I like takes . . . The more the better . . . I start to find more about the character . . .

Brian   Of course you do . . . you do. A human being is unlimited . . .

Alan (*quiet*)   We're not still wired are we?

Brian   No, sound man took them off . . . remember?

Alan (*shouts*)   Any more takes of this scene I shall puke all over his fucking lens!

Frances, **Charles**, **Eve** and **Debra** *burst in, rubbing hands. They rush to the coffee pots, pour coffee, milk, hunt for sugar, biscuits, snacks, etc.*

Brian   Bloody hell!

Frances   Never thought we'd ever finish!

Charles   My fingers are practically falling off!

Eve   Nor me, was frozen to my marrow . . .

Debra   Oh my God!

Alan   Even my piss was frozen.

Brian   Yet we had to pretend it was cold – didn't need to pretend!

Debra   My hands went numb!

Alan   Let me rub them for you . . .

Eve   Oops, be careful, darling. (*As if 'Watch out for that leery sod'.*)

Debra   Don't worry, I can't feel a thing . . .

Frances   Soddin' coffee's not very hot.

Alan   You'd think they'd make sure the bloody coffee was hot!

Debra   Poor girl didn't know what time we were coming back.

Alan   Isn't that the second assistant's job? I mean it is his job to tell her, ring through, tell her when we were released . . . ?

Brian   You'd think so, wouldn't you?

Charles   Of course you would . . .

Debra   It's bloody lukewarm, and I was dying . . .

Eve   Me too, just dying for a piping hot cup . . .

Frances (*opens door to kitchen offstage*)   Georgina, darling, could we have some hot coffee, please? This is a bit lukewarm, thank you.

Maid (*offstage*)   On its way!

Frances   Thank you.

Brian   Thank God for that . . .

Charles   This coffee's horribly cold . . .

Debra   It's not very pleasant . . .

Charles   That's for sure.

Alan   Couldn't believe it . . . Couldn't believe it today.

Brian   What couldn't you believe, Alan?

Alan   On come on, don't be such a goody-goody . . . You know what I mean . . .

Brian   Quite frankly I don't, no I don't, not really . . .

Charles   Of course he does, he's just taking the piss.

Brian   Now why would I do that?

Charles   'Cause you're a prize winder-upper, that's what you are . . . a prize one . . .

Brian   Oh, sorry about that, oh, do forgive me, I certainly don't mean to be . . .

Alan   Oh, no, of course not, no, I'm sure that butter wouldn't melt up your arse . . .

Charles   Hey! Hey! Tone that stuff down a bit . . . please. There are ladies present.

Debra   Oh darling, you are kind, I didn't think anyone noticed.

Alan   Sorry darling, just pissing about, no insult intended . . .

Debra   Don't be silly, who's offended? It was quite funny!

Eve   Fuck me, I hope we're not that precious . . .

Frances   Well, I hope not.

Alan   I was just saying that I couldn't believe it . . . you know, believe that we all had to do thirty fucking – forgive my French, but thirty fucking takes in freezing effing weather, of us entering the damn house, so I just said I couldn't believe it, and our young friend here says, in all innocence, 'Believe what?' as if there was some other event of monumental importance that happened . . .

Brian   Oh, that's what you couldn't believe . . . ? Sorreeeee. I thought you couldn't believe that the coffee was lukewarm, yet again, since it has been luke-fucking-warm every day we get in after work, if you hadn't noticed. Every effing day, so it's quite reasonable that I might have thought you were referring to that . . . And yes, I couldn't believe it either.

Charles   Believe it . . . Bloody hell, it was barmy . . . completely barmy.

Alan   Anyway each take looked exactly the same to me . . .

Frances   And me . . .

Alan   He didn't know what he was looking for.

Charles   But that's what they do, isn't it, that's what they do.

Alan   They don't know what they're looking for.

Charles   But think *it* will come on the next take.

Debra   A eureka moment!

Eve   That's the fashion now – billions of takes till you don't even know what you are doing or saying any more.

Debra   Feel like a walking zombie.

Eve   A robot.

Frances   A trained horse.

Alan   More like a laboratory rat.

Charles   That's what I felt like . . .

Alan   A laboratory rat?

Charles   Yes, that's exactly what I felt like . . .

Alan   As if being tested and at some moment somebody will have a breakdown.

Eve   Or do something stupid.

Debra   And then he'll have his precious take.

Frances   And I was freezing, and we stopped only once.

Debra   That's right, only once, that's hardly fair.

Eve   Totally, don't think our union would be happy about that . . .

Frances   Anyone know the Equity rules on this?

Brian   Oh darling, really, you don't think your union would do anything, would you?

Frances   They might.

Brian   Oh they might, might they?

Frances   Yes, they just might. I mean, I pay them at least five hundred bloody quid a year, darling, and they're obliged . . .

Brian   Obliged, maybe, but whether they lift a finger is very much up for debate.

Debra   Who wants hot coffee?

Charles   Oh please, I'd love some, is it really hot this time . . . ?

They all react with glee and excitement.

Debra (*taking plate from* **Maid**)   Oh, thank you, she's brought in some cakes!

More excitement and glee from all!

Brian   Cakes!

Frances   Oh goody!

Eve   Smashing!

Charles   I'm starvin'.

Debra   Mustn't spoil your dinner.

Charles   What, with that?!

Alan   Really I didn't know it could be spoiled . . . any further, I mean!

They all munch on cake with sounds of enjoyment.

Frances   Last night's dinner wasn't *too* bad.

Alan   Oh, you're *awfully* tolerant.

Frances   No, no, I don't think so.

Charles   I mean, the poor cow is doing her level best.

Eve   With a bunch of actors!

Brian   Such a sophisticated bunch of actors whose tastes are so elevated.

Debra   Oh darling, we're used to The Ivy, aren't we?

Eve   Of course, every night.

Frances   Or The Wolseley.

Alan   I prefer Scott's, that's smashing.

Debra   When you can get in.

Eve   Oh, I can get in.

All   Oooohh!

Frances   You're so famous.

Eve   That I'm not, but I know the head waiter.

Brian   Oh, how simply fab, she knows the head waiter . . .

Eve   Well he used to be an actor . . . I trained with him at RADA when Jonathan Pryce was there.

Charles   I love that actor.

Debra   So do I, he's awfully clever.

Eve   Never makes a fuss but just gets on with it.

Frances   He does, I do agree, he was lovely in that Terry Gilliam film *Brazil*!

Alan   Yes, *Brazil*.

Charles   Fabulous.

Alan   He's awfully good on stage too . . .

Debra   Better, I think he's much better.

Frances   So you trained with him at RADA, did you?

Debra   Was he good then?

Eve   Oh he was, he was one of the best, even then.

Frances   The others weren't too hot?

Eve   But he was . . . Showed great promise even then.

Brian   Except for the guy who became the head waiter at Scott's!

Eve   Oh, he was good too, he was, but I think he just didn't like being out of work.

Brian   Who does . . . ?

Eve   And so he went into catering instead.

Alan   Smart fellow, very smart fellow. I should have done the same . . .

Brian   Oh why . . . ? You were so good, getting in and out of that bloody car . . .

Alan   Oh God yes, it was simply fab wasn't it?

Charles   It was, you had such style opening the door.

Debra   And the delicate way you stepped out.

Brian   The director loved it so much that's why he had to shoot it thirty-five effing times.

Alan   Of course, that's why I spent three years at drama school.

Brian   Well, it obviously wasn't money wasted!

Debra   Cakes are terrific.

Alan   God knows, worth every penny.

Frances   More coffee anyone?

Eve   Oh just a dash, thank you, darling.

Brian   That's what you're paid for, that's what we do, as actors.

Coffee is poured for him.

Thank you, darling.

Charles   Yes please, darling.

Brian   I love acting . . .

Alan   Really?

Brian   I do.

Eve   We all do darling.

Brian   I mean I love film acting, and if that's what I have to do, so I do it, no big deal. He's a great director.

Alan   No doubt.

Brian   He's got a fantastic eye, an eye for composition.

Eve   Actually he does –

Brian   – and he knows what he wants from you . . .

Charles   True, true.

Brian   He knows exactly what he wants and he'll get it. That's why his films are so remarkable and I'm glad to be part of that vision . . .

Eve   Bully for you, darling.

Brian   Yes, I'm glad, I wouldn't want to do anything else in my life, that's what I want to do . . . So if he needs thirty takes there has to be a reason . . .

Alan   Oh, thanks for the lecture.

Brian   Wasn't meant to be a lecture.

Alan   Made me feel as if I'm some sleazy lazy actor who can't be bothered.

Brian   I didn't say that. Did I say that?

Alan   No . . .

Eve   No, not in so many words.

Alan   You didn't say that, but I felt that . . . that nobility to stick it out to the very last, the soldier on the battlefield . . . Loyal to *Mein Führer*.

Brian   That's right . . . In film the actor is a bit like a soldier, working in all weathers, in all conditions . . .

Charles   Oh, you're so noble.

Brian   And some days can be tough, so, yes . . . You have to have a positive attitude, keep your head down and obey, that's why you're paid 'silly money', or some of us are . . .

Alan   Ain't me, that's for certain.

Debra   Nor me.

Frances   I'd love to get some 'silly money'.

Brian   But that's not why you do it . . . You do it to serve a greater vision, to serve an idea that's bigger than just yours.

Alan   I just think, without saying I'm a raving anarchist, that thirty takes were excessive for a simple scene and it starts to rob the actor . . . of his sense of identity.

Charles   That's fair enough Alan, I can understand that . . .

Alan   That's all I'm saying . . .

Brian   Then, next time it happens, go to the director and tell him . . . Tell him!

Alan   Ha ha! Oh sure! And never work again. Good advice.

Debra   Isn't he meant to be a bit of a screamer?

Charles   Oh, I can just see his face.

Frances   Doesn't even know my name –

Eve   Yes he does, 'darling'.

Brian   Course you will . . . If you just say, excuse me, Stanley, or David, or Clint, or Joe Shmock, don't you think that we've done enough takes? I mean, not wishing to be rude but I'm an actor and wish to act. And I feel that what this does – all these takes – is draining my desire . . . He'll listen and he'll tell you the reason why.

Charles   And then you'll never work again!

Frances *does her loud shriek.*

Alan   Sounds good, but I don't wish to test your theory.

Brian   Then I'll ask him for you . . .

Alan   Oh no! Thank you very much, that's all I need.

Brian   I won't say your name. I'll just say the actors are somewhat curious as to why you need quite so many takes . . .

Eve   Don't include me.

Frances   Nor me.

Brian   No big deal, I'll take it on myself . . .

Debra   Oh sure, because you're playing a whacking great role and he knows it's not coming from you . . . Big deal.

Brian   OK then, I'll say it's coming from me, if you like. I'll say, 'Hey, Mr Director, you're exhausting me with all these takes but I'm happy to do them but are they really necessary?'

Debra   Course he'll say it's necessary, 'cause that's his life, that's the way he operates and he's good, he is good and so why not suffer a bit . . .

Eve   I don't mind, I really don't mind.

Frances   It's all the same to me. Once you've signed a contract for film your soul is no longer your own . . . Better get used to it.

Charles   That's true!

Eve   There's only so many hours in the day he can use or abuse –

Debra   – us.

Three-second freeze.

Moment of lull . . .

Charles   What time are we expected back? Anyone know?

Alan   They said they'd call us, that's what they said.

Debra   They had to break us for dinner; it's probably after dinner.

Eve   I hate to work after a meal and it means you can't drink and I love a glass of wine –

Frances   Or three.

Eve   – or two with my dinner, and now we have to effing wait.

Brian   That's the name of the game, my friend.

Debra   Oh, I know, yes, don't tell me . . . We do the acting for nothing and are paid for waiting . . .

Brian   That's the name of the game.

Debra   Who's complaining? I'm not . . . You just accept it.

Eve   That's what being a film actor is about. You're booked for a big movie –

Frances   – if you're lucky –

Eve   – and then you're whisked to places, wonderful places, places that you might otherwise never see, places you only imagined, read about, fantasised about. One minute you're sitting in some damp sodden flat, some dreary London suburb –

Alan   You've been to my place have you?

Eve   – the next you're on a sleek safe jet flying club class to some beautiful city in South America, or Australia, or New York or better still LA.

Brian   . . . Can't stand LA.

Eve   Or anywhere else, somewhere else like Rio.

Frances   . . . I love Rio! . . .

A flurry of reactions.

Charles   . . . Venice, have you ever filmed in Venice . . .

Alan   . . . Prague, the architecture is fantastic . . .

Frances   . . . Norway . . .

Brian   . . . Paris, I love Paris . . .

Eve   I had a film in Rio once and it was glorious, the film though was such absolute shit –

Alan   I think I saw it!

Eve   – but no matter, you're whisked away on a magic carpet and it is like magic . . . I think it's like magic anyway . . . And the agent says, would you like to do a film in Florida –

Debra   . . . I love Florida . . .

Eve   – and I'm like, hey, let's do it, and he says, don't you want to read the script, fuck that, just say bloody yes and get as much as you can, who cares about the bloody script, this is film, most of the scripts are shit anyway, as long as I don't have to take my knickers off, who gives a toss?

Frances *shrieks with joy.*

Charles   Some film scripts are brilliant . . .

Eve   Oh yeah, like one in a hundred, and I'm lucky enough to be in that one in a hundred? No, not yet, and it doesn't really matter, does it, it doesn't really matter, since you're not doing it for love. Not doing it because you care, you're doing it . . . mostly because of the fucking filthy lucre!

Frances *shrieks again.*

Brian   Speak for yourself!

Alan   I think she was.

Eve   . . . And I don't even read the bloody lousy thing, but I may have to because the nice sweet director might ask me, might ask me what I thought of his bloody masterpiece, ha ha ha! So I do a speed-read through the garbage just to get the main points so I can say . . . 'Oh darling! It's so . . . '

Alan   Deep!

Brian   Strange and edgy!

Charles   Mysterious!

Debra   I love the characters, how they interact . . .

Eve   The love theme is *so* touching . . .

Alan   It's sexy!

Brian (*American 'producer' accent*)   'Bound to be controversial.'

Charles   Oh yes.

Frances   Oh . . . Sorry I didn't quite get you . . . There's a nude scene? I didn't read a nude scene.

Frances *acts out the other characters or the other actors say the lines as a 'game'.*

Charles   We put it in . . . You didn't read the rewrite, those pages we telexed over to you?

Frances   Er, I don't think I . . .

Alan   Your agent said you'd love to do it, that's what your agent said; you were enthusiastic to do it. You didn't read the yellow pages? Well we FedEx-ed them over to you . . .

Frances   Oh, I am sorry . . .

Alan   No. No . . . no . . . no problem, no problem . . .

Frances   I'm sure it's . . . artistically necessary . . .

Charles   No, as a matter of fact I don't think it is artistically necessary . . . It's financially necessary – the producers want it in the film . . . It's only thirty seconds, that's all.

Frances   In that case, then it's absolutely no problem.

Alan   Ooh, that's good. I'll send the pages over to your room, don't worry, it will be a closed set . . .

Frances   Oh, a closed set . . . And what does she do?

Brian   She gives Larry, the hero, a quick blow job . . . It's subtly lit, you'll barely see it, very subtle . . . Or we'd get the wrong rating . . . Ha ha ha!

Frances   I have to do a blow job?

Alan   Hey, don't worry . . . We'll use a body double, it won't be you . . . You're an actress, we don't expect you to do it! You're a fine actress.

Frances   Oh, thank God, I mean . . .

Charles   No! Don't worry, it'll only look like you, so the audience will think that it's you . . .

Frances   Oh . . . they will?

Alan   Of course, I mean that's still quite a bold act, you'll be noticed, you'll get a lot of attention.

Eve   Oh shut up, very funny! Anyway it wasn't a blow job.

Three-second freeze.

Brian   Next time read the script . . . that's the least you can do, I mean, someone thought of you, thought enough of you to send you the script. So what if it's shite, maybe you can make something of it, there are no Shakespeares around any more . . .

Charles   That's for sure.

Brian   You're a pro, and if it's junk, turn it down. I know it's hard, it's money, sometimes silly money, but if you have the guts to turn it down, if you do, then something better will turn up . . . And you'll feel a lot cleaner . . .

Eve   Darling, thank you so much. Tremendously insightful!

She gives **Brian** *the finger.*

Frances *shrieks again.*

Charles   For some reason I can't bloody get through to New York . . .

Alan   Can't you get a signal?

Charles   No, not a bloody murmur, and my daughter flew there today and was supposed to call me . . .

Debra   What have you got?

Charles   What do you mean? Oh I see – a Nokia.

Brian   Do you have global roaming?

Charles   Global roaming? Bloody hell, what's that?

Debra   You should get an iPhone.

Eve   Gives you more apps.

Debra   I use my laptop, it's simply fabulous . . .

Alan   BlackBerry.

Eve   What have you got . . . ?

Debra   I've got the latest bloody Apple MacBook.

Eve   . . . No flies on you!

Brian   Bloody Apple MacBook!

All   Ooh!

Debra   Then all you have to do is download Skype, and once you do that you'll never look back and I can call and see my boyfriend every night.

All   Ooooh.

Brian   Oooh, Skype sex!

Debra   It's really bloody marvellous and it doesn't cost anything . . . or not much.

Frances   Not like my bloody iPhone . . . costs me a small fortune.

Debra   You must get Skype, you really must.

Alan   Has she got your mobile number?

Charles   Of course she's got my number, she's my bloody daughter!

Frances   Maybe she's got to call the country code?

Charles   Who knows? I'm just worried about her . . .

Debra   You can read books on it, download movies and I can read *The Times* in the morning!

Brian (*cynical*)   Wowee . . . Hey, I'm telling you!

Debra   It's brilliant, holds up to 20,000 songs, oooh!

They all take out their gadgets, mobes, laptops, etc.

Charles   But I only want to receive a call from New York . . .

Brian   You'll need global roaming enabled if you want to call the States, mate . . .

Debra   Unless you instal Skype on your mobile . . .

Eve   And if it's a Wi-Fi enabled mobile you can have a video chat, using Skype-to-Skype for free!

Debra   That's what I do on my MacBook.

Eve   Do you have AppleCare?

Debra   Oh yes! It's wonderful! The other day I dropped my phone, went to the store and they gave me another one free!

Eve   Oh, I love Apple!

Debra   I do too!

Alan   Maybe you should get an iPad – the tablet version of the Mac?

Brian *holds his iPad aloft . . .*

Charles (*reacts violently to it*)   Aaarrgghh! But I only want to hear that my daughter's arrived safely and I can't get through . . . I can't get through, and normally I do get through . . . And I'm sorry but I don't know what you're talking about.

Brian   Why don't you just use the phone at the hotel . . . ? Use the phone here . . .

Charles   Use the phone here?

Brian   Yeah, the ordinary looking phone in your room, that's attached to a . . . wire.

Alan   Because it could be that the signal is weak here in the mountains and she's trying and can't get through.

Charles   Oh yes, of course, a weak signal . . . Excuse me.

He exits.

Alan   Poor guy, it's tough for the older ones to cope.

Debra   My grandad won't even touch a mobile, won't go near it.

Eve   Funnily enough my ma's the same . . . I said I'd teach her but she says, 'Darling I have a telephone, a simple telephone with an answering machine on it, and it's the most beautiful thing in the world. And I even was persuaded to get a fax machine,' she says, 'and I love it, but best of all I love getting letters. Yes, real letters written with real ink or even typed . . . '

Brian   So sweet!

Eve   'Oh', she says, 'I just love that . . . '

Alan   What can you do? That's what the old are like – they can't cope with the modern world . . . Poor things just can't.

Eve   I said the moment you get a computer or even a simple laptop your life will change, you'll wonder how you ever lived without it, everything will be so easy, so simple and so straightforward, and you can pay your bills and book your flights and actually see who you are talking to . . .

Alan Oh, that's fab, sending picture messages on the mobile phone, I mean I'm not crazy about it but one of the crew, you know the guy on sound . . . Derek. He says that when he's missing his lady . . .

Debra On no, don't, don't!

Alan Hey, it's perfectly normal and reasonable what I am going to say.

Brian Oh do go on, let's have it in all its brutal glory!

Alan No, no, sorry maybe I'm getting just a little too familiar . . .

Brian So she takes her knickers down, does she, and gives you a big flash, a big juicy flash?

Debra Oh shut up, shut up please, Brian!

Brian And then he takes out his meat and two veg, standing at full attention and they both beat the meat . . .

Debra Oh, oh, did you really have to . . . ?

Eve Was that bloody necessary, Brian?

Brian Well, isn't that what you were going to say, the wonders of your smartphone? Ha ha ha!

Eve Loathsome.

Debra I do believe the man must be pissed out of his mind!

Brian No, darling, not pissed, maybe just a bit pissed off having to sit here and listen to people whine about this bloody film getting going.

Debra I'm not whining. I am deeply frustrated, but I am not whining.

Eve Well, I bloody am.

Frances   But let's not lose our social graces . . .

Brian   Oh wow . . . social graces . . . OK, I'm sorree, I was making a very bad joke . . . Sorry 'bout that, do forgive me.

Another lull fills the space.

Alan   What's holding us up?

Brian   We're waiting for the snow.

Alan   Oh, waiting again.

Brian   Yeah! The director wants that 'pristine white look'. Better than the artificial stuff.

Alan   Oh . . . I see. So we're waiting again . . .

Brian   'Fraid so . . . Shouldn't be more than an hour . . . That's what he said.

Alan   An hour . . .

Brian   Yeah. But maybe it's best to get into your costume . . . just in case . . .

Alan   Oh . . .

Brian   Yeah . . . It could be sooner . . .

Alan   Ah-ha . . .

Brian   The sound man will come after dinner to wire you up.

Alan   So we're doing the scene in the car?

Brian   No, no. I don't think so . . .

Alan   We're not doing it?

Brian   No . . . not today . . . No.

Alan   Is it going to be cut?

Brian   Cut? No, we're just not doing it . . . yet!

Alan   But later? We'll be doing it later?

Brian   No . . . not today . . . Today you just drive to the house . . . stop the car . . . You stop close to the house . . . Don't forget it's supposed to be 40 below.

Alan   So the 'scene' in the car has been cut from the script?

Brian   This I don't know, how would I know? Maybe.

Alan   But it's down on the call sheet . . . The dialogue in the car.

Brian   But we're not doing that dialogue today!

Alan   So why wire me up?

Brian   That's what they want . . . Who knows. Maybe it's just cover . . . Weather cover . . .

Alan   So we may be doing the dialogue?

Brian   I don't think so.

Alan   We're not?

Brian   I don't think so . . . No.

Alan   . . . No?

Brian   You'll probably be doing it to a blue screen in London . . .

Alan   So definitely not today . . .

Brian   No, not today . . . unless he needs it as a cover.

Alan   Well, I'd better learn it . . . just in case.

Brian   Yeah.

Alan   Yeah, but it's definitely not cut?

Brian   Today. It might just be cut today . . . Oh . . . you mean omitted?

Alan   Yeah . . . it's not omitted?

Brian   Oh no . . . You're just driving up to the house . . . Stop the car, but close as you can to the front door . . . it's 40 degrees below zero.

Alan   Yeah . . . You know everything, don't you?

Brian   I just listen.

Alan   So I've got time for a piss?

Brian   Oh sure . . . even more.

Frances   Anyone know what time we're due back?

Eve   Well, they did say after supper, that's what they said.

Debra   And since we're on nights, what time will they finish?

Brian   Well, they have to finish by five in the morning.

Debra   Bloody hell!

Group reaction.

Brian   But they could finish earlier.

Debra   They could, oh they could, could they?

Alan   But if our lovely star decides to work, if she manages to get on the fucking set, then he'll shoot our entrance and spend the rest of the time trying to exert a performance out of her . . .

Debra   So basically our lives, our bloody lives and well-being depend on our lovely leading lady!

Brian   She's the money, that's the name of the game, hey, don't you know that's why we're all working . . .

Alan   Oh yes, if you can call it that.

Brian   You put up or pack up, she's what the audience has come to see . . . You think they come to see us?

Eve (*to* **Frances**)   Is it still snowing, darling?

Brian   They don't give a toss for us, but she's our wages . . .

Frances   No, not at the moment.

Brian   That's what we're doing here, that's why you're getting paid, and well paid most of us.

Frances   Speak for yourself.

Brian   And it's still better than sitting at home, sitting at home scratching your balls and watching TV.

Alan   For sure.

Brian   I think so. There's some rough moments, I don't dispute, 'cause there are . . . But we're sitting here being paid and the director, poor sod, is trying to cope with a lunatic star . . .

Frances   What do I scratch, darling?

Brian   God knows, maybe your boyfriend's balls! You can scratch mine if you like!

Alan   Ha ha ha ha ha!

Frances   She's alright, she's just going through some issues right now, don't forget she made some cracking movies.

Eve   She's one of the reasons I wanted to be an actor . . . God, she used to burn up the screen, she was wonderful, and her Cleopatra –

Debra   Her Lady Macbeth!

Alan   Fan-fucking-tastic. But then she got on the bottle, big time, poor thing.

Debra   Didn't she go to rehab, wasn't it all in the press how she went to rehab?

Alan   They do rehab and then brag about it as if they just climbed Everest, big deal!

Frances   Now she's in AA.

Debra   The actors' club, that's a good place to network.

Frances   Well, she met her fourth husband at AA.

Brian   Can't stand LA.

Frances   Yeah, you told us.

Eve   I went to LA once. My agent said I should go and network, meet some agents and casting directors, but every night I was so lonely – I knew no one.

Alan   LA can be rough when you don't know people.

Eve   But one day an acquaintance took me to his AA meeting. I had to say 'Hello, my name's Eve and I'm an alcoholic', and then I had lots of friends.

Brian   When you're a piss artist you make friends.

Alan   But then you've got to go off the piss.

Eve   In Hollywood there's an AA group for the stars, that's where the agents go to network. You don't want to go where the down-and-out drunkards hang out.

Frances   God forbid.

Debra   Does she still do AA?

Eve   No, I think she went back on the piss, that's the problem.

Debra   Why did she ever do that?

Eve   Her lover left her.

Alan   Wasn't he a piss artist?

Brian   Piss artist and how, he was one of the best. He was out on the piss most of his life.

Eve   And yet she loved him?

Brian   Well, she adored him and joined him on the piss.

Alan   Well, aren't the Welsh all piss artists, isn't it in their blood?

Brian   Not necessarily.

Alan   But he was, he swam in it . . .

Brian   They're poets, the Welsh, great singers, writers, talkers, that's in their blood, but they get corrupted.

Eve   That's rather good, Brian.

Brian   He was the best actor on earth but he found fame and got corrupted, poor sod . . .

Debra   What corrupted him?

Brian   Who knows? Going to Hollywood, giving up the stage, giving up the place that defined him, that made him.

Frances   Stop pawing her, Brian!

Debra   You've got to be alert for the stage, alert, each night, and night after night, so you can't go on the piss or you'd soon be out of work.

Eve   I agree with you, darling.

Alan   You certainly don't sit in a trailer all day waiting to get out of a car so you go on the piss 'cause it doesn't really matter, you can cope with a two-minute or a five-minute take . . .

Eve   Too true.

Debra   The stage gives you stamina and guts. To me it's almost holy!

Alan   Oh come on!

Frances   Wish it was!

Eve (*rushes over to her*)   Darling, I love you!

Debra   It is to me . . .

Brian   What's so holy about it, darling, poncing about for four weeks rehearsing for some wanker director who believes the sun shines out of his arse 'cause he's doing the thousandth revival of *The Cherry Orchard* . . . ? Shitting yourself on the first night . . . Praying that the critics will love you . . . And then doing the same thing, the same bloody thing night after night, week after week, month after month . . . Ha! That's not holy, that's doing time, mate . . .

Three-second freeze.

A lull descends upon them – **Eve** *applies make-up,* **Alan** *is clicking his fingers, bored.*

Charles *re-enters.*

Frances   Did you get through, Charlie?

Charles   No! No, not yet, not even on the bloody house phone.

Debra   I used to sit in front of the mirror each night as I was making up and start sweating . . . sweating in fear in case I dried . . .

Brian   But you didn't dry, did you?

Debra   No, I didn't, but the fear used to make me ill, I'd imagine I was there in the middle of the stage, all eyes on me, and my brain would stop, it would stop, and I'd be there, just standing there centre stage, with nothing to say . . .

Frances   Actor's nightmare!

Debra   Imagine an actor with nothing to say . . . You don't exist, you've dried, like a lake . . . had dried up . . . And you were dead, empty, with no purpose and all eyes on you . . . What would I do!

Eve   Horrible thought darling . . .

Brian   Would what you do? You make a few lines up, that's what you do, you make some junk up until the other actors throw you a lifeline. It's not the end of the world, that's one of the hazards of the stage, no big deal. You cope, you're a pro aren't you . . . ?

Charles   I knew an actor who was playing Macbeth and he dried when he saw Banquo's ghost . . .

Frances   Who's Banquo?

Alan   The ghost of the man he murdered, dingbat. Don't you know *Macbeth*?

Charles   He dried and just stood there staring at him . . . Staring at him for ages. I think he thought it was the ghost's turn to speak.

Frances   It's not my favourite play.

Alan   But the ghost doesn't speak . . .

Brian   So he just stood there?

Debra   Horrible.

Charles   Yes he just stood there and the actors were staring at him, frozen and the audience were staring as him and they knew something was wrong, they knew this wasn't one of the Macready pauses.

Frances   Who's Macready, darling?

Charles   A famous Victorian actor renowned for his pauses . . .

Frances   Oh, how fascinating, I must Google him.

She opens her laptop.

Charles   So he stood there and the whole world seemed to stop, life stopped, in fact it felt that the audience stopped breathing.

Debra   Oh my God . . .

Charles   So you know what he did . . . you know what he did . . . you know what he did to solve this problem?

Eve   Go on, tell us.

Charles   He just walked offstage.

Huge reaction.

Yes he just did a bunk, walked off the stage . . . So they brought the curtain down . . . The stage manager apologised and said the actor had been taken ill and the understudy would be on in ten minutes . . . And so the understudy went on . . . But he was a lazy bastard and didn't learn his lines properly so he had to go on with the book in his hands . . . Ooow.

Brian   Theatre can be so embarrassing!

Alan   God, can it ever . . .

Charles   Anyway, the actor apologised profoundly to everybody and said . . . he had to leave the stage because it wasn't the ghost he saw but . . . the ghost of himself . . .

Alan   Bollocks!

Charles   . . . He saw himself as a dead man, that's what he said. That's who he said he saw, but we all knew that he fled the stage 'cause he dried, we knew that.

Brian   Wanker!

Alan   Course!

Frances   So what happened?

Charles   He didn't work for a while, and then he went into films and became rich and famous.

Brian   So now you know what you have to do . . . Don't work your bollocks off like a soldier on the battlefield night after night . . . That's for mugs . . . Just do a walker and, lo and behold, fame and fortune will come your way . . .

Alan   That I gotta try.

Debra   I still think that the stage is holy.

Brian   That's quite touching.

Alan   I wish it was.

Brian   Half the time, when I see a play I fall asleep.

Eve   Me too!

Alan   If you suffer from insomnia, see a play.

Eve   Ha ha! Cheap medication.

Frances   Not so cheap!

Alan   I never fall asleep at the movies.

Eve   Me neither.

Alan   Hardly ever.

Debra   I've had the greatest experiences in the theatre.

Brian   Good for you, I mean that sincerely.

Debra   It can be the most powerful event and a great performance can change your life.

Charles   I remember . . . that it happened to me.

Debra   It can, it can make you aware of the greatness, the power of human beings . . .

Eve   I believe you, darling.

Debra   And to be a servant of it . . . Like being a priest . . . in a church, serving the words of the great masters, feeling them within you, speaking those words, no more than that, *being* those words, expressing those feelings . . . It does something profound to you. To me . . .

Maid *appears.*

Maid   Excuse me, the dinner is ready . . .

All   Wahoo! / About time! / God, I do believe I'm starving. / Terrific! (*Etc., etc.*)

All move upstage to the table to fill their plates with food. **Debra** *remains on the sofa. They all return with their plates of food and eat throughout the following, entirely unaware of* **Debra***.*

Debra (*to audience*)   It can open doors in your own soul, open doors that have been fastened shut, have been nailed shut. It prises them open, something comes out of you, something deep within you, something even pure within you, something that you didn't even realise was there, like love, like an act of love, when those doors open, and it can even shock you, shock you that you could feel so much . . . And feel so much in front of a thousand complete strangers . . . You can bare your soul to strangers, and make them feel with you, feel for you . . .

Frances   Oh, I've spilled it all down my top.

Alan   That's not coming out in a hurry.

Brian   It's a good job you haven't got your cozzie on!

Eve   I hope it doesn't stain.

Debra   . . . feel for the thoughts of the writer which come alive in you. So you try . . . you try to touch the audience and when you do, really touch them, really move them, then something happens in that house . . . In the holy house of the theatre . . .

Brian (*to group, referring to the dinner*)   Hey! This is good.

Charles   Very tasty.

Eve   So much better than yesterday.

Alan   Bit on the dry side.

Debra   . . . Something happens, something strange and mysterious enters that large room, something like a spirit enters, yes. You summon . . . you have summoned up the soul of the writer . . . And those writers . . . Those great writers are in some way . . . in some way like prophets teaching us things . . . valuable things, things we need to know, to learn . . . to appreciate and I . . . I am the messenger . . .

Eve   Would anyone like some wine?

Charles   Oh, yes please!

Brian   'Bout time, darling.

Alan   Be rude not to.

Debra   . . . And I love to be the messenger of these prophets . . .

Eve   Red or white?

Charles   A dash of white darling.

All react in agreement.

Alan   White would be safer!

'Cheers!' during the following,

Debra   . . . these great playwrights that reawaken us, like Shakespeare, Ford, Marlowe, Sheridan, Webster, Molière, Racine, Sartre, Rostand, Goethe, Brecht, Chekhov, Gorky, Pirandello, Tennessee Williams . . . Arthur Miller, O'Neill, Wilde . . . Oh, I bless you all, all of you my beloved, you are like the most precious jewels . . .

Alan (*burps*)   Excuse me, sorry. Ha ha!

Charles   Such a pig.

Eve   So uncouth.

Frances   Vile man!

Brian   Compliments to the chef!

Debra   . . . I run my fingers through these most divine gems, worth more than gems, since they are without a price . . . They light up my soul . . . And there we are, our group of players coming together to re-create this special event, coming together each night, entering the theatre and waiting for that call, when the stage manager knocks on your door or calls through the Tannoy, though I love the knock on the door . . .

Frances   Do you think there's any pudding?

Charles   Oh surely, bound to be.

Alan   Hollow legs!

Brian   Where does she put it?

Eve   I'll never get my costume back on.

Debra   . . . for it's your call, your call to enter that stage, to calm your fears, to be unafraid, to come together with your fellow actors and raise the spirit of the play . . .

Alan   I'm bloody stuffed.

Charles   Very filling!

Brian   You've eaten that too quickly, Alan.

Eve   Far too quickly.

Debra   . . . and to do this again and yet again and yet again and I am blessed, blessed each time . . .

Charles   This wine is good! Because it's a Sauvignon, darling, that's why . . .

Debra   . . . So maybe that's what I mean when I say . . .

Eve   . . . that's why it tastes . . .

Debra   . . . it's almost holy . . .

Eve   . . . so good.

Debra   But I couldn't say this to them, I don't know why I couldn't, since I would have liked to . . . But I feel I can say it to you . . . It's easier to talk to strangers.

Frances   That wasn't too bad, I thought . . .

Alan   Better than yesterday.

Eve   The chicken was delicious and I adored the way she cooked the veggies with onion and pepper, yummy!

Brian   Strange, the poorer the country, the tastier the food!

Alan   I don't believe it's that great in Rwanda! Is it?

Charles   God, I shouldn't have drunk so much wine.

Alan   It wasn't so much . . .

Brian   I mean, we're only all climbing up the great stairway into the house . . .

Alan   Don't remind me . . .

Brian   So you can get away with it.

Frances   Hey, Deb, didn't you want to eat tonight? It was good.

Debra   Don't really like to eat before work . . . It makes me sleepy . . . Oh! But I will have something after . . . on the set.

Eve   Not much there, darlin' . . .

Debra   It will do, but thanks for thinking of me.

Alan   Well, when's our bloody call?

Brian   The second AD said he'd call us straight after dinner.

Eve   Right, I think I'm just going out for a smoke . . .

Alan   It's too friggin' cold to stand outside, just open the window, honey.

Eve   You don't mind?

Charles   Of course not, I think I'll join you.

Goes to window.

Oh, oh, just look at this, will you . . . Our star is taking a stroll . . .

All rush to the window.

Oh my, she looks totally out of it, poor thing . . .

Frances   Why doesn't she join us?

Debra   She eats in her room.

Eve   Anyway, she's with her therapist the whole time.

Alan   Never leaves her side.

Eve She's not even wearing a coat.

Debra Poor cow . . . She must be going bonkers.

Alan And this waiting around isn't helping her much . . .

Frances What's she doing now?

Brian She's just staring at the moon. Just staring at it . . .

Debra She's talking to herself . . . She's moving!

They move to the other window.

Brian She's just going over her lines and getting some fresh air.

Debra She doesn't look like that to me.

Brian She's going over her lines, that's all, why are you all so fascinated by her? Leave her in peace.

Debra Poor thing looks so lonely.

Brian Then ask her in . . . Ask her to join us for a coffee . . .

Alan You ask her?

Brian Why, are you afraid to ask this solitary woman to join us?

Alan I'm not afraid, don't be so goddam patronising . . . Just because she's a star, why should I be afraid . . . ?

Brian 'Cause you are, you all are, because a star isn't quite human, is she? They're not quite like us . . . are they? They live in a different stratosphere, or we feel so bloody inferior . . .

Alan Don't be so bloody absurd, nobody feels inferior, just because she's got more lines than us . . .

Brian It's not only that, they've got something else, something we don't have . . . And maybe never will have.

Frances Oh cobblers, you do like making an issue out of every little thing.

Debra   Doesn't he just?

Frances   You have to analyse everything, everything we say, or do, or worry about and turn it into some theory . . .

Brian   Not really.

Frances   Yes, you do. In fact I think that when you make these observations, such wise, such pithy observations about us . . .

Brian   Yes?

Frances   You're talking about yourself . . . Yes, you're projecting yourself.

Brian   Now why would I do that?

Frances   Why? I'll tell you why.

Brian   Go on then . . .

Frances   Because you see yourself in us, you see all the little fears, all the little tiny angsts, and you recognise yourself, but you can't bear it . . . No, you can't . . . In fact it even sickens you, that basically you're a simple humble actor just like us. Yes, but that's too much to take, that's too horrible, to think that you are like us, so you pick on us, chastise us, since this makes you feel that you don't belong here, you shouldn't even be here, shouldn't be in this room with us and *wouldn't* be with us but for the fact that there are no bloody hotels in this remote area so we are forced to be together, obliged to sit together in the one big room and put up with each other . . . Or sit alone in a small bedroom . . . Like that pathetic star . . . Who's standing in the cold, staring at the moon and talking to herself for company, since she's another who's afraid, afraid to see her reflection in us . . .

Eve   Well done, darling.

Brian   And cut! That's good, very good, that's the first time I heard you say something you really feel . . .

Frances   How bloody sanctimonious you are! You think
I would express my feelings to you, you loathsome little fart!

Charles   Don't upset yourself, darling.

Brian   My apologies, I was out of order.

Frances   Piss off!

Charles   Oh Frances, he was just winding you up.

Frances   I'm fine.

Debra   Look! Look she's turning her face to the window –
she's looking this way.

They rush back to the window.

Eve   Well, don't let's stare at her, move away . . .

*They move to the sides of the window and just peer from behind the
curtains.*

Charles   She's staring, she's staring at the window . . . at us.
I think she saw us . . . saw us staring at her . . .

Alan   Oh bloody hell!

Eve   What's she doing now?

Debra   Nothing . . . She's just staring . . . Wait, she's
smiling, she's smiling at us . . .

Alan   But she can't see us now, can she?

Debra   Not now, but she did . . . She did, that's why she's
smiling . . .

Eve   Maybe she's not smiling . . . Maybe she's laughing at
us . . . smirking at us . . . thinking we're all pathetic, for God's
sake!

Brian   Of course you're pathetic, course you are . . . She's
smiling just to be friendly since she saw you. She saw you in
the window, looking out . . . Or shall we say staring out . . .

Like she was the abominable snowman. So she's smiling just
to be friendly, but sadly to people like you –

Frances   Please cut it out, cut it out . . . 'People like you!'
Get off your high horse.

Charles   Good for you, Frances.

Frances   Please! Thank you.

Debra   She's just standing there . . . She must be freezing.

Alan   Wait, she's walking this way! She's walking towards us!

Charles   Well, bloody sit down, sit down. Don't all look
like we've been staring, ogling like brute beasts . . .

Brian   Which is exactly what you've been doing . . .

Alan   Like you haven't . . . ? Just like you haven't!

Frances   I do believe she's stopped . . . She's stopped, but
she's still looking this way . . .

Brian   Oh, for fuck's sake, I'll ask her in, obviously that's
what she wants . . . She'd like a bit of company like any
reasonably normal human.

*He leaves the room. They all rush to the upstage window and see him
walk past. They rush to stage-right window and see him in the distance.*

Eve   Look at him rushing over to her. He's almost running!

Frances   What's she doing, what?

Debra   She's walking towards him, she's slowly walking
towards him . . .

Charles   She's actually smiling.

Debra   She's smiling, that great big beautiful smile of hers.

Alan   What are they doing now?

Debra   They're just talking, I can see the breath from their
mouths . . .

Frances   She seems quite happy.

Alan   Are they coming this way . . . ?

Debra   No . . . no they're just talking and he's offered her a cigarette. Yes, he puts his hand over the flame to keep out the wind and their faces are really close . . .

Alan   Jesus!

Debra   Ah, it's finally lit and she takes a deep drag . . .

Frances   She closes her eyes as if she's in ecstasy . . . as if it's a hit of coke . . .

Alan   Maybe he slipped her something . . .

Frances   No, it was just a cigarette . . . from a pack.

Charles   Oops, they're looking at the window again, both of them . . .

Frances   Turn the light out. So he can't see us.

Alan   He's bloody pointing, bloody pointing at us.

Frances   And he's laughing, pointing and laughing, and she's laughing too.

Charles   Hey, they're laughing their heads off . . . at us.

Frances   Why? Why do you think they're laughing?

Debra   Why? Why? Isn't it obvious, all of us skulking behind the curtains . . .

Alan   The curtain twitchers . . . Ha ha!

Frances   Just stand in front of the window. Go on, just stand there and laugh back!

Debra   At least wave, like we're not creatures from another planet.

They all wave frantically.

They're laughing more than ever . . . !

Frances   They're laughing, laughing like it's the funniest thing they've ever seen.

Alan   Slimy little bastard, he's taking the piss . . .

Eve   Of course, now the star's given him her blessing he feels like a bloody immortal.

Alan   Bloody hell, so come away from the window . . . come away, don't give them anything to laugh at . . .

They shuffle back, but still keep darting odd looks.

Don't keep staring, you're encouraging them.

Eve   Encouraging them to what?

Frances   To take the piss 'cause you look like monkeys . . . Ha ha!

Alan   Speak for yourself.

Debra   Oh . . . oh . . . oh . . .

Alan   What?

Debra   They've stopped staring, they've stopped. And they're staring now at each other, but not laughing . . . Just staring.

Eve   He's taken his coat off and wrapped it round her shoulders, would you believe . . .

Frances   Jesus! Talk about cosy . . .

Alan   Arse-licker, working his ticket, rowing himself in.

Charles   Bloody hypocrite . . .

Alan   Course he is . . . The ones who talk the most always are . . .

Frances   Is she pissed? Does she look pissed?

Eve   She might be . . . She must be, just standing there freezing her tits off.

Charles   No, she doesn't look pissed at all.

All   Wooow . . . woweeee!

Alan   What? What happened?

Eve   I can't believe this, can't believe what's going on, come and see.

Alan   No, I don't want to be a monkey, I told you. Just tell me.

Frances   She's . . . she's put her hands, both hands behind his head . . .

Eve   Yes! . . . Yes!

All except **Alan** *react with huge excitement at what they've seen.*

Debra   Bloody hell, bloody hell . . .

Alan   What! What! Tell me!

Debra   She's pulled his head towards her and given him a big juicy kiss.

Frances   Jesus!

Debra   A big juicy kiss . . .

Alan   Oh, I've got to see this . . .

He gets up swiftly.

Debra   His arms are around her . . . Really pulling her towards him, really holding her, holding her like she was the last woman in the world.

Alan   Do you think his tongue's in her mouth?

Charles   Could be, could well be, dirty bastard.

He rushes to the window.

Alan   Lucky bastard more like . . .

Frances   Look, he's turned his head back towards us . . . with a big grin.

Debra   He's still holding her tight and grinning at us . . .

Alan   He's grinning . . . Wait . . . oh, you bastard . . .

Some have moved away.

He's giving us the finger! Giving us the finger, the slimy bastard. Cunt!

Charles   Giving us the finger, the prat.

Alan   Open the window and tell him to go fuck himself . . .

Charles   Why me? You tell him!

Alan   I will, I bloody well will, how dare he, the bastard!

Opens window . . . He just stands there.

Oi! Having a good time, are you? You both look freezing out there . . . Come in and join us for a coffee.

Shuts window.

Charles   Bloody coward, bloody coward you are.

Debra   I think that was the smarter thing to do.

Alan   Thank you.

Frances   They still staring?

Eve   No, they've parted . . . She's walking back to her place . . . He's coming here . . .

Alan   Oh, look at that smug look on his face – you asshole.

Frances   Well, don't let's look like we were in a state of hysteria. He took the piss that's all. Let's relax . . . just relax. Turn the bloody light on.

They all take up positions of complete normality, naturally overdoing it a tad.

Brian *enters. He's cold, rubbing his hands, etc.*

Brian   Bloody hell, bloody hell, it's freezing out there!

Charles (*laconic*)   I can imagine it would be . . . I think we were due for some more snow . . .

Brian   That would be nice, might even hold up filming for a bit . . . Then they could send us home . . .

Frances   Oh, just wouldn't that be super?

Brian   But I thought you loved it here . . .

Frances   Oh, of course, I adore it . . . But you can have too much of a good thing . . .

Alan   Poor thing, you're frozen, what happened to your jacket?

Brian   Hey, hey, just calm down, OK? It was no big deal.

Alan   What on earth do you mean, pal, we're perfectly calm.

Frances   Never felt calmer.

Eve   Shall I ask for some more coffee.

She gets up.

Debra   Oh I'd love some more.

Charles's *mobile rings.*

Charles (*phone*)   Hello! Hello! Hello! I've been waiting all day . . . all day and half the night for you . . . Haa! It's my daughter, my darling daughter . . . She got through from New York . . . Oh what *took* you so long darling . . . ?

Brian   Why are you so pissed off?

Alan   Who's pissed off? don't know what you're talking about . . . He thinks we're all pissed off . . .

Charles (*phone*)   I am so relieved, I can't tell you, so relieved . . . God, forbid, I thought something might have . . . What? You're breaking up . . . a bit . . .

Alan   Why on earth should anyone be pissed off? What for . . . what on earth for?

Charles (*phone*)   That's better . . . you're coming through now.

Alan   Just 'cause you had a mini-grope with that old slag out there, who's been holding up this picture for weeks . . . That hag who can't put a fucking scene together and why we're up working fucking nights . . .

Charles (*phone*)   Yes, darling, it's really going quite well . . .

Brian   Calm down, calm down . . . she's alright . . . she's really alright . . . She came outside just to wake herself up, so she shouldn't fall asleep . . . She waved to you . . . She was lonely and wanted some company, company of the actors . . . But you all looked so hostile, she said she was nervous to come by . . . And so I said . . . 'Listen, we all love you . . . '

Charles (*phone*)   Of course, there's a few problems but that's filming for you . . .

Debra   You said that? That we loved her?!

Brian   Yes, yes, I said that and then she was really happy . . . She was so happy she smiled, grabbed my head and gave me a big kiss! Amazing, what a few warm words will do . . . That was sweet . . . so sweet.

Alan   You're full of shit, do you know that?

Charles (*phone*)   Yes, it's a really nice company, a good bunch of actors . . . first class . . .

Debra   No, he's not, don't say that . . . That *sounds* so sweet, you see, she's just a really nice woman and I'm so glad you went out to talk to her . . .

Alan   So what was all that about . . . ? Giving us the finger? What was that about . . . eh? Like you were mocking us . . . both of you . . . full of contempt for us little players staring out the window like . . .

Frances   Monkeys!

Alan   Yes, like monkeys in a zoo.

Brian   Tell you the truth . . . I'll tell you why . . . 'Cause I knew you were all ogling, adding some choice verbals, and so it was a kind of 'fuck you'. If you can't take a joke . . .

Alan   You lying sack of shit . . . We saw you . . . You were both laughing . . . laughing your heads off!

Brian   Listen, idiot . . . She was so happy when I told her that we all loved her and I pointed to you, yes, I thrust my arm out and said, 'They all really love you', and she laughed . . . She laughed like a child, like a child in such relief, 'cause she knows she had some problems, she know that, and she thought that perhaps you hated her, yes she really thought that you hated her –

Debra   Oh no!

Brian   – and so laughed out loud in such relief and then gave me that big kiss.

Debra   Oh that's *so* sweet. I can't *wait* to talk to her, I'd really like to talk to her and tell her myself that I do *really* love her and have always loved her movies and that they mean so much to me . . .

Charles   My daughter sends all her best wishes for the film . . .

They all ignore him.

Brian   Then you should tell her that . . . She'd love that. We should all be a bit more friendly. Don't avoid her because basically you feel you can't talk to her . . . 'cause she's a star.

Frances   I don't avoid her, not a bit, but she's always trapped by that loony American woman who's her bloody therapist.

Eve   More like Svengali.

Charles   So glad my daughter got through.

Eve   Oh God, 'stars' are so bloody insecure, aren't they? They always need so much, need their fucking therapist, need their 'trainers', need their bloody managers, need their dietician, need their gurus . . .

Frances   Oh Christ, that's for sure, how they need their gurus . . .

Alan   If it's not one guru, it's another, just so long as someone is providing the answer for their pathetic shallow fucking lives.

Brian   Not necessarily.

Charles   Always, yes, necessarily . . . We all have needs, maybe theirs are bigger than most . . .

Alan   Oh sure . . . And their greed is bigger than most . . .

Charles   Hey, the coffee's here, thank God, what about some sarnies?

Frances   You've not long had supper, you greedy bugger.

Charles   Actually I'm not greedy, I'm bored. I eat when I'm bored!

Brian   Then have a nap, go to your room and have a nap, and I'll call you when they come to pick us up.

Frances   If they come to pick us up . . . If.

Eve   Of course they will, they said just after supper . . .

Debra   So we just stand by . . .

Eve   That's what we have to do.

Debra   Stand by . . . wait for the call.

Eve   'Fraid so . . .

Alan   They will call, they will have to . . . they've got to get the scene finished tonight.

Frances   And if they don't . . . ?

Alan   They have to, they just have to.

Frances   But if they don't . . . I mean . . . they've only got four hours left to shoot, and then it's back to the city, to the studio . . .

Alan   So they'll bring us back.

Frances   They can't do that because our star is booked for another film . . .

Eve   This is it . . .

Alan   This is it, absolutely it. The last throw of the dice, they've got to get it tonight . . .

Brian   OK, and so they will . . .

Eve   Unless they cut the effing scene.

Frances   They can't do that.

Eve   Why can't they? In film they can do anything, they can even bring the dead back to life.

Frances   Can you imagine, even the dead.

Alan   Like poor Oli Reed in *Gladiator*. He died before his contract ran out.

Frances   Very thoughtless of him.

Alan   Well, he was another famous piss artist.

Frances   Notorious, piss artist *á la crème*!

Alan   But amazingly sober on the set.

Charles   So they say – so they say.

Brian   So they used CGI, computer-generated images – you can't tell the difference. No, you can't. You don't even need to be alive . . . Some cynical wit made the comment that he was actually better dead!

Charles   I think that's in terribly poor taste.

They all agree.

Brian   They only need your image, and one day that will be all they need, just an image and your voice, put on a disc . . . Then piss off. Don't need you, mate . . .

Frances   No, don't need you needy, wheedling little actors, whining about your per-diems . . .

Charles   So glad my daughter got through.

Eve   Having to fly you and your loathsome needy egos round the world first class . . . put you up in expensive hotels.

Frances   Five-star hotels!

Eve   Chauffeur driven everywhere . . .

Alan   Oh, and darling, you must have an exclusive car . . . can't share a car.

Eve   Only bit players do that . . .

Alan   Course!

Frances   Filling your greedy stomachs every four hours.

Eve   And even then you'll always whine about the catering.

Alan   Oh, always.

Frances   Or the size of your trailer.

Alan   Or the size of your part.

Brian   But I believe they will do it . . . Tonight, they want to and they'll have to.

Charles   But . . . monsieur . . . just the possibility that they don't . . .

Brian   Then you'll have to stay . . .

Frances   But we can't stay, we can't, they're filming back in the studios tomorrow and all the actors are booked, the expensive ones . . .

Brian   Ah there you have it . . . The expensive ones, but we are not expensive, in fact by their standards we're cheap, we're expendable . . .

Frances   Even you?

Brian   Even me.

Frances   So, what are you saying about us *cheapo* actors?

Brian   They can shoot us when they like . . . We're booked in for the shoot . . . So they can keep us . . .

Alan   What about her? Your fabulous star whose lips you fed on so greedily . . .

Brian   They'll shoot her now, from our point of view, don't see us, just the back of a few heads, a shoulder or two, actually.

Charles   Don't even really need that, just a close-up of her talking to us . . . and then when they have time, the director will come back to us . . . but maybe not tonight . . . no not tonight . . .

Frances   Oh, OK, so worst case we'll have a few days of city life, civilisation . . .

Eve   Oh, thank God, thank God, a nice big hotel room with a giant plasma TV and space! Space . . . Oh, how I miss space . . .

Alan   A nice long bar . . . Oooh!

Eve   There's a fabulous sushi restaurant near our hotel . . .

Debra   Oh, please, please take me . . . I adore sushi!

Charles   Oh, so do I, so do I . . . so maybe it wouldn't be so bad . . .

Frances   Oh Charlie, did you get through to your daughter?

Charles   Yes, I did at last, thank you.

Brian   I'm not being a pessimist, but it's unlikely they'll let you go.

Pause.

Alan Why the fuck not . . . are we in a gulag?

Brian They'll need the shot of us arriving, that's right, but they'll have to do it at night when they're finished in the studio, so you'll have to stay . . . They don't want you going backwards and forwards . . . it would take too long, be far too costly. So I think they'd keep us here . . .

Three-second freeze.

Pick up the shot after work one night, but probably they'll send the second unit . . .

Frances Second unit?

Alan Second bloody unit, Jesus fuck!

Eve What difference does it make? Send the second unit and get it over with.

Alan What makes you think we're going to stay here?

Brian I'm just guessing . . . it's a possible option . . . It's her last day and they want to get the best they can, of course, and why not? That's why you're having to wait . . . Look!

He rushes to the window.

They're shooting her now but they haven't called you . . . have they? So they'll do you later . . .

Charles He could be bloody right. How could you know, 'cause we should be in the shot . . . 'head and shoulders'.

Brian It could be that she asked the director not to bring you in. So she could concentrate more . . . no disrespect, but some actors actually prefer, feel in fact easier doing their scenes without the other actors there. They do . . . It's not that she doesn't like you. She may just feel more comfortable without you there . . . some actors are like that . . . She can imagine you better without you . . . ha ha!

He collapses in mirth.

Frances   Oh how nice, she can imagine us better by us not being there . . .

Brian   It's OK, don't get on your high horse, she respects you, she does, but like some actors, they don't like to be watched . . .

Frances   Jesus!

Others react also: 'Crazy', etc.

Brian   Yeah, I know it's weird . . . it's the weirdest thing in the world that you don't like to be watched by those you're in the scene with, but she knows you're not really in the scene when she's in close-up. She knows you're only there to give her a focus . . . to help her, and that doesn't work for her and besides that it's not altogether necessary, so you may not be needed.

Four-second freeze.

Frances   I see.

Eve   We may not be needed.

Debra   Not yet.

Alan   Not needed . . . even if we were actors in the scene with her . . .

Charles   Flown out at great expense.

Frances   Not even needed.

Brian   No, not yet, but you will be needed.

Frances   *When* will we be needed?

Brian   That depends on the director. I'm only giving you suppositions . . . alternative possibilities . . . I don't know, we never know, how can we know? It's up to the director . . .

Debra   He's the god.

Eve   He creates the universe . . .

Brian   Well, at least the universe we function in . . . which is the movie. 'Our director, which art in movies, hallowed be thy name . . . '

Eve   In a way they are . . . you know, masters of the universe . . .

Debra   They are . . . they create alternative worlds . . .

Charles   So what are we, then? They direct us but it is *we* who are out there . . . on the screen. It is us the audience comes to see . . .

Debra   Couldn't agree more, Charles.

Frances   It is the actors that the audience love, not the directors . . .

Eve   That's right, us, the actors who sacrifice our lives, our souls, our minds, for the director who merely directs us into his vision.

Charles   Like a shepherd, he guides us to where he wants us to go.

Alan   We are but the meat, we keep the world alive, the world feeds on us.

Brian   That's what the great director Alfred Hitchcock used to say . . . 'Actors should be treated like cattle', that's what he used to say . . .

Debra   Horrid!

Alan   So we're like cattle, are we?

Brian   That's what he used to say, and he's famous for saying it . . . it's quoted all the time . . .

Alan   Listen, my friend, there'll always be tossers, always, who will never be short of words to abuse actors . . . it's the name of the game . . .

Frances   'Luvvies', how the press love that word . . .

Alan   Luvvies . . . try playing Hamlet eight times a week, try that, or Othello, or Macbeth . . . it would kill a coal miner!

Brian   You don't have to convince me, pal . . .

Alan   While those scumbags get sloshed every night on expenses, and shit out a column once a week . . .

Charles   True.

Alan   . . . and then they prey on us, like fucking filthy hyenas, and what do they know? Eh, what do they know if you're stuck in some ghastly rep company churning out a play every two weeks, busting your brains to get it learnt, hoping that you'll be good, that you give your best, your very best, and you do it, every night, never taking a night off, not even if you're ill, you make an effort, you go on . . .

Frances   I've done that.

Alan   You do it because you care for your audience who have bothered to come and see you, and you have to, and in all circumstances, even when my poor mother died . . .

Eve   Oh no!

Alan   Yes, even then, she died poor woman obligingly on a Sunday so I had the night off . . .

Brian   That was very thoughtful of her.

Alan   Yes, I had the night off. But the next night I was on 'cause I did it for her, and that's what we do, we're actors, a word to be proud of, like doctors, or soldiers . . .

Frances   No question.

Alan   . . . and like them we bring peace, harmony, literacy, even escapism . . .

Debra   Amen.

Alan   Luvvies! And so what, so what if they keep us for a couple of days more – it won't kill us. So what if we have to sit and wait, it's calm, no one's really forcing us to do this work, and what a relief, what a relief not to go in every night rain or snow, every night, and do it whether there's ten people there or a thousand . . . Here we're free, free to think, to imagine and yes, we will work . . . Oh sure, we will work.

Brian (*rather cynically*)   Bravo, Alan!

Debra   I hope so, I really do hope so, because I really don't know what to do any more, and that's why I like being directed, I like it so much, it gives me a purpose.

Frances   A purpose?

Debra   Yes, a cause, to make something worthwhile . . . I like the director telling me what to do, to make sense of my disordered and chaotic life . . .

Charles   Oh darling, don't upset yourself.

Debra   . . . The director gives me a goal, gives me a form, challenges me to be more than what I am. And what am I?

She begins to break down in tears.

A chaos of flesh and appetites, and so he pushes me, inspires me and then he actually directs me to the *real* me . . . by making me reach further, struggle harder . . . and then when, when sometimes I discover all those things that I am capable of . . . it's like a revelation, I actually see who I am and what I am and what a human being can be capable of and what we should all try so desperately to be capable of . . . and I love him for that . . .

Eve   Of course you do, darling.

Debra   I do . . . and he doesn't have to be the greatest director in the world . . .

Frances   Too few of them.

Debra   . . . just as long as he's of goodwill to you and to the author. And guides me, gently guides me and is there in case I fall, and you're not alone. And that's so important . . . you're not alone.

All   Yes. You're not alone . . .

Brian   Darling, darling, Debra, that was the most 'luvvies' speech I've ever heard . . . it really was.

He flings himself mockingly to the floor, followed by shocked silence.

Frances   Oh good . . . if that's what she is . . . if telling people what she feels . . . feels deep within her makes her a luvvie, then I'm proud, yes, I'm proud of that word . . . Because maybe people don't say what they think or what they feel . . . they disguise their feelings with cynicism, like you, Brian, cynicism, the great panacea for the dead souls, the walking zombies whose souls have long since died from neglect, from disuse –

Alan   You're a zombie, ha ha!

Frances   – from fear of using them, fear, but what you represent to me is fear . . . And those without souls, those whose souls are like dry and withered organs rotting inside them, love to spit at those who are unafraid to reveal theirs . . . Yes sometimes it takes some courage to say what you really feel . . . takes some guts.

Charles   Debra, darling . . . I love what you said . . . You remind me of my daughter . . . she is so much like you . . . she . . .

Brian   Who's coming out for a fag?

Charles   For God's sake, man . . . ! Please, I was just speaking to this lady . . .

Brian   Sorry, Dad . . . didn't mean it . . . Don't throw your toys.

Charles   Doesn't matter, nothing means anything now except your stupid needs and desires. And you can teach me all you like about your wretched Skype and 3G stinking mobile and broadband, but you haven't got one shred of manners . . . not one . . . not one shred of human decency in you, and I'm not your dad, God forbid! God forbid! God forbid! I would like nothing less on this earth! Go go go out and smoke your fucking fag . . . ! In fact I think I'll join you . . .

Pause.

Excuse my French, darling!

Charles *and* **Brian** *exit.*

Frances   I just can't stand it . . . can't stand it any more . . . all this waiting . . . It's like they're torturing us . . . like they have no regard for us, for what we are . . . for our feelings . . . we're just bloody cannon fodder . . .

Eve   Cattle, like he said . . .

Frances   I hate this man, I hate what this director's doing to us . . .

Debra   He's not doing anything . . . He's just as trapped as we are . . . But you are being paid, that's what you're paid for . . . for your time . . . How he uses our time is up to him . . . It's hard.

Eve   Some theatre actors do find it hard . . . They feel they're not being . . . properly used . . . they feel sometimes superior to the work, they feel that with all their iambic pentameters, they're just background, a filling, they feel humiliated . . . Unless you have a substantial role, that's often what you are . . .

Debra   It's not always like this . . .

Frances   It's not just that . . . it's this place, not having a decent place to hide away . . . all stuck in one room . . . all looking at each other, and that's the worst, all looking at how useless we all are . . . If we didn't have to view each others' humiliation it would be easier, having to make small talk, having to find things to do . . . filling in the time . . .

Eve   Our valuable time.

Debra   Our sweet and precious time . . .

Alan   He's paid for our time . . .

Frances   You've sold him your time . . .

The smokers come rushing back in.

Brian   He's coming!

Charles   He's just crossing the square.

Eve   Crossing the square?

Alan   Who's crossing the square?

Brian   The director of course . . . He's just crossing the square . . . he's coming this way! He's coming here . . . he's certainly coming here.

Frances   Well he sleeps here, doesn't he? Doesn't he sleep here in the big house?

Charles   But he's coming this way, towards us!

Debra   Towards us?!

Eve   What can he want with us?

Brian   He has to tell us something.

Alan   He *wants* to tell us something.

Brian   Calm down . . . calm down . . . just relax.

Eve   Don't let him see us, running around like headless chickens.

Frances   Why not, let him see us as we are . . .

Alan   What all this waiting has done to us!

They all sit and relax, pick up their books, magazines, open laptops, etc.

Steps are heard approaching, then the door to their room opens and the **Director** *walks in. He wears a loose leather jacket and smart jeans.*

Director   Hi, guys . . .

All (*eagerly*)   Hi!

Alan   Hi, how you doin'?

Charles   We've been missin' ya . . .

Debra   Wondering, like, when, you might need us . . .

Frances   Although we know . . .

Eve   God, don't we ever . . . that film is tough.

Alan   Making film.

Brian   Being at the helm, being responsible.

Charles   For all those people.

Debra   God, that's a job.

Eve   Hey, that's a job and a half.

Frances   Like being captain of a ship.

Alan   Taking care of the crew.

Brian   It's not a job that one would take on lightly. No sir, not a job to take on lightly . . . first to arrive on set.

Charles   Sometimes and more often than not at the crack of dawn.

Debra   And the last to leave.

Eve   More often than not.

Frances   With the producer breathing down your neck! God, that must be a pain.

Alan   So we don't envy you.

Brian   God knows we don't envy you.

Charles   But we admire you . . .

Debra   God that's true . . . how we admire you.

Eve   How could we not?

Frances   Dealing with the stars.

Alan   And their temperaments . . .

Brian   God, that must be so hard.

Charles   That must be a pain in the neck.

Debra   'Cause some stars –

Eve   But not all.

Frances   No, of course not, not all.

Debra   But some, yes some stars actually believe –

Eve   They're gods . . . !

Frances   Oh for sure, for sure!

Alan   That the sun shines out of their arses.

Brian   And you have to direct these creatures.

Charles   Ooh boy!

Debra   Shaping the shot.

Eve   Creating the image . . .

Frances   The final picture.

Alan   You know . . . so much to know.

Brian   Is it a slow pan?

Charles   Or shall we just dolly in?

Debra   A close-up or a medium close-up?

Eve   Or a crane shot, one of those epic shots?

Frances   Favoured by John Ford's great Westerns.

Alan   The wide panoramas, epic.

Brian   Like the making of America.

Charles   Or Dutch. I like Dutch when the camera tilts –

They all tilt their head slightly.

Debra   Like everything's skew-whiff.

Eve   Tense, out of synch.

Their heads straighten again.

Frances   So much to think about. God, yes . . .

Alan   So much to do . . .

Brian   And dealing with the scriptwriter.

Charles   They can be tough . . .

Debra   But not like the stars . . .

Eve   Never *like* the stars . . .

Frances (*referring to the writer*)   They're just glad to get a gig!

Alan   Course they are . . .

Brian   The stars trample all over their script . . .

Charles   Cut what they don't like.

Debra   And maybe add what they do like.

Eve   Make it up . . .

Frances   Improvise.

Alan   Lots to think about.

Brian   So much, we don't envy you . . .

Charles   But, you've got our respect . . .

Debra   Oh, that's for sure . . .

Eve   We know we sometimes –

Frances   – get a tiny tad impatient –

Alan   – with the number of takes –

Brian   – but we know you're a master –

Charles   – and you need those takes.

Frances   And boy, we have to get it right.

Eve   Oh yes.

Debra   I like a lot of takes. I do. I like the opportunity it gives.

Alan   It gives *us* to try different ways.

Brian   Kubrick did dozens of takes.

Charles   Oh yes – scores.

Debra   'Cause you're the master . . . You're the general.

Charles   In charge of the troops.

Frances   And we're proud to be soldiers in the field.

Alan   Never complaining.

Brian   Never whining.

Charles   Waiting . . . waiting patiently.

Alan   Film is a slow birth . . .

Brian   You create it slowly, patiently.

Charles   And what you have to deal with . . .

Debra   Nature, the firmament –

Eve   – getting the right sky –

Frances   – or the shots won't match up!

Alan   David Lean waited for weeks in Ireland for the weather to clear.

Brian   Imagine that!

Alan   Weeks.

Brian   Sitting around a dreary rainswept Irish village for weeks.

Charles   I'd go insane . . .

Debra   No, you wouldn't.

Charles   No, you're right, I wouldn't.

Frances   'Cause you're an actor.

Alan   A soldier in the field, so you do your time.

Frances   You wait . . .

Eve   Of course you do . . .

Debra   So, sir, we're happy to wait . . .

Charles   We know what you have to go through.

Brian   No one's ignorant of that.

Alan   But . . . but . . .

Frances   We would really like to know . . . please –

Eve   – when you're going to use us?

Debra   Since we *long* to work.

Frances   We're just busting to work.

Eve   To have once more a function.

Alan   I know . . . I know, and that's true.

Charles   I'm not complaining, God forbid!

Brian   But just to know, so we can prepare our minds.

Frances   Yes, to prepare our minds since in a way –

Eve   – in a way we live through the film.

Debra   We express ourselves through the film.

Frances   Without the film, without it . . .

Eve   We have no function.

Debra   No, none . . .

Alan   We come alive in your film.

Brian   That's true . . .

Charles   Like you bring us to life.

Alan   You do.

Debra   Like you give birth to us . . .

Eve   You and the scriptwriter.

Frances   Both, in a way give us birth . . .

Debra   Without you we are shadows.

Eve   Unknown . . . shadows.

Frances   Like scripts in a drawer . . .

Eve   Just waiting . . .

Debra   Just waiting for you to breathe life into us . . .

Alan   To say the word . . .

Brian   Action!

Pause.

*The **Director***'s *mobile goes off. He answers it as if the actors aren't even there.*

Director   Hi! Just taking a small break. Yeah, we're nearly there, thank God . . . We'll get our star in close-up and we're through. If she's been boozing, use a filter . . . No, no, we don't really need the others, not really, not enough time . . . No, otherwise they'll be on overages, not worth the cost for a ten-second reaction shot . . . So release them . . . Yeah, thank them from me, they've done a nice job, but we don't need them, no . . . No we don't, send them back now . . . OK . . . But don't forget to thank them . . . You know how sensitive they are, ha ha! No I can't . . . Gotta rush get the shot before it's light . . . Hey, we gotta big day tomorrow . . .

*The **Director** walks out as if the actors no longer exist, and for the film, of course, they don't.*

The actors are still sitting, frozen, just staring ahead, quite neutral, for at least fifteen seconds. They appear lifeless as if all energy has been drained from them.

Director (*offstage*)   CUUUUT!

Blackout.

BIBLICAL

Author's Note

There is something so vital and dynamic about our wonderful biblical stories, myths or parables that they lend themselves so easily to a modern interpretation. Of course their passion speaks directly to all of us and few of us are immune from the same problems and obsessions.

Adam and Eve

Characters

Adam, *young, lithe, masculine*
Eve, *pretty, innocent, cheeky*
Serpent, *cunning, sensual, agile*

Set

An empty white space. On stage left stands a thin tree; from one of its branches hangs a red disc, symbolising the apple, and two large fig leaves.

*We see **Adam** writhing under a great sheet and **Eve** suddenly appears out of him. Both are wearing flesh-coloured body tights, **Adam** wearing a sizeable phallus.*

Adam Sod me, you're a doll! Straight up, a living breathing, walking doll! And just out of one rib . . . Amazing! Triffic! Wasya name, doll?

Eve Eve . . . Yeah, Eve will do, OK? So this is where you live, yeah . . . Not too lively is it? Bit effin lifeless . . . So what's the nightlife like?

Adam What's the nightlife like? Oh darlin', you are a cute one. I am the effin' nightlife . . . Yeah, you're looking at it, so you'd better get used to it . . . It's a quiet but very nice piece of turf, don't get much better, and what's more there's no bad neighbours ta drive ya crazy, no stinkin' poxy teenagers partying all night . . . You're lucky, see, you're dead lucky that you got here first before the neighbourhood goes down, which it will no sweat. Whatcha gonna do when the fuckin' gorillas evolve, partying all night, in the street, all sodden night, smoking spliffs?

Eve Achally, sounds rather good to me.

Adam Oh yeah?

Eve Yeah it do . . .

Adam Well, darlin', you're still new, you've not acclimatised, you're just a new woman and like all new women you're into consumer trash, but once you've seen the marvels of this place, you'll forget all about that . . .

Eve Oh yeah, ya fink? So who are you? Wasya name?

Adam Adam.

Eve Adam?

Adam Yeah . . . Adam . . . It means blood, *adom*. Smart, right? So when the Boss made me he said let there be 'blood' . . . Hence Adam . . . It's the first language. Then he saw that I was moping a bit being on my tod, and being on your tod

can lead to bad habits . . . Didn't want me to waste away
giving myself hand shandies, so he made you . . . Nice one.
Of course he could have made you at once along with me but
then we'd be useless trying to sort things out, so he made a
bloke first as a sort of trial run . . . So it worked . . . Get used
to the place, sort out my patch to kip in, learn how to get on
with the orang-utan and the other livestock, so when you
come I could show you the ropes, get the place all cosy like . . .
He's not the Boss for nothing right?

Eve   S'pose. So you've got it sorted, 'ave ya? Gonna show
me around your gaff, are ya? Introduce me to the local
elephants and gorillas, yeah . . . Sounds triffic . . . Thanks . . .
So, wadya do at night? Just hang about?

Adam   What do I do at night, what do I do at night!
Blimey, you're a typical woman, you are . . .

Eve   How can I be a typical woman if I'm the first, ya daft
twat?

Adam   'Cause for some reason you're just what I expected,
don't know why but I had a sense that you'd come out all
needy, needing all the time, 'cause that's what babies are like
ain't they, at first, all needy, craving, something to entertain
ya, stimulate you . . . Some superstore with masses of useless
junk to make you happy, to piss about wiv.

Eve   Don't know what ya talking about, you gotta teach me
what those funny words mean. Don't forget I'm new, you're
already a tad past your sell-by date, but I don't mind, I really
don't mind, you're not exactly my dream bloke but then I
ain't got much choice, but you seem well equipped for some
fun and games, so that's alright I s'pose . . .

Adam   Oh, thanks very much, I'm sure, you're not bad
yourself, so we'll have a crack at it shortly, put you through
your paces, have a bit of a romp in the forest . . . Yeah, you're
a bit tasty, now I gotta moment to clock the equipment you
ain't come out bad at all . . . Hmm . . .

Eve Pooh! You don't half pong . . . Bloody hell, get yourself cleaned up a bit, can'tcha? You bloody reek like camel poo!

Adam No worries, no worries, didn't need to before, did I, had no one to tart myself up for, no. No nice little scrubber to spruce myself up for, but now I'm gonna scrub meself pink and clean my teeth . . . You won't recognise me . . .

Eve Thank God for that . . . And then I'll think abaht it . . . OK?

Adam That's cool, I'm not rushing ya into it, since we got all the time in the world.

Eve Oh God, that's boring me to death already . . .

Adam Eve, you won't be when you see just how amazing this place is, so I'll show you round the manor, you won't believe it, amazing, lots to see, lots, it could take you a lifetime, fruit, fruit like you wouldn't believe, and it's all at its ripest and juiciest and just hanging there all plump and full of the most delicious juice, and always ripe and ready to bite, delicious and juicy, just like you are, my pet.

Eve Hey! 'Ang on will ya, I can see ya getting a bit randy, so hold on to your horses. I mean I've only just arrived and don't want to be rushed, OK? So you can show me round the estate first.

Adam No problem . . . Luv to . . . And yes, you're right, there's no sodden nightlife, but what we got here is a nightlife that you'll never ever forget . . . There's a billion stars, twinkling, twirling and spinning like you can't imagine and shooting stars spewing into the blue velvet, and the aromas will knock you out, from all the flowers, and the herbs, the jacaranda and, oh, the sweet bursting oranges and persimmons and limes, and the waft of lilies hanging over the river, hanging like your delicious white pendulous titties, and then the sound, the music of the night frogs, their delicate sharp whistles as they yearn for each other and mate, and then comes the great lion's roar, like thunder rolling, in the distance, and the smell of their musk when they are mating, mixed with the scent of wild roses breathing in and out their odours into the heavy night air, oh and then the gentle music of the night owl, while the crocodile parts the silky river with its jaws, and you can just hear it, and these are our nightly visitations, out nightlife, our amazing, our wondrous nightlife, and then you won't say . . . not much effin' night life!

Eve   Well, I'm a girl ain't I . . . as you say, and I like things, sensations, happenings, a bit of a dance, I'm not like you, 'cause you're a man, you can sit just like a smelly lazy old couch potato and stare up at the stars, if that's what turns you on, good luck, if smelling some stinkin' old rutting lions rattles your cage, bloody good luck. 'T's OK for a night or two . . . But hey! I need a bit more sensory stimulation . . . Yeah.

Adam (*mocking*)   Yeah . . . I wonder why, after the Boss made you so beautifully, so elegantly, so perfect in every way did he leave your head with a vacant sign on it!

Eve   Vacant to you maybe, 'cause I got higher expectations than sleeping in a tent with grass under my bum and a spider crawling up there and earwigs in my nose, and then wait for my big bloody treat and that's for you to climb aboard . . . I just can't wait to see what that's bloody like, but I don't have high hopes, quite frankly, looking at you, even after you scrub yourself down, it's not really that much of a turn on, sorry to have to tell ya that, and what's that funny looking snake hanging between your legs?

Adam   You don't half 'ave a mouth on you, dontcha, and if you're a trial model of woman, I have a shrewd notion that the Boss had better get back to the drawing board . . . I mean, this is a bloody number-one paradise and you don't even have to do nuffin', nuffin', just sleep, wake to blissful sounds, eat from the choicest vines, swim in soft clear warm waters, drink delightful nectar, nibble from every single fruit and it's all free, all ya have to do is stretch out one lazy hand, it's all there and she's complaining . . .

Eve   Hey . . . hey . . . now that's an interesting-looking dude.

Adam   Where?

Eve   In the tree, over there, it's staring at us . . .

Adam   Oh him . . . Pay no attention to him . . . He's a
serpent . . .

Eve   A serpent?

Adam   Yeah . . . 'E just slithers around . . . Bit of an evil
bastard if you ask me . . .

Eve   'Ere, how come he looks like that thing that you got
hanging between your legs . . . 'Ow come?

Adam   Mystery to me, mate, maybe the Boss ran out of
new design ideas . . . 'E can't make everything in the whole
world different . . .

Eve   But he's ever so fascinating . . . Oh I love the way
he moves, like a long tongue, or like a wave, and what a
beautiful coat, it's simply gorgeous! Oh how I love his coat, it
shimmers and glows, I wish I had a coat like that . . .

Adam   Yeah, course, ya always wanting something arntcha,
especially something that belongs to someone else . . .
Anyway, I suppose you can't help it, you were made that way,
poor thing . . . Let me show you round the place and then
you'll see what's really beautiful on this Earth, and you can
take anything you like, 'cept one thing the Boss gave strict
orders not to touch.

Eve   Oh, what on earth can that be, I wonder?

Adam   Apples, any apple from that tree – you see, that's the
Tree of Knowledge, and you don't want to go anywhere near
that, more than your life's worth, and it'll give you a hell of a
stomach ache . . .

Eve   . . . Ooh, sounds fascinating . . .

Adam   Yeah, maybe, but it's not for you . . . Or me . . . Off
limits.

Eve   That makes it all the more interesting . . . Hmm . . .
Off limits . . . Now I just wonder why?

Adam   There you go, typical woman, as I always imagined
them to be . . . You have the choice of a thousand fruits but
you always want the one you can't bloody have! And the one
that will get you into trouble . . .

Eve   What's trouble?

Adam   Trouble, what's trouble . . . ? That's another word
for woman . . . You! You're trouble . . .

Eve   Another word for woman is curiosity, not trouble, silly
limited man. Oh never mind, I suppose you can't help it . . .
OK, piss off and get washed, can't bear your pong no more,
then we'll go for a walk . . .

Adam   OK, be back in a minute . . .

Eve   Take as long as it bloody well needs!

Adam *goes off.*

Serpent   Eve, Eve, my sweet young woman . . .

Eve (*startled*)   Oh! You speak?

Serpent   Indeed I do, and as a serpent I have a natural
understanding of woman, yes indeed I do. Of course you
have curiosity . . . You are a woman and it is natural for you
to wish to explore all the possibilities of life in this great and
wondrous Garden of Eden, unlike Adam, a simple man who
only does what he is told.

Eve   Yes, he's simple alright . . .

Serpent   His ignorance offends me, but he cannot help it
since God made his first model of man simple and obedient
to him, and without too much imagination. Why, knowing
that you were coming the poor man couldn't even bathe or
scent his body with beautiful odours to make himself attractive
to such a beautiful woman.

Eve   Ooh! Thank you . . .

Serpent   And you are beautiful, for God has now refined his model, while poor Adam being a first draft so to speak is always a little rough round the edges, and his simple mind will never understand the subtle complexities of your sex, oh my God no.

Eve   But I sense that you do, Serpent . . .

Serpent   Of course, we two have much in common . . .

Eve   We do?

Serpent   No question of it, we are both graceful and curvaceous, not like that lumbering idiot, we're silent at times but know how to hiss when the occasion calls for it, and naturally we have a forked tongue, yours figuratively of course, and most importantly have a venomous bite! Ha ha ha!

Eve   Oh, I haven't had a chance to try it yet!

Serpent   Oh you will, believe me, you will . . .

Eve   What did Adam mean about not eating the apple, why not the apple?

Serpent   It's from the Tree of Knowledge, that's why, and knowledge can be dangerous . . . For some people, particularly the stupid ones . . . So he won't go near it since God forbade him, but knowledge in the right person, in a bright person, in a woman such as you, Eve, would give you astounding riches beyond your wildest dreams. You would be able to do anything, anything that you wish, for there is nothing that you cannot achieve with knowledge.

Eve   Anything, anything at all?

Serpent   Yes, yes, anything at all . . . You need not live on the level of animals, just to eat, sleep, shag and stare at the stars, night after night . . . Oh no, for one day you could actually go to the stars . . . But don't let me tempt you . . .

Eve   Oh . . . You're not tempting me . . . You're just showing me a few options, and I'm weighing them up.

Serpent   Of course you are, oh what an intelligent woman . . . A woman who cannot be tempted . . .

Eve   Listen, Serpent, you truly truly think it wouldn't hurt me, to bite on the apple . . . ? Adam said it would give me a stomach ache . . .

Serpent   Ha ha! What he means is that knowledge would give him a headache . . . I mean, what could an oaf, a simple gardener, do with knowledge . . . ? It would confuse the poor man . . .

Eve   But it wouldn't confuse me?

Serpent   Don't you see, Eve . . . the apple of the Tree of Knowledge was made for you . . . It will open your eyes, it will help you to fulfil those dreams that you as a woman are born with . . . I see when you are sorely tempted, but I promise you the rewards are beyond description . . .

Eve   It may be too much.

Serpent   Eve, come on! For a woman, nothing is ever too much . . . Fulfil the needs of your divine sex.

Eve   Well . . . I'll just take a small nibble . . . OK?

She mimes taking the apple.

Serpent   As you wish . . . Just sink your teeth into it . . . see how gloriously sweet it is . . .

Eve (*bites*)   Oh, oh, it is glorious . . . What a sublime taste . . .

Serpent   Yes, yes, knowledge does have a sublime taste . . . Just as ignorance has a dull taste . . .

Adam *returns, cleaned up . . . Senses immediately what has happened.*

Adam   Eve, Eve, what have you done? What have you done, oh God!

Eve   What do you think I've done, you daft prat? I have eaten of the tree of knowledge, of which you feared . . . Yet you feared for nothing . . .

Adam (*snatches the apple*)   Give it to me, you stupid wicked woman. When you had so much to choose from why on earth would you take this one thing you were forbidden to take? Oh God, why did you make her so wicked!

Eve   Wicked?! Wicked to taste the fruit of knowledge you foolish man . . . ? Look at yourself, you're stupid . . . you know nothing, live like a goat in a barn, do what you're told, like an obedient mule. You should try it, Adam. Don't be afraid, nothing that God makes could be dangerous or he wouldn't make it in the first place. Don't you see, he put the Tree of Knowledge there to tempt you, as a kind of test, to see if you've got the bottle . . .

Adam   Oh Eve . . . Oh well . . . (*He eats of the fruit.*) Hmm, it's pleasant . . . Yes, it's very pleasant . . .

Serpent   Of course it's pleasant, knowledge is always pleasant . . .

Eve (*suddenly cries out*)   Oh Adam, Adam! For God's sake you're starkers, you're bollock bloody naked with your dong hanging out like an old turnip . . . For God's sake cover yourself up, man . . . It's disgusting!

Adam   Eve! I can see everything! Your body is full of funny shapes and bulges and hairy bits, so cover yourself up too. How can you walk around like that in front of everything that moves, you shameless hussy!

Eve   Oh my God, yes! Ow, it's like a bad dream when you're walking around the street with no knickers on . . . Oh my God . . . Quickly, get some leaves!

They both grab some oversized leaves from the tree and cover themselves.

Eve   Don't know why, but I didn't notice that I was naked before . . .

Adam   Neither did I, neither did I . . . You know what? I was living in a fool's paradise, and Eve, you helped me to wake up. Tell you the truth, I was getting bored here, same old thing day after day . . .

Eve   Oh, you're bored after all these years on your tod, staring at the stars. I'm bloody bored already, mate . . . And you know what?

Adam   What?

Eve   It just could be that God wanted to give you a bit of a nudge and so made me . . . See!

Adam   Hey! You could be right, my old darlin' . . . So what shall we do now?

Eve   Get out, mate, the world's our oyster. I just can't wait to get out there, go shopping in those huge shopping malls, that's a real Garden of Eden . . . Get some high-heeled thigh-length boots . . . yeah, in that bloody snakeskin, and some Versace jeans . . . Oh goody!

Adam   I fancy a nice streamlined Porsche, 1000 horsepower and a high-powered computer with all the extras . . . Hey! Baby!

Eve   I want my hair styled by Sassoon and to have lingerie by 'Rampant Filth', a miniskirt and black thongs . . . Oooooh!

Adam   IPod, BlackBerry, mobile . . .

Eve   Giant plasma TV!

Adam   High-power speakers.

Eve   First-class travel . . . everywhere!

Adam   Five-star hotels . . .

Eve   A diamond watch!

Adam }
Eve   }   Ah, knowledge is a wonderful thing! Wonderful!

Fade.

David and Goliath

Characters

David, *young, virile, confident*
Saul, *middle-aged roué, opportunistic*

Set

A table and two chairs, an outdoor café. Modern music playing, could be in Tel Aviv.

David   So you say he's a big fucker, this Goliath geezer?

Saul   You've gotta believe it. A bloody giant, massive, muscles like branches of oaks, fearless . . .

David   Yeah, well, he would be with all that height and weight going for him.

Saul   Yeah, well it's true that sometimes the Philistines produce one of those bloody gigantic beasts, something in the blood, in their history, they lived and thrived on war and conquest, they drink the gore of their enemies . . . It's rare these days when our beautiful women produce such a monument of size and muscle . . .

David   Samson?

Saul   Yeah, Samson, God bless him was a one-off, but he got done in by a tart. Jewish weakness, tarts. They'd sell their mother for a shicksa, you know what they're like, it's the forbidden fruit, it's a weakness . . .

David   No, not just a weakness, the Jews love a bit of variety, that's all, they've got exotic taste buds. Sure Jewish girls are beautiful, but you'd sweat your bollocks off before you get a pinch of tit. Whereas those delicious Philistine shicksa are free and easy, liberated, love men, sexy as cats, randy as monkeys, who can resist that . . . ? I mean you can't, right?

Saul   Yeah, I see what you mean . . . I'm wrapping myself around a few tarts myself, I can't deny . . . Oh yes!

David   No, you can't . . . It's going round the whole camp that you pull some very tasty scrubbers . . .

Saul   Hey, David, chill! Don't want to be known just as a cocks-smith.

David   'S not so bad, come on . . . The soldiers quite like that – that at heart you're one of the lads, spreads your rep around, makes them feel they've got something in common with you . . . You're one of us, hey! That's good.

Saul   What about you?

David   What about me?

Saul   You slinging your hook anywhere . . . ?

David   I'm OK . . .

Saul   OK? What's OK?

David   OK, yeah . . . I'm not going out of my way like some of those mad fuckers, who'll stick it in anything that moves . . . They think they'll get a medal for how many scrubbers they've pulled . . . Anyway, I'm busy with my writing . . .

Saul   What writing?

David   I'm writing, that's what I love to do . . . Like psalms.

Saul   Psalms . . . What's psalms?

David   Like poems if you like, just jotting down my feelings . . . My joy, joy of life, the little things I notice when I'm out with the herd, the wonder of God, exultation, it just passes the time when I'm out all day alone with the flock . . . It gives me time to reflect . . .

Saul   Well, don't be too much of a loner, it's no good for you, and then people might start to entertain some daft ideas.

David   What ideas, Saul, what are you talking about . . . ? If a man sits alone and reflects on his world and writes, writes about the little stirrings in his soul, what harm is there in that?

Saul   Oh! What harm, hey, some of the most dangerous radicals were men who sat alone with a pen in the hand . . . Anyway, I know you are no radical, so I'll tell you as a mate, as a good mate – forget that I'm a king, I'm just a good mate who loves ya . . .

David   Yeah, so go on, spit it out . . .

Saul   Well, Dave, there's talk, just talk, that you might be turning the other cheek, that you might be a bum-bandit!

David   Whaaa?

Saul   A bum-bandit, call it what you like, turd-burglar, pillow-biter . . .

David   You gotta be bloody kiddin', just because I don't go round pulling Philistine scrubbers and shouting my big drunken mouth off about how many 'hits' I've had, you've got me down as an iron hoof?!

Saul   No! No! Not me, Dave . . . It's just a bit of loose talk that's floating around . . .

David   Listen, mate, sure I'm a bit careful where I sink my shaft, I don't want it covered in boils, carbuncles, running sores . . .

Saul   OK! OK! I know that, I know you, Dave, and I know that the last thing you are is a meat grinder, but let's cool it for a bit . . . It's only stupid gossip, you know how men gossip, lazy soldiers with nothing better to do and not much up there in the first place . . . But they see you hanging out in the fields with this guy Jonathan . . .

David   Jonathan! He's my mate, he's a good bloke, lots of laughs . . . And sometimes we play together . . .

Saul   Play together!

David   The harp, the harp, you dirty old lecher . . . I write the words and he composes the music, he's got a really fine ear . . . We might even do a few gigs when we get better at it.

Saul   Oh I see, well, that's pretty neat and maybe you guys could do a couple of gigs here, so the guys could, like, check it out, you know, and then of course they'd see that you're both straight kind of blokes . . .

David   You mean John and I gotta get up, do our gigs, play, sing them our beautiful romantic songs, just to reassure a bunch of meatheads that we get groupies hanging off the end of our dicks . . . ?

Saul   Might help, Dave . . .

David   Nah . . . It might even make it worse, confirm their suspicions, then what you gonna do?

Saul   Forget it . . . You're right. I'm with you, Dave, why should you prove yourself before idiots?

David   Now you're making sense.

Saul   So let's talk about Goliath . . .

David   Yeah, let's get real and talk about Goliath, so you wanna take him out?

Saul   Not quite that simple . . . The Philistines have issued a challenge . . .

David   Oh, for a change, so what's new?

Saul   Yeah . . . Their army has challenged our army to a one-on-one . . . No more mass slaughters and weeping widows . . . Something far more civilised, and I can't deny that it is . . . Just one of *their* best versus *our* best, the winner takes Gaza! It makes sense and as I said I can't deny it's more humane, but the bastards know they're on to a winner, 'cause we don't breed the kind of muscle to take on Goliath. Now if I say, 'No mate, it's not on,' then I look like a warmongering villain . . .

David   At least they won't think you're a pooftah . . .

Saul   Dave, forget all that shit . . . I need your help, you're a smart guy.

David   You're right, we don't breed muscle any more, not like we used to . . . We produce brains.

Saul   For sure, brains like accountants, dentists, tailors . . .

David   Investment bankers, jewellers, hairdressers . . .

Saul   Optologists, cosmetic surgeons, doctors . . .

David   Movie producers, playwrights, singers . . .

Saul   Pianists, violinists, conductors . . .

David   Novelists, tailors . . .

Saul   I said that already, tailors . . .

David   Stockbrokers . . . But you get one stinking, dirty thieving bastard and the smell they send out covers all of us, the whole Hebrew race is smeared by one lowlife thieving scumbag.

David   Wasn't it always the case . . .

Saul   Don't I know it? Now listen, Dave, about Goliath . . .

David   Yeah, Goliath, I'm listening . . .

Saul   I've heard of your reputation with the slingshot . . .

David   Yeaaah . . . ?

Saul   Now don't think I am barmy and you can shut me up . . . But . . .

David   Yeah, go on, I'm listening . . .

Saul   Well, word on the street is that you can knock the shit out of a thieving fox with a well-aimed shot from your sling at a hundred yards . . .

David   Yeah, maybe so?

Saul   Well, you know what I'm getting at?

David   You know what, Saul, I haven't the faintest . . .

Saul   Oh yes you do, Dave baby . . . Yes you do . . .

David   . . . I do?

Saul   I think you do . . .

David   OK, so you want me to go out there and kill this brute Goliath for you in a one-to-one and in this way avoid all the bloodshed of two armies knocking the shit out of each other . . . Of course your army is far superior, and you would easily overcome them but then you would look like a prize turd and a coward to boot . . .

Saul   You're a mind-reader.

David   Well, for one, his skull is like a rock . . .

Saul   So use a heavy stone.

David   But to use a heavy stone with any force I will have to get closer . . .

Saul   So get closer.

David   And if I miss?

Saul   You never miss . . .

David   But if I do . . .

Saul   So you reload . . .

David   But at that distance he'd be on me before I could get my stone in the sling . . .

Saul   You won't miss.

David   You've got a lot of faith in me!

Saul   'Cause you're the best . . . I've heard all about you . . .

David   I'll think about it.

Saul   Look, Dave, what I am saying is . . . the Jews need a tough guy, alright, a hero, a young man with the guts to do this thing or we look like a race of chicken-noshing wimps . . . Show 'em, Dave, show 'em that we've got the guts, Jewish guts! You can't imagine what that will do for our image, let alone everything else, and last but not least . . .

David   Oh yeah, what's that?

Saul   Think what that will do for your rep . . . You know what I'm saying . . . You do, dontcha? No one but no one will ever raise the subject, ever again . . . about you being maybe a little left of centre, they won't even dare to breathe it . . .

You and Jonathan can go about playing ya harp and singing to your hearts' content, and no one will dare to utter a dickie bird, especially after you floor that giant ganuff . . . I mean that's worth a go, kid.

David   OK . . . No sweat . . . Let's do it!

Saul   Hey! You're a cool character . . . You sure now?

David   Sure as I'll ever be . . . OK, Saul, I'll catch you later. Set it up.

Saul   Hey, where you going?

David   To find some nice smooth heavy stones, where else!

Blackout.

Samson's Hair

Characters

Samson, *strong, beautifully built, long thick hair*
Delilah, *young, dark, lithe and very attractive*

Set

Open white stage. Door, stage right. Music.

Samson *and* **Delilah** *move slowly across the stage, intertwined like two dancers.*

Delilah   I love the way you make love to me, my darling man, you're so strong, yet so gentle . . . You could break me in two like a twig . . .

Samson   And why, my sweetheart, would I want to do that?

Delilah   Instead you hold me in your hands as if I was as delicate as a butterfly . . .

Samson   That's exactly how your soft slim body feels to me, a beautiful soft butterfly.

Delilah   Having your great strength with me . . . within me fills me with your power, I feel it coursing through me, I feel exalted, I seem to float on the wings of your love, my darling.

Samson   And when I join myself to you, my precious angel, I feel as if . . . I am complete, made whole . . . It's as if magic has entered my veins, flowed through my entire body.

Delilah   Oh, my wonderful Jew, Samson, my powerful and handsome Jew who can confront any number of Philistines and slay them all . . . just with the jawbone of an ass! You amazing man. How strong you are . . . How did you become so very strong, my noble warrior?

Samson   I have never questioned it, Delilah, or sought the answer, since my Lord God gave me this gift of strength so I might defend our tribe from our enemies, and even if they are your own tribe, I cannot fail to defend our people, Delilah.

Delilah   My dear Samson, there is no need to defend your actions in front of me, my darling one, for I do hate them, even if they are my brethren, for always seeking to fight, and never to speak and offer peace, but only happy when they are spilling blood . . . Oh, how I do hate them, Samson.

Samson   But you must not hate them, darling, for they are misguided, and are led by foul-minded men, and one day they will realise that, and I will hurt them no more, I will kill them no more, for believe me it gives me no joy to slaughter my fellow man.

Delilah   Oh what a good man you are, Samson, and yet still they shiver in fear whenever they see you, when they see you appear out of the ranks of the soldiers, oh how they blanch, for they know that they cannot hurt you, my beautiful darling man . . . They even believe that you are blessed by God . . . Some even believe that you cannot be hurt!

Samson   . . . Yes . . . Perhaps . . .

Delilah   And he, your blessed God, will always protect you . . .

Samson   Yes, for I bless him, every moment of my day for giving me this gift.

Delilah   I am so happy, so very happy that he protects you my darling, for I should be loath to lose you . . . I would indeed be so full of grief to lose my champion, I think I could not endure to live . . .

Samson   You will not lose me, my loved one, while my Lord stretches out his arm over me . . .

Delilah   Like you do me, my sweetheart, as you do me . . .

Samson   Yes, my heaven, as I do, thee.

Delilah   The Philistines are so jealous . . . How they would love to know the secret of your strength . . . But they never shall . . . It is your secret . . . and you will never tell anyone, I know, not even your beloved . . .

Samson   No, not even to my beloved, no, not to her, for what if one day the impossible were to happen, and they capture you and torture you for it . . . How horrible that would be, to think of you suffering for me . . . too horrible . . .

Delilah   No! No! Not horrible, oh you don't know your Delilah, Samsa, you don't know your little butterfly for I would gladly die for you, gladly, and even if they tortured me, I would never ever speak . . . because no pain that they would or could inflict could ever match the power of your love . . . Besides I will always be with you, always be protected by you, so that they cannot capture me, and even when you are in battle I am safely protected amongst your tribesmen.

Samson   Good Delilah, you will always be safe here amongst my tribe, always.

Delilah   You know, don't you, my sweet and lovely man that you could always trust your secret with me . . . You really could . . . You could, darling, and you know it would make me feel even closer to you, even closer that you have trusted me, with such a precious secret . . .

Samson   Oh my darling, if only I could, but one must never reveal the intimate secrets of the soul less they perish in the open air, and, more than this, much more than this, it is a treasure, a gift from my Lord, and so I must not boast, or expose it. For then I would betray my Lord and how could I ever do that?

Delilah   Of course, my sweet piece of heaven . . . Of course, and I respect you so much for what you have just told me, for being so faithful to your Lord whom you love so much . . .

Samson   Thank you for being so understanding, my beloved.

Delilah   Do you really love me, Samson – really, from the bottom of your heart as I do thee?

Samson   Oh my Delilah, how can you ever doubt such a thing. I love you with every pore of my flesh, with every beat of my heart, with every hair on my head, oh do I relish and love thee . . .

Delilah   Oh yes, my darling, desire and relish, and how beautiful that is while we are young and drown in each other's ardour, but love, true love also means trust, a deep lasting trust, that goes beyond desire or even love. It is a belief in your loved one, a belief so strong you would entrust your life to them, as I do you.

Samson   Oh darling wife, you can trust me until the end of time . . . .

Delilah   Oh yes, sweet words, but would you trust your life, trust your life to me, my strong warrior, would you, my strong warrior, would you . . . ?

Samson   Only in God can we really trust our lives, my beloved.

Delilah   Oh . . . Oh . . . Samson, I feel you slip away from me, just a bit, oh my darling, like a chill wind suddenly brushed my cheek . . . Oh darling, I'm so sorry, but I can't help feeling this way . . . that your love for me, though strong as you say, but does it really go down into the very root of your being, and then I feel this coldness . . . like some part of you is held back from me, and that part, that part that you hold back hurts me . . . that you don't love me with the whole of your being . . .

Samson   Delilah, my angel, oh, how your words hurt me too, for I do love you with all of my being, with every single part of me, and what you believe I hold back, I hold back because there is a part of every human being that belongs to God, to him and him alone . . . And this I hold back for it is not mine to give. It is my Lord's, who trusted me with his gift, and so I hold nothing back except that which is his gift to me . . .

Delilah   I understand Samson and I bless your honesty, your integrity and your faith, and what a wonderful faith, but still . . .

Samson   Yes, Delilah.

Delilah   I can't help but feel . . . This coolness, like while you protect me, and you do, there is a small fissure, a small tear in the fabric of your love . . .

Samson   No, Delilah, there is no tear . . .

Delilah   Yet, when we love each other and when you enter me and pour all your love into me are we not then as one being?

Samson   We are, of course we are, sublime one . . .

Delilah   Yes, we are, for husband and wife are of one flesh, and do you not think that your God would not bless you for sharing everything with me, everything . . . ? Your love, your pain, your sickness and even your secrets, for I am you . . . And then you would trust your life, your sacred life to me, and then, Samson, I would love you till the end of time . . . And the cold wind would be for ever shut out.

Samson   And would this . . . knowing this secret would make you so happy?

Delilah   The happiest woman in the whole world, for then I would know without any doubt that I had your love to the very deepest recesses of your soul . . .

Samson   Oh woman, woman, how could God have made such an idyllic wonderful but strange creature . . .

Delilah   Not so strange darling, not so strange, for what men call strange is our willingness to reveal our souls to the men we love, and that is strange to men who always must retain some little secret, like children fearful lest they lose something, but with me you still retain it since I am part of you . . . And I'm willing to bare myself to the very depths of my being, for I am yours, and there is no greater gift that I can give to you but myself, my whole self I sacrifice to you, and happily . . .

Samson   And in the same way do I sacrifice myself, all of me . . . Happily, yes happily . . .

Delilah (*teasing*)   Oh loved one . . . I cannot persuade you, and I will never try. I will never ask you again, never, for to be denied hurts me too much . . . But I do understand you . . .

You are a great man . . . And it behoves you to be cautious and keep your secret . . . Even from me . . .

Samson   Delilah . . .

Delilah   Even from me who trusts you with her body and soul, but I understand . . . I do . . . You are simply a man and like so many men, who fear to open up their hearts to their women . . . Oh my wicked Samson . . . Are you just like other men?

Samson   Oh Delilah, my darling Delilah, you torture me . . .

Delilah   God forbid I should ever do that, you torture yourself with your silly secret, but as I have already said, I will ask you no more . . . No more . . .

Samson   Delilah, I will give you my whole being, my life and soul to you, since I do trust you, I do, so I will . . . I will tell thee . . .

Delilah   No! No! I don't wish to take anything that is not freely given, and I was wrong to beg . . . Forgive me . . . You see, I could only accept it if you really wished to, really deep in your heart, really wished to, I want you to desire to tell me, not because a silly girl made demands on you, or you were cajoled, but because you cannot bear to hold something back from your loved one.

Samson   Darling one, darling one, I really do desire to tell you, I do, very much.

Delilah   Then, my most beloved if you really do I will allow you to tell me your little secret, for a secret is only great when it is kept private, locked up in a dark place, when you let it out to your beloved it is really very small.

Samson   Hush now, my child, and I will tell you my 'little' secret and you must bury it deep deep down inside your soul, never to see the light of day, for if it did my enemies would feast upon my flesh.

Delilah   Oh! Oh! Oh! How you spoilt it by even needing to say such words, as if such things were possible, oh how small a thing you make of me, oh Samson, I now do not wish to know, not now when you trust me so lightly . . .

Samson   Forgive me, my honey, for I am sometimes weak in my mind when I am so strong in my body, I often wish it could be reversed . . .

Delilah   No, darling, that is not true, for you are not weak in your mind, God forbid, you are just very cautious, and so you should be with such a gift, a gift from God. I had no right to demand such knowledge from you, and it was not even the secret that I wanted, no, it was your trust, your trust in me that I was greedy for.

Samson   Then, my glorious Delilah, whom I do trust above all creatures on Earth, you shall have it, you shall . . . I will tell you the secret of my strength . . .

Delilah   Oh Samson, please . . . Please, dear one, are you sure? Please be very sure.

Samson   As sure as the hand I see before my face . . .

Delilah   Oh . . . Oh . . . Oh . . . I even tremble a little . . .

Samson   Delilah, my darling, it is locked in my hair . . . ! My hair. That is the source of my strength . . .

A shadow like a cloud falls over the stage.

Delilah   Your hair?! Oh, how strange, Samson . . . Your hair, your thick beautiful hair, your mighty power lay . . . in there.

Samson   Yes, I do not question why it should be thus, but our Lord works in mysterious and wonderful ways, doth he not?

Delilah   Oh Samson, what a treasure you have shared with me, and this has opened up something within me, a torrent of love flows through me that I never dreamed I had . . . Oh darling, my love burns deep, so deep inside the very chambers of my soul, where your secret will for ever be kept, for now I know, know so very well, that you love me, with your life as I do thee . . .

Samson   Delilah, yes, you know now, without any doubt that I love you without restraint, for now you carry my secret within you . . .

Delilah   And that overwhelms me my darling champion and mighty lord and you know how safe your secret is with me, and none would ever prise it out of me, not even if they ripped the tongue out of my head, not even if they threatened my life, since I would gladly lay down my small insignificant life for my mighty Samson . . .

Samson   No, not insignificant, for now you carry my God's secret within you . . .

Delilah   And I feel blessed for it . . .

Samson   Oh Delilah, your skin is soft as the lilies of the valley, and your breath is like honey mixed with myrrh.

Delilah   But now to mark this moment, the special moment that we share, and before we share our other delightful God-given secrets, let us drink some wine, as a toast.

She pours the wine. **Samson** *drinks copiously.*

Samson   Oh Delilah, I am so happy . . . I so ache for thee my dearest flower . . . But suddenly my head grows heavy . . .

Delilah   Rest my angel . . .

Samson   How strange but a sleep seems to wish itself on me.

He lays down.

Delilah   Then sleep, sleep, my darling, you have given so deeply of yourself . . . It is natural that you feel a sleep coming on, so sleep my darling, sleep, and when you wake I will be in your arms . . . waiting for your caresses, my sweet one.

Drugged with the wine, **Samson** *sleeps.*

Delilah *moves to door right, which very slowly opens. An arm appears with shears. She takes the shears, gently lifts up a strand of* **Samson**'s *hair and begins to cut.*

Del (*as she cuts*)   Oh my darling, you poor simple man, to trust a woman who you crave so much, how simple you are, my darling warrior, to fall like all simple men to the wiles of women . . . But I do have love, I have love for my own people whom you have slaughtered with wild abandon. I too have a secret, but you could never prise my secret from me, never. For I am a woman and have the cunning that you poor beasts lack, for you only have the stupid strength of a carthorse, and soon you will not even have that, for I will avenge my tribe and I am proud to do so, so farewell my dear lord. I do love you, Samson, but I love my own God more, and you, poor soul, betrayed yours . . . (*To someone offstage.*) He's ready . . .

Slow fade over the sleeping, shorn **Samson**.

Two hooded men enter slowly and ominously, carrying rope and chains.

Moses

Characters

Pharoah
Moses
Pharoah's Son, *the actor who played Samson*

The son acts as Pharoah's bodyguard, and we only know it is his son when he is struck down.

Set

Empty white stage.

Pharaoh *reclines on rug and cushions, as does* **Moses**.

Pharaoh   So what's your beef, Moses, or can I call you
Moisha?

Moses   Call me wotcha like, pal, but you know the beef,
I mean, let's be cool about it, and work it out . . .

Pharaoh   Hey, what's to work out, you want to take my
slaves, which are my labour force, out of the country . . .
That's robbing me of my assets, my wealth, my manpower.
And why . . . ? You suddenly caught the religious bug . . .
Hey, that's seriously uncool! You have a good life here,
Moses. Why be concerned about slaves? They're happy,
well-fed, they wouldn't thank you for it . . .

Moses   Hey, Pharaoh, let me tell you something, these
people are Hebrews and always were Hebrews and always
will be Hebrews, and even through the centuries, as wretched
slaves they've never abandoned their idea of their one God.
So this was no new born-again crap that suddenly hit me like
a thunderstroke; this is my enlightenment, an eye-opener for
me, to bring meaning into my life . . . So let them go, let my
people go, 'cause they're only gonna be a shitload of trouble
to you . . . You know that . . . Look, I've lived and flourished
here all my life, thanks to you, Pharaoh, you made me
comfortable, sustained and nourished me, but now I have
a dream, to lead them into a land where they are free to
worship as they wish, and no longer be slaves . . . So let my
people go.

Pharaoh   Hey, Moses, my man, I find that whenever
people get the religious bug that's when the trouble starts,
they get a sense of entitlement, even a dash of superiority, like
'my God is better than yours' crap. But let me tell you they're
OK with us . . . They're fed, they're safe, they've even got
their own houses, let's say shacks, OK? But whenever did
slaves have that? They even grow their own food, have their
own cattle . . . eat according to their own custom, and even
have a day a week off! And you want to take them out away

from security and comfort into a harsh, ruthless desert, no easy food, little water, no shelter. You're totally one brick short of a pyramid, mate.

Moses   OK, OK . . . Just listen up, we'll make a deal . . . My Lord, with whom I have the privilege of conversing, will give you an opportunity to reconsider by giving you a little demo of his powers . . .

Pharaoh   Oh yeah, like a taster, sounds like a right bully-boy, your God.

Moses   No, by no means, that is why he doesn't just strike you down by a bolt of lightning, which he could, but gives you time to think.

Pharaoh   Yeaaah?

Moses   He will show you a little of his power and fill your entire land with locusts – they will eat your hard-laboured crops, they will ravish your fruit, and deplete your granaries, leading to famine and starvation, they will darken the air like hail if you do not repent!

Pharaoh   Hey, listen to you! We always get locusts, at least once a year they swarm all over the land, we put up with it, we always do, we bring the harvest in before they arrive, so what's new? Don't bullshit me, mister, with your phoney threats.

Sounds of locusts – **Pharaoh** *and his bodyguard react violently.*

Blackout . . . Lights up after the first plague.

Pharaoh   They ate half the nation's crops you slimy stinking old trickster . . . You had word somehow that they were on their way, didn't you? I don't know how, maybe a messenger or several and teams of horses in relay to speed you with the news, so you had advance notice, you con artist. Piss off!

Moses   Please Pharaoh, let my people go or it shall go much worse for you and I don't want you to suffer when it is not necessary to suffer . . .

Pharaoh   Not necessary to suffer – you're asking me to release fifty thousand strong bodies, healthy slaves and who will do their slave work? Who will take their place and pave our avenues and haul the rocks and dig the tunnels for the water and collect the harvest . . . Us?

Moses   Please let my people go or it shall go worse for you for the next will be a plague of frogs.

Pharaoh   Frogs? Frogs?

Moses   Yes, frogs – they will fill you with disgust and loathing, they will invade your chambers, your beds and leap on to your table, into the cots of your children, they will crawl, leap, hop, jump, slither, squelch into the most unexpected places. They are slimy and sticky – their slime will cover your cloaks, they will lay eggs in all possible crevices, even in the places you least expect. Also they will carry infectious diseases, diseases from the swamps, from the mud, from the thick filthy eddies of the Nile . . . At night they will crawl in their thousands into your homes, frogs will be your daily visitation, they will be the first thing you see in the morning and the last thing you see at night . . . They will revolt you . . . They will eat the few crops the locusts have passed . . . Now, Pharaoh, do you want this, can you suffer this??

Pharaoh   Phaah! Frogs! Small simple squashy things . . . That's nothing, since it's the season when they breed and migrate from the cooler reaches of the Nile . . . This is nothing new, you fool, since we have the wretched frogs each year. We're used to it. Fake! Trickster! You time your threats to come with the seasons – you fool and then attribute it to your 'magic' power. Fraud, I suppose you make the sun rise each morning . . . Go tell it to a child . . . Tell it to them . . . Not me, so go! Go!

Lights out . . .

Sounds of frogs – **Pharaoh** *and his bodyguard react violently.*

Pharaoh (*disgustedly*)   Ooh! Yuk! Yuk! Yuk!

Lights up.

Moses   Let my people go, put an end to your misery. Get slaves if you must from elsewhere . . . My people have done your bidding and been under your whip for centuries, Pharaoh, so spare yourself, pal, more misery than you can possibly imagine . . .

Pharaoh (*recovering*)   Oh, the frogs . . . The frogs, that was very good, a very clever piece of timing, that I congratulate you on . . . And oh, the cats loved the frogs and chased the slimy hopping things and, OK, they did eat the rest of the crops but then we ate the frogs, a new dish, certainly, but spiced up not without a certain piquancy . . . Yes, very nice, and now I suppose you are threatening me with more of your tricks . . . It's the rainy season soon so how about threatening me with storms, with a deluge, that you'll bring down the heavens upon our poor heads, tell us that, you cunning conniving Hebrew!

Moses   No, my Lord has something else in mind for you, Pharaoh, and yes, to do with water, but in a way that is unimaginable. Poor Pharaoh, what grief you bring upon your people . . . By tomorrow you will taste no water!

Pharaoh   Oh really, we are always prepared for the drought, our wells are full to the brim with water.

Moses   Yes, but by tomorrow it will not be fit to drink, not sweet water, not the luscious sweet water to bathe and cleanse your limbs, not cool sweet water to quench your throats, not water on which your flocks depend on to survive, not water to cook your food, to wash your houses, but a water that will horrify you, for all your water will be turned to blood – to blood, do you hear? Blood, blood, salty, horrible, undrinkable blood . . .

Pharaoh   Blood! Blood! Blood! You disgusting viper, you wretched Hebrew, how dare you threaten the welfare of our great country with such a loathsome vile threat . . . You dog! Get out of my sight before it is your own blood that is shed!

Blackout.

Sounds of horror. **Pharaoh** *and his bodyguard react violently.*

Lights up.

Pharaoh Stop it! Stop it! Moses, stop it!

Moses Will you let my people go?

Pharaoh Yes, yes, yes, anything, but stop it.

Moses It is stopped . . . The water is as it was . . .

Pharaoh It is?

Moses Yes, yes, as it was. You stopped it yourself by allowing yourself to give way to the needs of others. And when man listens to the needs of others . . . When man listens to their wishes, heeds their pain, their hopes, then the Lord blesses him, but those who fail to take heed, who oppress them when a gesture of kindness would be so easy, then such people will be cursed. And he who causes pain to others shall be cursed for fifty generations, he who causes anguish and lamentation in small children shall also and for ever be cursed. In the eyes of God.

Pharaoh Oh Moses, you fill my stomach with loathing, you have the talent of a leper since you poison wherever you go . . . And we took you in, we gave you shelter when you were plucked out of the bullrushes where you were hidden, hidden from your murderous hunters, made you into a prince of the realm, and how you repay our kindness . . .

Moses Pharaoh, I appreciate every single thing that you have done for me and believe me when I say that the last thing in the world I wish is enmity between us.

Pharaoh These Hebrews for which you suddenly have such anguish for are our slaves, our property, and even our nourishment, and we treat them well, feed and clothe them, and as you well know each and every country has slaves. It balances our economy so our children can be skilled and creative, be masters in their chosen occupations, which makes our nation great. But for you to come out of the woodwork like some half-baked revolutionary and try to cause rebellion and chaos when we gave you so much is treachery that I have never before witnessed.

Moses   Then let my people go and all will be well and you still will prosper, I promise you.

Pharaoh   I have said . . . I have said . . .

Moses   Oh Pharaoh, why must you bring more suffering on yourself, you swore to let them go, you swore, and the rivers of blood were turned sweet again, and now you refuse and by refusing you bring down the wrath of God upon your head.

Pharaoh   Moses, my magician told me different, they told me that it was not blood that the water had changed into . . . It was the season for pollination and the red pollen of the poppy seed poured over our land, it was unusually great this year and the wind lifted from the great farms and it stained our waters. It thickened and stained our waters, so again, cunning trickery to coincide with nature . . . Yes, that is cunning . . .

Moses   But Pharaoh, do not be deluded, did it not stop when you gave your word?

Pharaoh   Ha! The wind dropped and by then the pollen dissolved and so you were lucky in your trickery, my friend.

Moses   But Pharaoh, open your eyes, the fish all died in the rivers and a great stench rose up and covered the land, and the rivers turned foul and the fish swelled up and burst their skins, and you believe this was caused by pollen!

Pharaoh   I believe what I believe and what my magicians tell me . . . So go . . . Get out . . . Think of some more tricks, you Hebrew huckster!

Moses   Then, my dear Pharaoh, you, by your own actions will bring down on your country such horror as you can never imagine. It will shock you beyond your wildest dreams. It will make you wish that you had never been born . . .

Pharaoh   Oh yes, of course, what else have you discovered that will torment us, plague, disease, hail . . . What horror will you align yourself with? I think, clever as you were to detect these flaws in our elements, you have run out of calamities so do your worst. We have survived all and will survive more, but whether you survive will be another matter, and now let me warn you for once, for I too, am capable of unleashing horror upon horror on the slaves you call your people, so beware Moses, beware . . .

Moses   Oh, do not force me, my Lord Pharaoh, to invoke God's anger, for it is an anger that will devastate you and I feel for you and your people . . .

Pharaoh   Feel for yourself, big man . . . Feel for yourself, so what treats, do you think, trickster, you have in store for us?

Moses   I will warn you Pharaoh that my Lord only asks from you only what is possible, only that, only freedom for others which really would cost you so little, and he who can give, who has great vast wealth, and yet can give so little will be punished so much. For we do not demand your land, nor your cattle, nor your gold, not your palaces, not your women . . . but only freedom, freedom to be. The simplest and most basic requirement of man. Freedom to live, unhampered, unafraid, to live in peace, to grow, to thrive, to make families, to love and honour our children, to know that their future also will be a life of peace . . . That is not so much to ask . . . In fact it is nothing to ask. It is only asking you to be kind, and this only blesses you, and to allow us to believe in our one God, our God who is the father of all blessed things.

Pharaoh   Go, you slug of mankind, do you not think we do not live in peace, adore our children, love tranquillity and harmony, or how we have created one of the greatest empires on Earth whose art will live for ever while you crawl in the mud . . .

Moses   Know, Pharaoh, that our Lord does not wish to torment you beyond endurance but this is to show that each time you choose to deny his bidding you will unleash a greater and greater force of destructiveness upon you.

Pharaoh   Unleash . . . My magicians can watch your magic, so do your worst, you vain cheap sorcerer.

Lights out. The voice of **Moses** *in the darkness.*

Moses   Alas a darkness, alas a darkness will cover the Earth, which will confuse you and set your people in panic and terror. The dark will weigh heavily on you. You will not be able to work or to feed yourself or your family or your livestock; livestock and your wives and children will be blind to you as you are to them.

Pharaoh (*in darkness*)   Moses! Moses! Do not do this to us, rescue us from this plague which obliterates our loved ones from us and when we try to light candles a mysterious wind snuffs them out . . . Moses, Moses, my friend, my brother whom we plucked from the Nile and cared for, spare us . . . Spare us . . .

Light returns.

Moses   And I shall never forget the sanctuary you gave me, never, but now, Pharaoh, let my people go . . .

Pharaoh   Oh, oh, thank the gods. Light, how beautiful is light. I can see again! Your magic is strong, Moses, but we can endure darkness, hell, horrible as it is . . . So I had a moment of weakness and became a beggar to you and now I feel shame.

Moses   There is no need to feel shame, Pharaoh, for I too would beg relief from these torments which you have no need to suffer, but since you now have sight, Pharaoh, all you have to do is let us go and be in peace

Pharaoh   I'll think about it . . . OK!

Blackout . . .

Lights up. **Pharaoh** *has covered his face with a hood.*

Pharaoh   Aaach! Your God is a filthy vindictive God, to cover our flesh with boils, our poor wives, our mothers and even our small children . . . Is this the work of a just God? To let loose in our flesh poisons and loathsome pus, to deform us, to contaminate us? Our wretched boils make us loathsome to each other, this filth that your God unleashes is like the eruptions and chancres that come from a whore, that seeping wound that stinks are from prostitutes . . . So your God is a foul contaminated whore or maybe it's just a plague carried on the wind that again you claim credit for, but I see your face is clean . . . Heal us, Moses . . .

Moses   Let my people go, Pharaoh . . .

Pharaoh   Yes, yes, yes, take them, take them, go, get out of my country with your abominable tribe and your grotesque God!

Moses   You are healed.

Pharaoh   I am?

He pulls up his hood, his face is clean.

Moses   You see whenever you give, you are rewarded

Pharaoh   Yes, I am rewarded when I am tortured to give, is that giving? I think not.

Moses   Then no more torture, which you bring upon yourself, so let my people go . . .

Pharaoh   Let me ponder, Moses. Let me ponder, Moses, for it is much you ask . . .

Moses   Pharaoh, you and your ancestors have kept our people as slaves, who have enriched your kingdom for four hundred and thirty years . . . Isn't that enough . . . ?

Pharaoh   Moses, please just let me ponder . . . if they have been waiting for four hundred and thirty years, to wait just a little longer will not hurt them.

Moses   Pharaoh, do not play with the wrath of God, I warn you.

Pharaoh   So tell me, you slug of your God, what have you in mind of us?

Moses   Alas, your first-born, the treasure and kingpost of your house, will be struck down this very night. All the love you have bestowed on this child will dissolve in dust, and you, Pharaoh, will be responsible, as if it were your own hand that did it, which in a truth it will be, so please, for your sake and your children's sake, let my people go!

Pharaoh   Bluffer, filthy trickster, do your worst!

Moses   So be it

(*To the people.*) Now this very night I wish every one of our tribe to take the blood of a lamb and smear it upon the doorposts of your dwelling, for the Lord hath ordained that this angel of death will pass this way and strike down the first-born of the Egyptians, since Pharaoh still has refused to let you go. So every doorpost that is stained will be a sign for the angel of death and he will pass over it! This is something that you must not fail to do, for this is a sign from you of your covenant with the Lord. And you may say, why doth our Lord wish this from us, since the angel of death must surely know us, would know us from the Egyptians, since did he not spare our water from being turned into blood, hespared our crops from the locusts, the darkness was not upon our eyes. But know ye that the Lord wishes you to identify yourself, and never be ashamed to declare your faith . . . To be proud and not to disguise who you are, and even if others abuse you, and torment you and even, yes even if they kill you, never hide yourself or who you are, for you are Hebrews and be proud. So let the sign on your doorposts be a sign of your pride and acknowledgment of the one God who created Heaven and Earth.

Blackout.

Howls and lamentations . . .

The bodyguard slowly collapses, thus revealing that he is the **Pharaoh's Son.**

Pharaoh (*weeping*)   How you torture us . . . Not man-to-man, army-to-army, with bravery, guts, endurance, in the honest heat of battle where man has a chance to redeem himself, defend his country and protect his family. No with you it is with the unleashed powers of a fiend . . . Go! Go! What a foul God is your God, no God but a monster, a loathsome filthy beast who would murder our innocent ones to achieve his ends. A filthy murderer . . . Oh what a God to have . . . Our gods are kind, beneficent, are gods of growth, life, light, stars, sea, wind, gods of the fishes, the birds, the flowers the glorious butterflies, the rain; a god for each and every one of them. A god for everything, for every insect, every beast, a god of love, a god of music, a god of poetry . . . But you . . . you sinister cruel Hebrews have only a god of death. Death! One God. One! So there are no gods on behalf of your children, or your cattle who are sick, or for rain when the land is parched. You just have one God to listen to you all and therefore no wonder he is such a cruel God, that cruelty comes so easily to your God, cruelty and death, so go, go, to your God of death.

Moses   I will go, Pharaoh, and I will go with a heavy heart for you . . . Our Lord made an example of you, so that others may learn to pay heed to what is right and just, but sadly you paid the price, for you have abused our nation mercilessly and the Lord sent a stern warning to others that says whatever nation abuses our race, now and for ever, will face the wrath of God, for whosoever does this, out of malice, jealousy, greed or for whatever reason shall perish, but whosoever offers the hand of friendship shall find this reciprocated tenfold, whosoever wishes to leave us in peace will find us a friend until the end of time.

Pharaoh   Go with your speeches Moses! And just remember your time will come . . . ! (*Weakly.*) You have helped to destroy our beautiful nation . . . ruin our great society by robbing every family in the land of their precious first-born, and even the first-born of the beasts – even the beasts which did you no harm, did *your* great beast slay . . . What monster is this God of yours?

Moses   I warned you, Pharaoh. I gave you the opportunity to release my people – for keeping them in perpetual slavery is a kind of death for them . . . You were given warnings first, warnings that you chose not to heed, but now you are the one who is wise after the event . . . You could have prevented all that has happened, but in fact you chose to test our Lord, but only a fool would ignore such warnings and you, Pharaoh, are not a fool, you are a wise and clever man, but your arrogance and pride blinded you . . . For these tragic deaths, you, Pharaoh, must take responsibility . . . You, for you had eyes but looked not, you had ears but heard not . . .

Pharaoh   Go! Go to your wretched beast God . . . You are his arch devil . . . Yes, I did ignore his warnings . . . I cannot surrender my will, my kingdom, like a spineless beggar, for I am Pharaoh and will risk my life and the lives of my people, poor people, that your cruel God murdered, in just the same way as the Egyptian tyrant murdered the new-born in fear of a rival, but what did we do? We saved you and drew you out of the rushes, we saved your young life and gave you comfort, and this is how you repay us . . . And you expect me to go down on my knees at your first threats . . . This is not what a Pharaoh does and, yes, now we have paid the price, but you, Moses, chosen of your Lord to be his scourge, have won a hollow victory, for you are a people without true courage, and reliant on a villainous God-beast and his whim . . . But one day the beast will not be there for you . . . And then what will you do, for you are a weak and needy people . . . What will you do then, Moses?

Moses   Our Lord is our Lord for ever and all time, and will never betray us if we keep his covenant and do not betray him, and we will not . . .

Pharaoh   You will see . . . Yes, you will see . . .

Lights fade slowly out.

PERSECUTION

How to Train an Anti-Semite

Characters

Dot, *a middle-aged bigot*
Sid, *a totally indifferent bigot but only when it suits* him

Set

Small living room in a terraced house in Tottenham.

Dot They're at it again!

Sid Who?

Dot Sod me, they're bloody at it again . . .

Sid Who, ya cunt?! Don't just fuckin' wind me up!

Dot Cunt yaself, y'old bollock. The Jews! The fuckin' Yids are at it again.

Sid Wadja mean, 'at it again'?

Dot Knockin' shit outta them poor fuckers in Palestine.

Sid Oh yeah . . . Well they're always fuckin' knockin' shit out of each other . . . It's their way of life . . . innit!

Dot Oh yeah . . . Course it don't mean nuffin' to you, sittin' here all fuckin' cosy . . . But imagine you're some poor cunt in Gaza!

Sid Gaza? Wossat?

Dot Gaza! Gaza, you prat! That's where they keep 'em in a big fuckin' concentration camp. 'T's 'orrible, fuckin' 'orrible!

Sid Oh yeah. I saw a bit on the news . . . So why they doin' that for . . . this time?

Dot 'Cause its easier to fuckin' thump 'em . . . 'cause they're trapped in this big fuckin' park . . . living in squalor . . .

Sid Fuck me, that's a bit much . . . They sound worse than the fuckin' Irish . . .

Dot Worse, I should say it's fuckin' worse, and they're bombing schools and 'ospitals . . .

Sid Get on, they're not, are they?!

Dot Yeah, course they don't care, see, to the Yids them Arabs are just fuckin' animals!

Sid Yeah, don't sound too good to me . . . But why would those Yids do that? Did those fuckin' Arabs get stroppy . . . ?

I mean, they must have stepped outa line or somefink? I mean, why fuckin' bomb them poor cunts to bits? Eh?

Dot   There's no why, you moron. It's just 'cause they 'ate 'em. They 'ate the poor fuckin' Arabs and more to the point they want their fuckin' turf, want that fuckin' big park they squat in . . . Gaza, it's called Gaza.

Sid   So why don't they bung them a bit of dosh and buy the fuckin' Gaza park off 'em? Save all that dosh on guns and jets . . . Buy off the cunts. I mean, they got the dosh, don't they? Yids always got the fuckin' dosh! Save a lot of punch-ups, wouldn't it!

Dot   Yourra real prat, Sid . . . You are . . . You're 'eartless! It's their fuckin' bit of land . . . Innit? Owdja like to be kicked outa your fuckin' bit of turf . . . Eh . . . What if some long-nosed cunt came round 'ere wiv a wad of cash and said OK mate, piss off!

Sid   What?! This fuckin' slagheap in Tottenham? Fuckin' luvly. If some Jewboy said, 'Piss off . . . I'll bung ya a hundred grand for this pisshole,' I'd be off like a fuckin' shot! I would! Off to the Costa Brava . . . Luvly.

Dot   Yeah . . . OK, but they've not bunged anything, they wannit for free by bombing 'em to bits. 'Oping to scare 'em off first . . . by bombing women and little innocent kids . . . Owdja like to come 'ome one night after work and see me lying in little bits. Eh . . . Owdja like to see that?!

Sid   After work? I ain't 'ad a job for two years, 'ave I? Been on the fuckin' dole ain't I? So I'd be bombed too, wouldn't I!

Dot   I'm just saying, suppose you came 'ome, OK after the pub, and you find yer 'ouse in smithereens and . . .

Sid   You blown up into little bits. (*Smiling.*) Oh, it would break my fuckin' heart . . . Not half . . . I'd be fuckin' gutted . . . (*Bursts out laughing.*)

Dot   Sid, sometimes you're a real cunt, aren'tcha? You don't give a fuck for anyone but yaself, just like them fuckin' Yids!

Sid   Hey! Cut that 'cunt' shit out, OK? You're spewing it out just a bit too much! So shut it! OK? Just shut it!

Dot   You laughed dint ya, ya c – (*Catches herself.*) When I said you might find me in little bits, you laughed, like it was funny . . . That ain't nice, is it?!

Sid   Didn't mean it, didn't mean nuffin' by it! Course it's not real, it's one of yer fantasies 'cause no one's gonna bomb this shithole we live in. Where they don't even collect the garbage from one week to the next and ya got a whole family of golliwogs for ya fuckin' neighbours, and the stink of their cooking makes you fuckin' sick!

Dot   OK . . . It's no use talking to you, 'cause you don't sodden care, 'bout me, the world, 'bout nuffin except ya stinking pub each night!

Sid   Course I don't fuckin' care . . . I don't, I don't give a monkey's shit, and ja know why, 'cause it's not my fuckin' business what those cunts do to each other, halfway 'cross the world. 'S not my business. 'S not!

Dot   That's why they get away wiv it . . . That's why them Jews get away wiv it 'cause of people like you!

Sid   Oh, so it's all my fuckin' fault now is it, you soppy tart?!

Dot   You don't care if someone just comes and takes your turf . . . You fuckin' would, ya know, you would if someone came over in boats and took over!

Sid   You're a barmy prat you are! Look around ya, open ya fuckin' eyes, you dumb fuckin' moron, this country already been taken over . . . ain't it?! There's a mosque down the fuckin' street. The Greeks and Cypriots have taken the whole high street. And the fuckin' Pakis occupy half the council flats and the Irish the other, and half of them are on welfare, so what the fuck ya talking about, 'alf the world away . . . It's happening here! Here! Here!

Dot   Yeah, but they're fuckin' working . . . most of 'em, they're not bombing you to fuckin' bits, or shoving up giant concrete walls so you can't fuckin' move . . . They're giving you a nice doner kebab when you come home late from the pub, yeah, they're bombing you with shish kebab and chicken tandoori! You don't mind that do you . . . ?!

Sid   Nah, I don't, as long as they stuff my stomach and don't shove a bomb up my arse I don't give a monkey's toss.

Dot   You don't care 'bout nuffin but yaself . . . I'm alright, Jack!

Sid   'S right! I don't fuckin' interfere wiv others and don't let them fucking interfere wiv me . . . Course if they do . . .

Dot   . . . If they do . . . What then? Wotcha gonna do? Eh?

Sid   You'll see. Don't you worry, mate . . . Keep your nose clean and I'll keep mine . . . That's fuckin' British . . . Right! We let them in, all those bleedin buggers from the four corners of the fuckin' Earth we let in. Can't turn back the tide. So, do your work and don't be a ponce and we'll get on just fine.

Dot   So you don't care what them Yids are doing as long as you can stuff your face?

Sid   You got the picture!

Dot   Others care . . . Others march 'cause they know that those little kids dying could be their kids.

Sid   Yeah but they're fuckin' *not* their kids!

Dot   But they feel for them as if they were 'cause they got heart and want to stop it. They march and demonstrate, even smash a few Jew shop windows . . . to show their anger . . .

Sid   Smash Jew shop windows, what's that going to fuckin' do?

Dot   Show they care! Sends a message that they care, then more and more smash Jew windows, and then they start to get the message, yeah, they get the fuckin' message to bloody leave off! Fuckin' leave off or it will get worse! Much fuckin' worse! I mean windows are still only windows, they're not fuckin' heads!

Sid   Yeah, Dot, I see ya point, yeah, you 'ave got a point. I tell you what . . .

Dot   What?

Sid   If we get any more fuckin' pimps and liggers from Albania, Poland, Latvia, Bangladesh, Africa, Russia I'll fuckin' march! Yeah, I'll march, I'll march my fuckin' legs off . . . OK! I'll march if I see one more Polish plumber taking away my job, I'll march to kingdom come! Ha ha ha!

Dot   Yeah, your job? Don't make me laugh, you been on the dole for two years . . .

Sid   Disability benefit!

Dot   Oh yeah, but they're not killin ya are they . . . They're not burying you alive in a bombed-out house. The ones here are mostly working, and they know 'ow to fuckin' work, and keep the trains fuckin' runnin' and the bleedin' 'ospitals, and the fuckin' buses and God knows what else . . .

Sid   They're not killing ya?! Where you been, you suppurating douchebag! Who stuck a fuckin' bomb in the fuckin' underground, eh? Oo fuckin' did that?! Who blew up that bus? . . . Eh, you silly twat . . . It weren't the fuckin' Yids . . . Or was it . . . Ya think?

Dot   Nah! Nah! It weren't the fuckin' Yids, but it was *because* of the Yids, because of what they did in Palestine, in Gaza park!

Sid   Oooh, I see, so they bomb us . . . not the fuckin' Yids, not them! That really makes fuckin' sense! Sure!

Dot   They did it to punish us! For *'elping* the Yids. America gives the Yids arms, don't they??

Sid   I s'pose so, so what's that got to do wiv us?

Dot   'Cause we 'elp the Yanks, right, we're partners wiv the fuckin' Yanks, right, we're one of their limbs so natch they strike at us . . . Get it?

Sid   Oh! Yeeah! I gotcha, the Yids are beating up the Arabs so the Arabs kill a few hundred Brits . . . Oooh, I see . . . Yeeah. Sure . . .

Dot   Look, dopey, course the Yankees bunged all that dosh to their Jew cousins in Israel, the Arabs paid the Yankee back by giving them a kicking in New York . . . 'Cause that's where all the Jews hang out . . . New York.

Sid   Yeah, butcha said, or I said, they give us a bloody nasty kicking too! And we ain't bloody Yids, why fuckin' us, we're fucking innocent, aint we?

Dot   Nah, not really, 'cause we joined in, didn't we? We joined in so we get fucked over . . . Yeah? Get it?

Sid   Sounds bonkers ta me . . .

Dot   'S not bonkers, 's not at all. The Yids got billions, countless billions, so it's easier to bung some of it ta Israel, they buy arms and whack the Arabs . . .

Sid   Wot about those Arab sheiks wiv the oil wells? Ain't they got money too, big dosh, oil dosh . . .

Dot   Yeah, they bung dosh to their Arab mates, they do, course they do, wadya fink? But the Yank Jews got even more.

Sid   What, more than those oil sheiks?! How they got so much dosh then?

Dot   They stick together, ya see, they stick together like shit to a blanket and they don't give the money to no one but themselves, right, like a club, right, and they're very cunning in business, they know all the tricks . . . Wherever they are they drain the country of money and squirrel it away . . .

Sid   Oh yeah, well, how about those banks, those fuckin' scrounging banks that just took billions off us . . . Are they Yids? Those pigs in a trough who give themselves huge bloody bonuses even after they sunk our dosh into a shit-hole . . . They fuckin' Yids? I thought they were Scotties . . .

Dot   Yeah, maybe, but they're only the tip of the iceberg . . .

Sid   You dopey prat, they practically ruined the fuckin' country, tip of the fuckin' iceberg! So 'ow the Jews get their fuckin' money then?

Dot   You wanna know how they got all their dosh apart from fiddling?

Sid   Go on, surprise me, I might learn something.

Dot   OK, I'll tell ya . . .

Sid   I'm listening . . .

Dot   By screwing the Germans, yeah, by screwing the Huns!

Sid   Ow?

Dot   Through the big lie.

Sid   The big lie?

Dot   That 'Itler gassed millions of the fuckers, the more they say he bumped off, the more dosh they get, can you believe that . . . ? Eh?

Sid   That's a bit strong innit? Fuck me!

Dot   Sodden right it is! And now it's all coming out . . .

Sid   It is?

Dot   Yeah, it is, all that Holycaust shit is a myth, a money-maker. It's all coming out, even a priest, a holy priest from the church, he said only 350,000 died . . . And 'e's a man of God, so 'e should know . . . Right?

Sid   I thought 'Itler 'ated the Yids and killed them *all* off . . .

Dot   Course he hated them, course . . . I mean everybody 'ated them really but didn't let on, like the Brits, we're too polite, too decent for our own good, but 'Itler had the guts . . . 'E 'ad the guts to do wot no one else had the guts to do . . . Oh fuck, did that man 'ave guts . . . So 'e got rid of 'em . . . Yeah!

Sid   Yeah . . . So 'e killed them off!

Dot   Yeah . . . Right, but not as many as they claim . . . Not that many, not six mill! That's not even possible, not even fuckin' possible . . . I mean, I know the Germans are efficient . . . I know that, but that's not fuckin' possible!

Sid   So how many do you reckon?

Dot   Well, I'm not an expert but I'd say around half a mill, top whack, the rest were pooftahs, gypsies and maybe left-handed people . . .

Sid   So the Jews say 'Itler bumped off six mill and cop the guilt money from the Huns.

Dot   Course! There weren't even six mill Yids in the whole world . . . Everybody knows that . . .

Sid   So if everybody knows that, right . . . why are the Krauts paying Yids all that money, eh?

Dot   Guilt! Just guilt! They feel guilty for 'Itler and starting the fuckin' war so they just coff up! Those heebs have made millions, no fuckin' billions . . . It's a scam, see? And half of them that claim ain't even been in the camps . . . They just make it up and cop a whole heap of dosh!

Sid   How do you know so much, eh? I mean, how do you know 'ow many got topped or baked in the ovens?

Dot   'Ow do I know . . . 'Ow do I know?

Sid   Yeah, 'ow come you know so fucking much?

Dot   'Cause I keep my eyes and ears open, don't I? I watch the news while you're playing darts in the pub . . . And . . . I see it on the World Wide Web!

Sid   Ha ha! You're like a big fat spider in the middle of her web!

Dot   Just 'cause you're too stupid to use it . . . If you weren't so stupid and made an effort to use it you would learn something too . . .

Sid   I got the radio, I got the TV, I got the papers . . . I don't need to stick my head into a screen, fanks very much!

Dot   That's the difference between us . . . I like to know stuff . . . Ya see . . . we could do wiv another 'Itler 'ere . . . Couldn't we?

Sid   Ya fink?

Dot   Yeah . . . I mean another spring clean wouldn't do any harm . . . I mean would it . . .

Sid (*dawning*)   Wait a min . . . You're fuckin' right, Dot . . . We coul do wiv another 'Itler . . . Right now . . .

Dot   You fink there's enough Jews left to make it worth his while?

Sid   No, you daft prat! For the Asians, for the Blacks, the fuckin' Chinese, no strike that, I love my chop-suey, no, all those scum from Eastern Europe, those fuckin' Albanians, Latvians, Poles, Cypriots, bout three or four mill all told! Nice one! Come on, 'Itler! Come back, ya cunt! We need ya, darlin'! Ha ha ha!

Dot   Ya barmy, y'are! Ya just 'ate everyone dontcha . . . You're not selective . . . You don't fink abaht it!

Sid   Like you do . . . eh?

Dot   Yeah, I do . . . I fink abaht it . . . I fink abaht those poor little kids blown up in Gaza park, that never 'ad a proper decent life that we 'ave . . . And ya know what that does . . . ? Makes the whole of the Arab world fuckin' mad, mad wiv us! And all 'cause of them heebs, and ya know what that means, dontcha?

Sid   You tell me, Go on . . . tell me what vibes you get sitting on ya fuckin' Web . . .

Dot   World fucking war, mate 'cause of them! 'Cause of them Yids, world fuckin' war!

Sid   Gedadavit!

Dot   Yeah . . . That's right . . . Listen, jug ears, world fuckin' war!

Sid   Naaaah!

Dot   Naaaah? Naaaaaaaa? Listen, the Yids are bashing up all those fuckin' Arabs . . . Wot's gonna happen . . . one day some Arab state nearby's gonna get pissed off rotten and lob a fuckin' nuclear bomb in the middle of Tel Aviv, and then the Yids will have to lob one back, and then the other Arab states lob theirs . . . And then the Yanks who are in the pay of the Yids jump in an' all, and then we're fucked, we're all fucked!

Sid   Then we gotta keep out of it! Keep out of it, like I said.

Dot   Oh yeah. Very handy like, but we're locked in with the Yanks, we're all in the same fuckin' soup.

Sid   I see, yeah, fuck! So them Yids have gotta give the Gaza park back . . . yeah?

Dot   No, you prat . . . The Arabs got the park, already live in the park . . . In Gaza park, it's theirs, it's just that they're locked in the fucking park, locked in like a fucking jail, yeah!

Sid   So why they locked in the fuckin' park?

Dot   'Cause, 'cause, they got pissed off with being locked in, no food, no work, no travel, 'elpless, so they bunged a few rockets at the Yids, yeah, like you know they were desperate, fuckin' desperate, so they bunged a few rockets, 'ad no more

effect than fireworks . . . And this gave the Yids the excuse
they wanted to bomb them to bits, to fuckin' bits!

Sid   Oh I see, they went apeshit 'cause the Arabs bunged a
few squibs at them . . .

Dot   Nah, you see that's why the Yids locked them in the
park . . . Ya see. To provoke the Arabs, this gave them the
excuse to wade in . . . You see . . . It's just a clever plot!
Geddit!

Sid   So 'ow d'ya know all that?

Dot   Listen, ya got to be blind not to know it aintcha . . . Ya
gotta wake up, Sid . . . Check the Web . . .

Sid   Oh yeah, the fuckin' Web . . .

Dot   Yeah, if you could be bothered, you might learn
somefink . . . Yeah . . .

Sid   I thought the Web was for ponces who looked up porn
channels and jailbait kids . . .

Dot   Oh! Yeah, that's all it is . . . To people like *you*, maybe,
who sit in front of it, wanking ya brains out . . . But for people
like me, we learn somefink!

Sid   About the Yids . . . ?

Dot   Too fuckin' right, gotta be on their case, don't want ta
end up crucified like them poor fuckers in Gaza . . . Don't
want that, do you . . . ? So you gotta be on ya guard . . .
Be alert, mate . . . They're crucifying them poor fuckers in
Gaza . . . Just like they did to our Lord Jesus . . . See, 'istory
repeating itself . . .

Sid   I thought the Romans crucified Jesus, didn't they . . .

Dot   You don't know nuffin', Sid, that's all whitewash,
bloody 'ell . . . The Jews turned him over to the Romans,
right . . . They turned him over and the Romans, yeah,
technically they nailed him up, but they did it for the Jews,
see, read it in the Bible, you ignoramus!

Sid   So the Romans did it for the Jews, like as a favour –
you wannim topped, we'll do it for you, no sweat . . .

Dot   Look, Sid, the Romans 'ad to do it, didn't want to, but
they 'ad to, to keep the peace, 'cause Jeez was a troublemaker,
I mean for the Yids! See?

Sid   Oh now I see, yeah. You're clever, Dot, really clever.
Now I know (*Yawns.*) Well I 'ope they get their Gaza park
back then . . . Oops, I'm a bit late for the pub, better get goin'
or my mates will crucify me, ha ha ha ha ha ha ha!

Dot   On ya way back pick up a nice dona kebab for me will
ya . . . Ya dope.

Sid   Wiv chilli?

Dot   Course wiv chilli!

Blackout.

Roast

Author's Note

The appalling tale that *Roast* describes came from an anti-Semitic medieval collection of stories that were current at the time.

Characters

Mummy
Boy, *her son*

Set

A child's bedroom.

Mummy I've got something to tell you, darling . . .

Boy Ooh! Is it a story? Is it . . . You going to tell me a story, Mama?

Mummy Yes, my darling, I have a little story, about a small boy, a good and honest boy, just like you . . .

Boy Oh! Oh! Tell me, Mummy, please!

Mummy Shh now! I will, be patient . . . Then you'll go to sleep, OK?

Boy Yes, I will . . . I promise, Mummy.

Mummy Very well, I'll tell you a special little story, about a special little boy.

Boy Oh good . . . Good . . .

Mummy Now you know when you go to church on Sunday and take Holy Communion . . .

Boy Yes! Yes! I like that bit . . .

Mummy Shhh! . . . When you put the holy wafer in your mouth . . . Jesus is in that wafer . . . You're really putting the flesh of Jesus our Lord in your mouth – you know that, don't you?

Boy Yes, I know, I know, and the wine is his blood, I know that too, but they say I'm too young to drink the wine, but I will one day . . .

Mummy Of course you will, my darling boy, of course you will, because our Lord told us at the Last Supper that he is in the wafer and the wine, so that we may have our beloved Jesus within us . . .

Boy But how can Jesus be in every wafer and every drop of wine in the while world?!

Mummy Now that's a good question my clever boy . . . You see, his love is infinite, it goes to everyone, to every human being in the whole world, and Jesus is like that love, he is in every tiny grain, every little grain of the wafer, in every drop of the wine . . .

Boy   'Cause he's the Son of God!

Mummy   Exactly, of course he is, sweetheart . . . Now listen, many years ago, oh a long time ago, there was a little boy just like you, except for one thing . . .

Boy   Oh, oh! What thing, Mummy, what thing, tell me . . .

Mummy   Shhh! This little boy was the son of those poor Jews who rejected our Lord, and who have been punished ever since . . . They rejected him and cast him out, you see, they betrayed him and so our beloved Jesus died on the cross . . .

Boy   That's horrible, horrible . . .

Mummy   Yes, yes, indeed it must have been for that poor, poor man . . . But this little Jewish boy was innocent, he couldn't help that his parents were of the condemned race . . .

Boy   Of course not, of course not, poor little boy!

Mummy   Exactly, he was still innocent, a poor innocent boy who could not choose his parents. Anyway his father was not a good man, in fact he was a very wicked Jew . . .

Boy   Are all Jews wicked, Mummy?

Mummy   Not all, darling, not all, but they cannot help it since they rejected our Lord, but Jesus tells us to forgive, so we must learn to forgive, even the wicked one . . .

Boy   How was this one wicked, Mummy?

Mummy   Well, darling, I'll tell you . . . You see, he hated us Christians as I suppose sadly most of them do, even though we pray for them and let them be baptised as Christians when they see the light of the Lord.

Boy   But why was this Jew especially wicked, Mummy?

Mummy   He wanted revenge on Jesus, he so badly wanted to hurt our dearest Lord Jesus who he blamed for all their misfortunes. Imagine, he blamed our innocent sweet Jesus for all their pain, rather than themselves for rejecting him. For rejecting God's son . . .

Boy   Oh! How horrible, and Jesus was so beautiful, so full of goodness . . .

Mummy   Yes, darling, how well you put it, but sometimes it is said that pure people shine so bright a light that wicked people see their own spots, and blemishes, and the impure feel frightened at what they see and full of self-disgust, so they want to shut out that pure light, they want to smash it, to darken it for ever.

Boy   Oh, that's terrible! So how did they do it, Mummy? How did the wicked Jew do that, Mummy, since you can never put out the light of Jesus!

Mummy   Oh my little darling, how right you are . . .

Boy   So tell me, Mummy, what did the wicked Jew do who was the father of the innocent little boy?

Mummy   I will tell you . . . I will, so you will know, darling. Now I told you how our Lord is in the wafer and the wine . . . And you remember how the wicked Jew had a sweet innocent son . . .

Boy   Yes, of course, the small boy just like me . . .

Mummy   Right . . . Now this small Jewish boy had made a friend of a Christian boy in the village . . .

Boy   Oh that's nice . . . That's nice . . .

Mummy   Yes, and the little Christian boy felt sorry for the little Jewish boy and since they played together, he asked the little Jewish boy if he would like to come into the church one Sunday . . . And being really curious the little Jewish boy did . . .

Boy Oh, the little Jewish boy went to the church where I go every Sunday! He went to my church!

Mummy Not ours, darling, but one like ours, one just like ours, with beautiful coloured windows and a figure of the Lord in his agony . . .

Boy Oh, that's so nice for him . . .

Mummy And the little Jewish boy was so happy, he heard the beautiful hymns and was moved, and then the priest came round to give Holy Communion, and the little boy was offered the wafer, but he was afraid . . . So afraid to eat the wafer . . .

Boy Oh! Why was he afraid, Mummy, why should the Jewish boy be afraid to eat the wafer?

Mummy Darling, who knows what goes on in his small Jewish head, what terrible things his father had planted in there about us Christians, terrible ugly lies that made the little boy afraid, so after the priest passed him, he took the wafer and slipped it into his pocket.

Boy Oh what a shame, because then he wouldn't have Jesus inside him . . .

Mummy No, darling, no, not quite inside him, but maybe with him as you will see, in a moment . . .

Boy Oh yes, tell me, I long to know . . .

Mummy And so you shall, my little angel . . . After the service the Jewish boy ran all the way home, ran so hard because he was so excited by what he had seen and wanted so much to share his adventures with his mummy and daddy . . . to tell them what he had seen and done.

Boy I do that! I do that, Mummy, when I run home from school and tell you of my adventures of the day . . .

Mummy Yes, darling, just like you, running home and wanting to tell me, to share all your adventures with me . . .

So he ran home, all excited by his wonderful new discoveries and told his mummy and daddy about the church and the songs and the incense, those heavenly smells, but his father's face grew dark . . . Oh, it grew so dark with rage . . .

Boy   Oh, that's awful! That's awful . . . When the little boy only told of his adventures!

Mummy   Of course, that's what all boys do, they need to share their world with you, but this man was not someone to share anything with, except hate, and his face grew darker and darker and even his horns seemed to grow . . . since, you know that some of them do have horns!

Boy   Oh, how horrible . . . that's frightening. Is that why when you see them in the street they always have their hats on . . . ?

Mummy   It is, darling, so be very careful and keep far away from them, won't you?

Boy   I will . . . I will, now if I ever see them in the street I will always cross to the other side of the road.

Mummy   Good boy, good boy, 'cause they may try to tempt you, and offer you some fruit or sweet things, but never ever accept it, since they have been known to snatch little Christian children and eat them at Easter time . . .

Boy   No! No! I will never ever go near them, Mama, never. Oooh!

Mummy   Good boy, good boy. Anyway, darling, this boy, the little Jewish boy told his father how he visited the church and how at the church he was given a wafer and how, not to upset anyone in the congregation he put it in his mouth . . . But before he could tell his father that he spat out the wafer and put it in his pocket . . .

Boy   Yes, yes, Mama!

Mummy   Before he could reassure his angry father that he'd spat out the holy wafer . . . his father raised his eyes to heaven, uttered a terrifying curse and screamed . . . He screamed and raged and struck his poor innocent son . . .

Boy   Oh no!

Mummy   Yes, the old Jew screamed and raged like he had a nest of demons inside him, because he was so ashamed that his innocent had taken the wafer, had put Jesus, his bitter enemy, in his Jewish mouth, that his anger knew no bounds . . .

Boy   Oh that poor, innocent, little Jewish boy! Oh! Oh! That's horrible, *horrible. (Starts crying.)*

Mummy   Shh! Darling . . . Shh! I know it's really horrible, but wait . . . wait . . . The father, that wicked Jewish father, who hated our Lord so much, so very much, that even the thought of his child putting Jesus in his mouth turned him mad! Mad! Mad!

Boy   Oh! Oh! Oh! What did the Jew do Mummy? Oh! What did that bad man do to his poor little boy?

Mummy   I will tell you, I will tell you, darling, but I can't tell you unless you're going to be brave . . . and not cry . . .

Boy   I promise not to cry, Mummy, I promise . . .

Mummy   Because you know that Jesus is our saviour, don't you?

Boy   I know that, Mummy, yes I do know that . . .

Mummy   Well, darling, the Jew went mad, mad with rage and seized his beautiful innocent child, and screaming, 'This beast is no child of mine,' screaming at the top of his voice, he then opened the gates of the oven . . .

Boy   Oooh nooo!

Mummy   Be brave now, darling . . . He threw open the gates of the oven and hurled his little boy into the flames and slammed the gates of the oven shut!

Boy   Oooh! I'm not crying, Mummy . . . I'm trying not to cry!

Mummy   Good, darling . . . Well, his mother ran, she ran howling into the street for help . . . She ran crying, screaming, 'Help me! My husband's thrown my child into the oven! Help!'

Boy   Oh, how terrible . . . What happened? Did the little boy die . . . ? Did he die, Mama?!

Mummy   Well, darling, some townsfolk rushed into the house, they rushed and saw the oven blazing, they opened the gates of the furnace . . .

Boy   Yes? Yes? Yes?

Mummy   The furnace was blazing hard, blazing hard, but the little boy . . . (*Sobs a little.*)

Boy   Yes, yes, oh tell me, Mummy, quickly!

Mummy   The little boy was not even singed!

Boy   Aaaah!

Mummy   The little boy was not even singed, since the flames had made a space around him and the men carefully drew him out of the oven . . . They thought they had seen a miracle!

Boy   Oh they had, they had!

Mummy   And when the men asked him, when they asked him why on God's Earth had his father thrown him into the oven, the boy showed them the wafer, the wafer that was still in his pocket.

Boy   Of course, the wafer, the holy wafer!

Mummy   The boy was protected by our Lord Jesus, our Lord Jesus was next to him . . .

Boy   Oh Mummy, how wonderful, how wonderful . . .

Mummy   Jesus was with him, beside him, in the wafer that he'd carefully put in his pocket and when the little boy showed the men the wafer, they dropped to their knees and prayed . . .

Boy   Aaaah!

Mummy   They prayed, thanking our beloved Jesus for this deliverance . . .

Boy   Oh Mama, I'm so happy for the little boy!

Mummy   Of course, my darling, stories of Jesus always make us happy . . .

Boy   But Mama, what happened to the wicked Jew, the father?

Mummy   Of course, they threw *him* into the oven!

Boy   Oh goody . . . Ha ha!

Mummy   But he, the poor old angry Jew . . . burnt to a cinder . . .

Boy   Oh good! He deserved it! But what happened to the little boy . . . and his mama?

Mummy   They took him away, cleaned him and baptised him as a sweet little Christian child . . . But the mother went far away and was never heard of again. I think she went to her family in a far-off village

Boy   But the little Jewish boy was saved! Oh, Mummy, that's wonderful.

Mummy   Yes darling, he was saved, he had the wafer of Jesus close to him and our Lord's love protected him, just as he protects you. So now go to sleep . . . Go to sleep, my darling.

Boy   Mummy, I do love Jesus . . . So very much . . .

Mummy   I know you do my sweet and he loves you too . . .

Boy   Do you really think he loves me?

Mummy   Of course he does, darling, of course he does . . .
As long as you're good . . .

Boy   I will always be good . . . Good for Jesus . . .
Goodnight, Mummy . . .

Mummy   Goodnight, my angel . . .

A long loud scream.

Fade out.

Line-up

Characters

A
B

There are two men in a queue shifting forward very slowly.

A   Some are going to the left and some to the right.

B   See how the Nazi pig looks at them for a couple of seconds, makes his decision . . .

A   Do you have to insult pigs . . . ?

B   I think the ones to the left . . . are the rejects, yeah . . . to the right . . . they're workers . . . Yeah, definitely the rejects are on the left . . .

Who go to their graves . . .

A   Via the gas chambers!

B   Do you believe that shit?!

A   Keep your eyes open . . . Most of all your nose . . .

B   Sure it stinks . . . It stinks of death alright . . . Could be they incinerate the dead, animal carcasses, waste products . . .

A   Believe what you want . . .

B   I will, can't believe that any nation, and human being on Earth could do that, not even the Germans, who may be capable of any crime under the sun, could stoop so low . . .

A   What's that stink, man, that filthy stench and that foul yellow smoke pouring out of the chimneys . . . ? I was a chemist once, that smell is a poisonous gas . . .

B   Shh, not so loud, you fool, you're not arguing in your dirty Viennese coffee house . . . Keep alert . . . Look, the ones on the *right* seem to be the rejects, look, the old and the women are being sent to the *right* . . .

A   OK, OK, so try to look fit, look alive, don't stoop like an *alta cucker* . . .

B   After five days in a stinking shit-filled train with little to no water, no food, what do you think . . . I can barely stand . . .

I'm rotting, my trousers are crapped up . . . I stink to high heaven . . .

A   You think it's different for me . . . ? But you make an effort, stand straight, just for a few minutes more or that filthy bastard will turn you into grease.

B   Maybe that's better, get it over quickly . . .

A   Coward, face it . . . Stand up, put some Yiddish spirit in your spine, must survive to tell this story, take a deep breath, have faith, man . . . !

B   Faith! You make me sick with your eternal faith . . .

A   You make me sick with your constant whining, there are children here with more guts than you and women still with pride on their face!

B   I know I'm a weak bastard . . .

A   You're a crazy bastard, not a weak one, anyone would be crazy by now. I'm crazy . . . You've got strength . . . strength you don't even know . . .

B   Don't, you'll make me cry, you bastard . . .

A   You've got strength . . . And you know why? So you can speak, so you can tell the world what these filthy brutes are doing, the world will know . . . !

B   Oh, they will know, believe me, they will know . . .

A   Yeah, but only if you stand up, stand up straight, or you won't be able to tell the world . . .

A   Look, that big guy went to the left! He's a worker, obviously . . . On the left is life, fight for life!

B   It's left . . . You're sure it's left?

A   Yes, yes! . . . I'm sure . . .

B   But I saw someone who looked . . .

A   Yes, sometimes he sends a young fit one to the right . . .
Maybe he gave him a bad look . . .

B   Oh, you die if you give the bastard a bad look . . . !

A   Bet your life you do . . . If you give an officer a bad look,
now, in this situation, then you're a sign of future trouble,
they don't want trouble.

B   OK, I'll smile, I'll say good morning . . . nice day . . .

A   Keep moving . . . And stand straight, don't look at the
filthy bastard, just stand up straight, normal, don't look at
him or he will see the hate in your eyes . . . You just look
ahead . . . !

B   Ahead . . . OK . . . OK . . . My knees are buckling . . .

A   No they're not . . . Just a few yards to go . . . a few yards,
then life . . . You'll be chosen to work, they always need
workers, free slaves like all those poor dogs around us,
gathering up our possessions . . .

B   Try to catch the eye of one of them . . . to indicate which
line . . . to be on the safe side . . .

A   NO! They won't look at us . . . They dare not glance at
us, not for a second, the guards are watching, watching all the
time, and the dogs . . . the dogs are watching too . . .

B   Even the dogs are trained to hate us . . .

A   Fuck 'em, don't whinge . . . All sub-species hate us, didn't
you know this by now . . . ? Fuck 'em! Stand up straight, go
on, it's just a few more paces . . . If you can live through this
hour, you might live another year, and beyond that . . .

B   I don't think so . . .

A   Well, I do . . . You have to live to tell this story, expose
these brutish bastards to the world . . .

B   Some won't even believe this, there will be those who just
will not believe . . .

A   Fuck them! There are diseased dogs everywhere . . .

B   Ooh, I smell the gas, I can smell the gas now . . . Do you really think . . . Do you . . . ?

A   Noo . . . ! They're just cooking up their dinner . . .

B   There's the woman, the crazy woman from the train still clutching her dead child, poor thing, they'll just shove her in a pit, along with it, poor woman . . .

A   Look, the trooper is trying to tear the dead child from her arms, but she won't let go of it . . . Yet if she did, it might save her life . . . Ow! Ow! He shot her . . .

B   It's what she wanted . . . She's at peace, she's on the way.

A   But you're not . . . You've got to live . . . Got to tell the world, tell the world what sub-humans are capable of . . .

B *(cynical)*   Yeah . . . sure . . .

A   Yeah, sure . . . Stand up, God damn you! Hold yourself up and you'll live . . . Only a few yards left . . . Then you can sit, then they'll feed you . . . They'll even let you wash . . . They have to . . . They need workers . . . workers without typhus . . .

B   Workers . . . What a foul misuse of a word . . .

A   OK, you intellectual shmock . . . Tonight you'll be in a bunk . . . You'll have some food in your stomach, you'll get stronger, look at these Jew workers in their striped suits . . . They don't look starving . . . They're fed!

B   I hope my wife's still breathing . . .

A   She's breathing . . . She's breathing . . . They didn't take her . . . You're lucky . . . You should be so lucky . . . Look what you have to live for . . .

B   If she's alive . . . She escaped under the fence with the children, the Polish underground helped . . .

A   God bless her . . . God bless them.

B   Yeah. if they're still alive, please God . . .

A   So stand up. Stand up! God damn you, for them . . .

B   What happened to yours?

A   No children, thank God, my wife died on the train on the fourth day . . . God bless her, she died in my arms . . .

B   I'm so sorry . . .

A   Better that she perished then, my poor darling wife . . . So I want to stay alive to avenge her . . . her memory . . .

B   I understand . . .

A   Keep moving, just a few yards more . . . Look, see, the old ones and some women are going to the right . . . Look up, keep your head up, man, stop staring at your feet.

B   What are you talking about . . . ? I'm marking out my grave.

A   Fool, a few more minutes . . . and you'll live.

B   Oh, sure . . . How easily we got on the trains, how easily we were pulled out of our homes, how easily we line up to be shot . . .

A   Gassed in this case!

Beaten, burnt . . . Easily? Not so . . . It was gradual . . . We were given hope, that's the trick, a little bit of hope, so we believed that when we were hungry we weren't starving, and then when we were starving we were still living and still they gave us hope until the end when we were too weak to fight back . . .

B   Weak Jews!

A   Not so weak, not so . . . They fought back in Treblinka, bravely, and demolished much of the camp. In Warsaw our brothers held off the Nazi war machine for a month . . . With hand-made grenades . . . faulty pistols . . . with their bare hands . . .

B   So I heard . . . These were indeed brave men.

A   And women . . . Some of the women were the bravest . . .
They fought back like men . . . They made the grenades, they
fired machine guns . . . They didn't paint their nails or wear
lipstick . . . !

B   The legend of Warsaw will live for ever!

A   Only if it were alive to tell it . . . Move . . . Keep your
head up . . . Stop looking at the ground . . . measuring your
fucking grave . . .

B   Why not . . . What use am I . . . ? I can hardly stand . . .

A   You can stand for two more minutes . . . Just hang on,
they need men, you're vital to them, for their filthy war
machine, you're a watchmaker, you can repair the tens of
thousands of gold watches they've robbed from our dead
bodies . . . It'll pay for the bullets!

B   So I'm to help the bastards!

A   Pretend to help, pretend . . .

B   And you . . .

A   I'm a dentist . . . Very valuable, extracting gold from old
teeth, and swiftly without a lot of mashed teeth to be filtered
out . . .

B   Good for you . . .

A   Nearly there, nearly there . . . Hold your head up!

B   Even their filthy dogs are slobbering for your flesh . . .

A   Window-dressing just to scare us, no more!

B   Good luck, my friend . . . Good luck . . .

A   Good luck to you . . . And hold your head up and we'll
drink soup together tonight! Maybe even smoke!

B   I love you my dear friend . . .

A   I love you . . . I love you with every fibre in me . . . I love you, so hold your head up . . .

B   I will . . . Yes . . . I will . . . my honourable brother . . .

The lights slowly fade, as one goes to the left and one to the right. They cast one last glance at each other.

Blackout.

Pound of Flesh

Characters

John, *average young man*
David, *average young man*

John I think, I really think it's appalling . . . What they did. What those bloody Israelis did to those poor people in Gaza . . .

David It is appalling, there's no other word for it . . . I know they were provoked, but I mean . . .

John Provoked is one thing, but overkill is another . . . They knew those Palestinians had no damned military power, no jets, no navy, just a few hundred lousy rockets . . .

David It's a Jewish thing . . .

John How do you mean . . . ? I'm not anti-semitic, God forbid . . . I like the Jews . . . let's say most of them . . . It's those Zionist fanatics!

David When I say it's a Jewish thing, I'm not in any way some Nazi either . . . I mean that's how they make you feel . . . I mean carrying that fucking Holocaust cross prevents you from opening your bloody mouth!

John Bloody hell, don't I agree . . . And I can't accept what they feel is their God-given right to occupy lands they haven't put a foot in for two thousand years . . . If that's not a bloody piss-taking liberty I don't know what is . . . Take that to any extreme and Mexico would be invading California . . . It would set loose an avalanche . . . The Aboriginals would arm up and invade Sydney . . . There would be no end.

David As I said, it's a Jewish thing . . .

John Yes, I see what you mean . . . Working off our guilt trip so we say nothing . . .

David Oh, do they ever, but it's more than that, the Jews seem to lack the middle notes . . . It's treble or bass, they lack the modifying centre . . . I suppose that years of persecution have shaped them . . . Have polarised them, north and south, hot or cold, happy or tragic . . . persecution or freedom . . . No middle way, hate us or love us . . . Take Shylock, God! Shakespeare really knew his Jews. Shylock risks losing his money but then is offered more than twice the sum he's owed, but he insists on his pound of flesh . . . Even when he is offered the loan back many times over there is something so deeply ingrained in him to cause pain . . . to take revenge . . .

John   You think that's a Jewish thing?

David   It seems to be, yes, it's not altogether their fault. It's a mixture of cause and effect. Even a certain amount of Christian provocation has stewed something inside their guts . . . like a poisonous germ, perhaps.

John   Possibly, yes possibly, it's something that fermented in them and they can't actually help it!

David   That's right, that's what I'm saying, and Shakespeare instinctively senses that, when he wrote the Shylock character, the poor man is poisoned, poisoned with desire for revenge . . . Although today he's played more of a hero. Again that bloody guilt we carry around on our shoulders.

John   Oh my God, yes! Absolutely. It's appalling since it does tend to numb genuine and even helpful criticism and if you're brave enough to offer it you're likely to be branded as a bloody racist or worse . . .

David   Look, there's no doubt there's a few crackpots, lunatics, Holocaust-deniers, like flat-Earth zombies, who conveniently slag off Israel as a handy mask for their bile, and there are quite a few as we have seen . . .

John   And so we, that is some of us who have genuine criticism to make, get bracketed with those yellow-faced bastards!

David   That's the worst thing, that's the curse, you become nervous to open your bloody mouth.

John   So how do you get round it? I mean, one can't be silent out of fear of being thought an anti-Semite when one reacts to those disgusting land-grabbing bastards turning poor

Palestinians out of their homes . . . Even burning their olive groves . . . And all in the name of God! Can you believe?

David And they're not even Israelis . . . Some of them are barely Jews, they're immigrants from Russia and most of them have never stepped inside a synagogue in their lives!

John Or they're from Brooklyn, Golders Green, and now they strut around like pioneers with an AK47 around their shoulders! And with their loathsome Brooklyn accents they claim that God granted them the land . . . God?! I can't even hear it.

David Nobody can . . . Nobody can and the truth is that it can only end badly . . . There's so much pain and resentment in the Arab world . . . It stirs every young Arab's heart.

John I'm afraid you're right . . . The seed of revenge is so deep inside them and one day it will explode with devastating effect . . .

David It will, and I'm amazed that the Jews can't see it, or maybe some of them do, some of them are wise to it . . .

John Of course Jews as a whole are a very bright people . . . They're not stupid.

David But they have this flaw . . .

John Exactly, they become blinded by their own overwhelming need, blinded by it until they can see nothing else . . .

David Nothing else, exactly . . .

John Except their own obsessive needs . . .

David Even if they take the whole world with them . . .

John Oh my God yes, yes . . .

David I mean, militarily their superiority can only last so long, only so long, and there are quite a few more Arabs than Jews or Israelis . . . Like over two hundred million, and there are only six million Israelis, if that; and a hell of a lot are getting out!

John   It must be like hell, it must be like living in a war zone . . . Can you imagine living in a small country where you have to erect a giant wall to keep the assassins out . . . What an appalling way to live.

David   I can't begin to imagine it . . . It's unimaginable, especially near the borders where rockets are lobbed daily as your morning wake-up call . . .

John   It doesn't even bear thinking about, and then half the population are fastened to the radio all day . . . All day, whether you're in a cab, going to work, going out, the constant radio for news, for the next disaster, the next bomb on a bus . . . in a café . . . in a disco . . .

David   And whom do I blame? I'll tell you who I blame . . . Those idiot zealots armed to the teeth in those fucking settlements like Hebron . . . Just a few hundred surrounded by a sea of Arabs and protected by the army, while they can abuse the locals!

John   And each settlement is like a small boil on the face of Palestine . . . it's like a putrid sore and the Arabs hate it, and not only do they hate it . . . it unites them like no other cause ever did. It gives them a goal . . . a goal to live . . . or die, as it happens.

David   I'm amazed at the Israelis' stupidity . . . It's the Shylock psychosis . . . Why not take what they were given in '48 . . . Even, OK, '67 . . . It's more, far more than they ever dreamed of, a dream come true. and if only they settled with that, if only . . .

John   Well in '48 they did and were happy beyond their wildest dreams, at last a land of their own, but the Arabs didn't want these strange Europeans filling their land, a land given as a guilt-offering for the crimes of the Nazis, and before them the crimes of the Russians . . . It wasn't Arab crimes.

David   Well, I suppose they had nowhere else to go . . . Not really . . . No one else even wanted them . . . No one . . .

John   True . . . No one wanted to take in the Jewish refugees, and tragic as that sounds, and I can't believe I'm saying it, but can you really blame them?

David   Hey, John, what you said might be construed as having the true whiff of an anti-Semite . . . I mean, look at the vast contributions the Jews have made to whatever society or country they settled in . . . In the sciences, medicine, commerce, far beyond any comparable minority . . .

John   And money, don't forget that . . . money!

David   Oh, we're back to the Shylock syndrome.

John   And what about the Indians, Asians, Scots . . . They've all punched far beyond their weight . . . It's the nature of minorities to far exceed the achievements of their host countries.

David   In '67 four major Arab nations lined up to destroy Israel for all time . . . They actually lined up, a massive collective army whose sole purpose was the destruction of Israel, and not just the destruction of the state but its total annihilation. It could have been another monstrous Holocaust, but the invaders were sent packing. Israel's military superiority overwhelmed the Arabs since the Jews were fighting for their very lives, for their existence, while the Arabs were not. So Israel drove them back and occupied the West Bank almost as the spoils of war. Gaza was the result of the '48 war. All the land occupied by Israel since '67 was the result of Arab aggression and that's a fact, John, aggression to retain their ancient lands . . . Isn't that quite understandable? No one's denying it . . . No one. Least of all the Israelis, so all they have to do now is to remove their nasty little settlements and there would be a strong possibility of instant peace.

John   . . . I doubt it . . . I doubt that very much . . .

David   No question, there would suddenly be worldwide support for Israel . . . the Jews would start to lose that Shylock stink and anti-Semitic attacks would shrivel, leaving only the putrid shrieks of the psychotics and Nazis.

John   Yes a good dream, but you leave out the fanatics, the religious psychos who interpret the Old Testament as a wish fulfilment of their deepest desires, like a contract from God who acts as their super real-estate deity . . . People who have the most loathsome contempt for Arabs and who never can be influenced or enlightened. They only want their pound of flesh . . . Offer them the '67 borders and lasting peace, even a slight adjustment, border-straightening . . . Make peace with Iran, Jordan, Egypt, Lebanon, but they will never be content . . . They will hold out for the dream of the entire nation and if they could only think back that in the ghettos of Warsaw and the camps of Auschwitz, when even a foothold in the Holy Land would have been a joy beyond imagination.

David   Yes it's beyond greed, it's the dream of the impossible, like waiting for the Messiah who will never come – their intrinsic Jewish need will destroy them, I fear. They could have everything, everything minus a few plots of land in the West Bank and for this they will sacrifice everything. Everything! It's pathetic, it's the pound-of-flesh psychosis . . . Shylock could have taken twice, three times his original bond but his greed overcame him and he ended up with nothing . . . What a prophetic tale . . . Shakespeare knew his Jew, did he not?

John   I believe . . . I do believe that it's a kind of death psychosis . . . For whatever reason, Jews were discriminated against and, more than not, persecuted right through history, from the beginning of time you might say, and why? Yes, why? That's something everyone has a theory about but whatever the theory, the effect of all this cruelty, harassment and even killing of the poor victim Jew was to make them see life as a constant struggle between life and death . . . There is not too much middle ground, it's only life and death and a waiting for the Messiah who will never come. Waiting for the whole land of Palestine which can never be theirs, and so they are always in a state of hunger.

David   Yes, it's the need, and it's far worse than the greed for land, their own land – their biblical land . . . It's like the most terrible hunger . . . hunger for the past . . . hunger for the old world before the Romans came and destroyed it . . . And so two thousand years later they start over again, for a moment let's say they retrieve the old world, but the foundations are so fragile that soon it topples, it cracks, it shudders and then once more they go into exile and the thing starts all over again . . . 'Next year in Jerusalem.'

John   As so it goes on . . . throughout the years through the centuries and they hunger for suffering . . . It's manna, like manna to them . . . It tells them that they have a goal and that their suffering is for a cause, they accept or seem to accept that they must suffer for the ultimate reward, which is to come . . . No other race has accepted suffering like they have done, and even when the Nazis rounded them up in the cities where they lived for centuries, from the ghettos, how peacefully they obeyed the order to leave their homes . . . To march down the street, to get into those stinking trains . . . Yes, there were a few rebellions . . . How could it not be, but when? . . . At the end, when it was almost over, a few valiant Jews did make a stand, a heroic stand . . . But only at the end, when millions had already calmly obeyed their fate and walked like zombies into the gas chambers. Isn't that shocking . . . ? They almost seem to crave the pain . . . This restores their sense of purpose. But they survived and regrew and found their destiny. Israel. And now they live for war, a war that they have to win each and every time since the first time they lose it will be the end of them.

David   Yet Israel is also a great sanctuary, for every Jew, every Jew will have a home, their home . . . a miracle of survival, the sweetness of it you can never imagine, never imagine what it must have been like to hear those jackbooted bastards marching down the streets marching up your stairs, ordering you out of your home. And now no more, no more, ever and if anyone tries they will be wiped out. The boot is definitely on the other foot. But now they crave peace, but then what's the point, what's the purpose? Coffee shops? Cinemas? Shopping? Going to the theatre? How lovely . . . It's what we, in the gentile world, call home . . . A place where we complain if the price of beer goes up or our petrol, and we get garden catalogues and shoot foxes on Sunday. How very nice. And this is what they in Israel would like . . . But if they did one day achieve such a state, what then? Soon their demons would get restless . . . Let's shake it up a bit, let's test it . . . We could even get more . . . A pound of flesh nearest the heart is the required amount.

John   Yes, the West Bank.

David   Is that the pound of flesh?

John   But then Shylock was offered three times the loan he made . . .

David   But he insists on the pound of flesh . . .

John   And then they lose everything.

David   Everything.

John   When they had everything.

David   Sad isn't it?

John   Yes, it is.

David   Could they not just stop . . . stop this spiral, be content with what they have?

John   If only . . .

Fade.

Gas

Characters

A
B
C

Four people in a gas chamber in a Nazi concentration camp. A chamber with three or four bodies twisting around each other. Vapour pouring in as 'gas'.

A   Oh God in Heaven save me . . . God in Heaven save me . . .

B   Shut up! No one's there . . . You're praying to no one. Soon you'll be gone . . . Idiot . . .

C   Shit on them! Shit on them for ever! . . . Curse their eyes . . . their hearts, their children . . . Curse that filthy drek for ever . . .

B   Shut up! Breathe in . . . Breathe in deeply and soon you'll sleep . . . Breathe . . .

A   I'm so afraid to die, I don't want to die, no! No! Help me . . .

B   Breathe, just breathe in . . . Breathe deeply . . .

C   Fuck 'em all . . . Mad dogs, filth, scum, human shit . . . Disease . . . Live! Live!

B   You waste your energy, you're dying, suck it in, it will be better for you, die peaceful . . . Don't fight, suck it in . . .

A   Say the *Shema* . . . Say it . . . Please say it . . .

B   You say it . . .

A   Say it! Say it! I don't know Hebrew . . . Never learned, please I beg . . . you . . . please . . .

C   *Shema Yisroel, Adoni Elahaynu, Adoni echod*!

From now on they all say the prayer and join in for several repeats.

A   Good, good, I love you, I love you, my God, love, love, love you . . .

B   Shut up! Die in peace, just die in peace . . . Shut your fucking whining mouth . . .

C   No! . . . Filthy Nazi bastards, you filth and shit of the world, I shit on you . . . In your eyes, in your mouth, I'll rip you off the face of the Earth, you're cursed for ever . . .

B   Shut up, shut up, just die . . . At least die with dignity . . .

A   Oh Mama, Mama, boobala, my kindala, I love you, love you, your popa always love you . . . love . . .

C   Somebody will come after us, someone will come and burn that Nazi shit off the face of the earth . . .

A   I'm breathing it all in . . . but no peace yet . . . no dying, but it burns so badly, it burns my lungs . . .

C   Stew them in hell, rip them to shreds, those faces like yellow wax with their ice-blue eyes, scum of hell, the puss of the devil and all who follow them . . .

B   Oh God, shut up and die!

A   Say *Shema* . . . again . . . Say it one more time . . . please . . . please . . .

They all do so.

A   It's coming . . . coming . . . I feel weak. I feel death coming . . .

B   Good . . . good . . . I do too . . . Oh, comes peace, then comes happiness . . . And blue skies . . .

A   Happiness . . . happiness . . . happiness . . .

B   Yes . . . yes . . . yes . . . Soon peace . . . soon, soon . . .

C   Shut it you dog, compliant Yiddish dog. They pull you by your chain . . . You easy Yiddish dogs . . . These insane devils in that sewer called Germany . . . That dustbin of plague rats . . .

A   Yes . . . Yes . . . But now . . . go with love . . . go with love in our heart for each other . . . We are together . . .

B   I'm fading, I feel myself fading. God bless you all . . . my brothers . . .

C   Shit! Shit! Shit! Shit! Fucking filth . . .

A   Shhhh! Shhhhh . . . It's coming now . . . Soon . . . We'll be . . . together . . . with family . . .

B   Together . . . I see my beloved . . . Yes, I do see her . . . So . . . (*Gently.*) Quiet now . . . shh . . . quiet now . . .

C   Yes . . . It's growing dark . . . dark . . . growing dark . . .

A   Good . . . Soon . . . soon peace . . .

B   Soon . . . soon happy . . . Don't struggle . . .

A   No, it's growing dark . . . *Shema Yisrael, Adoni, Elahaynu . . . They all start joining in.*

C   Dark . . . dark . . . Hand . . . hold my hand . . .

A   I love you, brother . . .

B   I love you . . . Oh, how I love you . . .

C   I love you . . . love you . . .

They continue as the light fades.

REJECTION

Guilt

Characters

Henry, *married to Polly*
Polly, *married to Henry*

Two fat middle-aged Jews are sitting eating a nosh at a table.

Henry I love this herring, herring with a bagel, you can't beat it, my life, I go mad for it, I get this yen!

Polly Don't I know it . . . I'm also mad for it but with some cream cheese and smoked salmon, hmm, divine, and some sliced pickle . . . ayeyai . . . and then some black olives, the fat black olives, not those shrivelled ones. Feh! Awful . . . hate them!

Henry No, I know, the fat ones with flesh on them, not the shrivelled salty ones. Can't stand them either.

Polly No. The fat, plump, tasty, oily ones.

Henry Yeah, that's what we normally get, that's what we get normally, normally that's what they used to have in the shop, in Rogg's . . .

Polly Not always, no, not always, but what he had, what he had, yeah, what he made, were wonderful fishcakes . . . wonderful!

Henry Oy! Oy! Oy! Specially when they were fresh and just out of the oven, yeah his fishcakes were the best . . . who's arguing, they were the best and all the taxi drivers went there 'cause they know where the best is, 'cause they know, they go everywhere . . .

Polly Of course. They go everywhere, they're taxi drivers!

Henry So sometimes when I was buying salmon he'd say, the fishcakes are just out of the oven and he goes in the back . . .

Polly Oy! God knows what it was like back there . . . I don't like even to imagine, feh, what a greasy dump it was back there, ugh . . .

Henry But his deli was wonderful, I mean the fishcakes you couldn't beat!

Polly Who's arguing?

Henry His cheesecakes were divine too!

Polly   Divine! I agree.

Henry   So he used to go in the back and come out with half a fishcake in a paper serviette . . . and the smell was divine, it's divine, what can I say . . .

Polly   What can you say, you can only say it's divine, that's all you can say, and shut your eyes to the filth and muck.

Henry   Hey Polly, it wasn't so wholesome, but it's not filth and muck . . . it was . . . er, just a bit grubby . . .

Polly   Grubby?!

Henry   It was a bit grubby, that's all . . . it had the feel of the old ghetto, you know he carried the feeling of the old East End ghetto, you know, the old market place and the chicken entrails on the pavements, and God forbid you slither on it . . . It's the old world, what can I say, the old world, but you couldn't beat the fish cakes . . . you *cannot beat those fishcakes*!

Polly   No one's arguing, if it wasn't for the fishcakes I might not have gone back to that *v'shtinkiner* shop.

Henry   Hey that's a bit harsh, it was bit grubby, that I admit, and he hadn't even changed the large pickle tins on the shelves in years . . . Ha ha ha! . . . They'd been there for years and they were all rusty . . . I just can't believe how he got away with it . . .

Polly   No one can believe it, who can believe it! No one . . . no one can believe how he got away with it . . . Maybe he thought it's got charm, like museum pieces . . .

Henry   Don't know how he got away with it! It amazes me . . . I even used to say 'Barry, how long you gonna keep those old pickle tins up there?'

Polly   Doubt if they're full.

Henry   And he laughs like he thought it's funny, they might have been there twenty years!

Polly   At least!

Henry   And they were all sitting there rusting away . . . it's unbelievable.

Polly   He's *mishiga* . . .

Henry   Course, he's *mishiga*, but he still made wonderful fishcakes . . .

Polly   That was why he still got customers, that's why, and his sweet sour cucumbers were unbelievable.

Henry   They're unbelievable . . . like the recipes from the old country . . .

Polly   From Poland, Warsaw maybe.

Henry   Of course, who knows?

Polly   The thing is they were so crunchy!

Henry   Ooooh, delish!

Polly   Crunchy and delish, specially the new green. I'd go crazy for the new green! Yum! Yum!

Henry   Inside a heated bagel, with cream cheese and salmon, inside a crunchy toasted bagel . . .

Polly (*ecstatic*)   YAAAAAAAH!

Henry   OOOOOOOHHHHH!

Polly   Hey . . . what about the latkes . . . !

Henry   OWWWWWW!

Polly   Tucker, no one made latkes like Barry, there's no one in the world made latkes the way he made latkes.

Henry   Those potato latkes were the best . . . Mind you, my mother used to make wonderful latkes, I mean wonderful, crisp with a hint of onion and then shake a bit of OK Sauce on them.

Polly   YEOOOOOOOW! Now I've got a craving for latkes
. . . You've got me going with your talk of latkes! Now all I
can see in front of me is a plate of latkes!

Henry   I wish I could go out and buy half-a-dozen latkes.

Polly   We used to send Les out for latkes, 'member, but
when he got back he'd eaten half of them.

Henry   After that we couldn't send him out for latkes.

Polly   No – not latkes, he was addicted to latkes – 'Les don't
eat the Latkes!'

Henry   Shame Rogg's has gone, dead shame he's gone, he
was the last little bit of the old East End . . . !

Polly   He was . . . oh, he was, yeah it's a great shame but
they would have closed him down sooner or later 'cause of
those rusty tins . . .

Henry   The shop was a museum piece, they could have put
it complete in the Victoria and Albert Museum.

Polly   Oh sure, what, are you crazy!

Henry   I kid you not, Polly, nowadays these old *v'shtinkiner*
shops are now relics of a bygone age. They're relics, bits of
old history.

Polly   Don't make me laugh – what, with the rusty pickle
tins and all!

Henry   Even with all the rusty tins on the shelves . . . those
old tins are now collector pieces!

Polly   Shame then you didn't buy those old rusty tins . . . !
Ha ha ha ha! – old rusty pickle tins, the latest treasure of the
Yids!

Henry   His salmon was first class, I tell you it was first class.

Polly   It was! It was!

Henry   You wouldn't have got better at Harrods.

Polly   No question . . . They used to smoke all the salmon in the East End. That was the place . . . no one could smoke salmon better . . .

Henry   Years ago, you could barely afford it, a fortune it cost, like you can't believe.

Polly   So who are you telling, like I don't know!

Henry   I mean it was a luxury taste, oooh! It tasted of luxury . . . slippery, smoky, salty, pinky.

Polly   It was like a 'Jewish' taste . . . that's a Jewish taste, the smoked salmon, like that's what I imagine a Jew would taste like . . . like smoked salmon.

Henry   You're funny, Polly, but you could be right . . . it's certainly a Jewish dish . . . and years ago we would queue up, queue for the salmon but we could only afford a couple of ounces or maybe a quarter, four ounces and we'd watch Barry slice the salmon . . . so finely, so thin to make it go further 'cause it cost a fortune then, before fish farms, cost an arm and a leg, and so we'd stand behind the counter and watch him slice the salmon and cut away the brown bits to be sold later as salmon scraps.

Polly   Oh how I loved the salmon scraps, 'cause they were cheap!

Henry   And with tweezers he'd pull out the fine bones if they were still there and he'd dip his razor sharp knife into a long oil jar and then oh so slowly pull the knife against the firm pink smoked flesh and it would come away like a veil, like a thin pink veil . . .

Polly   Ooooohhh!

Henry   So fine, almost transparent, and when he shaved a perfect slice he'd carry it on the flat blade of the knife . . . and deposit it on a fresh sheet of grease paper, and then he'd start again and all eyes were upon him and nobody was impatient even if they were last in line, 'cause it was a ritual . . .

Polly   That's right . . . that's right, it was . . . a ritual.

Henry   Almost like a religious act . . .

Polly   Oh for sure.

Henry   And then he laid the next slice of salmon and then the next until your order was fulfilled.

Polly   I remember so well, and if Les was with us he'd cut a sliver and hand it down to him. Oh, Les would love that! He would. Remember his face?

Henry   And at the end, when there was no more slices and you'd only bought four ounces, he'd then cut off a piece of the skin, and on the skin there'd still be a thin layer of salmon clinging to it, and so he'd give you the skin.

Polly   Oh how I loved the skin! Loved it!

Henry   Course! We all loved the skin, and we'd stand and watch to see how much of the skin he would cut off . . . and sometimes there was even chunks of salmon on it . . .

Polly   Of course there was, there was . . . I remember that.

Mimes chewing.

Henry   There was an atmosphere, like even when you just stepped inside Marks of Wentworth Street.

Polly   Tucker, that was a deli!

Henry   Oh my God.

Polly   That was a deli and a half.

Henry   Brilliant! When you went in . . .

Polly   When you stepped inside the door . . .

Henry   The atmosphere hit you . . . DELI! Kosher DELI! Hmmm!

Polly   All the sides of salmon laid out like a treasure chest.

Henry   Like a pirates' hoard . . . marvellous – like jewels.

Polly   A treasure trove. You walked in there and just breathed in . . . aaaah!

Henry   Wholesome, fresh, tingly, the smell of the Yiddish soul . . . aah!

Polly   Herrings, rollmops, pickled onions, chopped herrings, schmatzed herring.

Henry   Gefilte fish, black olives, green olives, pickled cucumbers . . .

Polly   Red peppers, green peppers, cream cheese, cottage cheese . . . ahh!

Henry   When you walked in there, the atmosphere hit you and you waited, you waited patiently, everyone waited, 'cause there was always a queue.

Polly   Always, I never was there when there wasn't a queue!

Henry   You know it may sound a little *mishiga*, but to me the staff had the faces of . . . saints! They did!

Polly   You're *mishiga*, but in a funny way I know what you mean . . . wholesome, benign, I know what you mean . . .

Henry   Like they were so happy to serve you, they had a look.

Polly   Tucker, when I think of it, you're right, they had a look.

Henry   Like a *haimisher* look, like they were pleased to serve you, like they were happy selling you wholesome food of the soul.

Polly   Holy food . . . even.

Henry   You could say that . . . holy fool, soul food and it made them happy to feed your soul.

Polly   Of course.

Henry   That young Mr Marks always gave me a smile when I came in, like he was so pleased to see me . . . pleased to see me come back.

Polly   He had that look, like a saint, tucker, you're right . . . you *are* right!

Henry   He smiled, a sweet half-smile, and pleasure was all over his face . . . and you know what . . . once when I was in Marks, just once when I was waiting . . . to be served, I felt my eyes water up.

Polly   I know you're a bit *mishiga*, Henry, but I believe you . . .

Henry   Couldn't help it, like it was the manna of the gods, our food, Mama's food, home food, all the food of memory, from childhood, from Friday nights with Mamala, with the Shabbas candles, such good food, wholesome food, tasty delicious food, special food, and so when I saw the younger Mr Marks with his pale, sweet, soft, gentle face, I had to bite my tongue . . .

Polly   Gavolt, you're sentimental, what can I say . . .

Henry   I am, you're right, I'm sentimental, a heart of shmaltz.

Polly   Heart of shmaltz, that's what you are, chicken fat runs through your veins . . .

Henry   But now Marks of the Lane has gone . . . it's gone, gone for ever . . .

Polly   And that's the biggest shame, how could that go? It doesn't seem possible, doesn't seem possible . . . Marks of the Lane . . .

Henry   Where our parents would shop and then *we* would shop and then where our children would shop, like it was there for ever and it was always there and you knew nothing else and Mama would say, 'Kindala, be a good boy and go to Marks and pick up some bagels and cream cheese,' like it was there for ever and always had been there since the beginning of time.

Polly   That's what it felt like . . . it did!

Henry   And now it's gone . . . oy vey.

Polly   Is gone, what can you do?

Henry   Remember the old man who used to sit outside the shop with a big sackful of bagels?

Polly   Course I remember, course I remember, with that face like he was full of kvetches.

Henry   All gone. Gone, I can't face going down the Lane any more.

Polly   So don't go, who's telling you to go.

Henry   When I used to walk past the shop, all I could see were the lights and the old staff and Mr Marks behind the counter, like ghosts I could see it all and it shook me up, it did, such a beautiful thing to pass on, such a lovely piece of our lives, to die.

Polly   Things die, even sometimes beautiful things die.

Henry   One day we're going to die . . .

Polly   Oh, shut up . . . don't be so mournful, can't stand it when you get mournful . . .

Henry   We make room for the others, for the *shnorrers*.

Henry   So you got any more herring?

Polly   You finished the last of the herring . . .

Henry   Hmmph!

Polly   You want I should run out and get some more!

Henry   Where can you get some more?

Polly   Rinkoff's, Rinkoff's in Vallance Road, they have herring.

Henry   Rinkoff's! Of course! They're still there?!

Polly   Of course they're still there, they're always there!

Henry   Oh, wonderful, of course, I forgot, Rinkoff's are still there! Wonderful!

Polly   What's wrong with you, you know they're there, they're always there and as far as I know they'll always be there.

Henry   Oy, what a blessing, what a blessing, it's just that we never went there, not so much . . .

Polly   Because we always went to Rogg's in Cannon Street, we didn't need to go to Whitechapel, but anyway they're still there.

Henry   What a relief . . . I thought it was all over, oh thank God, there's a bit of us still left . . . *dunken gott.*

Polly   So you want me to run down to Rinkoff's . . .

Henry   I'll go tomorrow, tomorrow I'll go down and get some chopped herring. Don't want to spoil my appetite for dinner . . . So what's for dinner?

Polly   I thought I'd make some chicken soup.

Henry   Ayye!

Polly   What's the matter with you today, you losing your marbles? It's just chicken soup . . . you going *m'shiga* or something?

Henry   I dunno, today I just feel nostalgic. Yeah, you get a squirminess in your gut. Yeah, I feel nostalgic and so everything sets it off . . . so kill me, what can I do, I get emotional.

Polly   Yeah, I thought I'd make chicken soup for a change. Anyway, Les might come by. He sometimes comes by on a Friday.

Henry (*controlling his feelings*)   So why not, yeah, not had chicken soup for a while, nice . . . yeah . . . Good girl.

Polly   So tonight we'll have chicken soup . . .

Henry   With dumplings?

Polly   If you want with dumplings, so I'll make with dumplings.

Henry   Oy, oy, oy, I'm crazy about dumplings!

Polly   So tonight we'll have dumplings!

Henry   Lovely, so now I've got something to really look forward to . . .

Polly   *Mazeltov.* I'm glad that your night is settled.

Henry   Look, Polly, don't dampen my enthusiasm just 'cause I love chicken soup with dumplings . . . it's a wonderful dish, it's special, and it brings back memories of my mother, bless her soul, 'cause she could make chicken soup to make your eyes pop.

Polly   So my chicken soup doesn't make your eyes pop! *M'shigana!*

Henry   Listen, your chicken soup is amongst the best . . . the best in the world, nobody can make chicken soup like you and your dumplings are to die for . . . no question. I'm not comparing your chicken soup with my mother's, no way . . . it's just when you're young you carry a memory, and the memory is coloured by emotion, but I remember when I sat down at the table and gently slipped my spoon into that soup it was as if I was scooping up liquid gold and the taste . . . ayye! That flavour was not of this world . . . It's hard to describe . . . And the kneidals, the dumplings were firm but not hard and the taste was unbelievable . . .

Polly   So we'll make or try to make it unbelievable, but I can't compete with the memory of your mother . . . Up to now you've always been satisfied, I've not heard you complain . . .

Henry   Course not, Polly. I told you, yours is the best . . . it's just Mum's was the first, that's all, the first, and so I'd go every Friday night or Sunday morning for ma's chicken soup . . . In the end I somehow saw her as a chicken, always clucking away in the kitchen. But the weird thing was, if you had a problem, if you had some tsouris, some grief, or your boss was giving you a gavolt, or something in your life was going bad . . . once you dipped your spoon in the soup, the problem slowly melted away . . . Isn't that the strangest thing . . . ?

Polly   You should have marketed your ma's chicken soup . . . like Paul Newman's Salad Dressing!

Henry   Believe me, you're not kidding . . . could have made a fortune . . . No, but it could never be the same because it wouldn't have the . . . feeling . . . the love she put into it.

Polly   I thought she put carrots and onions into it . . . !

Henry   And love . . . *that* makes the difference!

Polly   So now I know, I'll put some love into it . . . along with the dumplings.

Henry   Listen, don't get sour just 'cause I talked about Ma's chicken soup . . .

Polly   Who's sour? I'm not sour, my mother also made the best chicken soup in the world.

Henry   Of course, every child believes their ma's chicken soup is the best . . . it's natural.

Polly   Course it is, but my ma also made the most amazing borsht in the world, people would come from far and wide just to taste her borsht . . .

Henry   I remember it was . . . it was an amazing borsht, no question.

Polly   The colour, the colour . . . ayyyyye! It was like the deepest crimson, dark, rich, like ancient velvet, a colour you could only imagine . . .

Henry   True, it was a fantastic colour.

Polly   When Houdini, the world's greatest magician, came to the East End, he tasted my mother's borsht and he said . . . never in his life, in all his travels throughout the world, not even in Moscow, where he entertained the Czar, had he ever tasted or even seen anything like this! And his own mother was a goddess to him, but couldn't compete with Ma's borsht!

Henry   It's a wonderful story and I never get tired of hearing it . . . no matter now many times you have told me that story, for some reason I never get tired of hearing it . . . but why would Houdini go to your old ma's grubby old East End flat? I mean he was staying at the Savoy.

Polly   That's why, you gloomp! He came from the ghetto and wherever he went in whatever city, he'd visit the Jewish quarter . . . the slum. He loved it. It was in his blood . . . that's why he visited my ma's and pa's flat . . . I'll never mention it again!

Henry   Hey, Polly, don't get so serious, I mean it, I love it . . . the great Houdini . . . it's an amazing story . . . it is. But you *also* make a mean borsht, there's no one can make it like you . . . so you had a good teacher.

Polly   She was, she was a wonderful teacher . . . but in those days we had chickens in the back yard . . .

Henry   Of course, no battery chickens, God forbid . . .

Polly   The chickens had a good life, a proper life, strutting around, pecking all day. The battery chickens look like concentration camp victims!

Henry   Oy, God forbid! A happy chicken tastes better . . . it tastes –

Polly   – of happiness! You want a bagel . . . to get on with before dinner . . . ?

Henry   Nah, I'll wait . . . it'll do me good to wait, but to tell you the truth I wouldn't mind just a piece of matzo, that's all, a half slice with –

Polly   – a slice of cheese . . . ?

Henry   Perfect, and that will do me nice until dinner.

Polly   I've got a bit of smoked salmon left in the fridge . . .

Henry   Hmm . . . OK, just a sliver, no more.

Polly   A sliver is all there is . . . Anyway, Les said he might drop in.

Henry   That'll be nice – not seen him in months.

Polly   He wasn't sure . . . said he might.

They sit silently for a while.

Henry   You know what I miss sometimes . . . just sometimes?

Polly   What do you miss, Henry?

Henry   Well, I miss your wonderful fishcakes. Sometimes you forget to make them, or you go off them for a bit . . .

Polly   So open your mouth and tell me that you want fishcakes, that's easy to do, you know how to ask, don't you? You put your lips together and drool!

Henry   Ha ha! Polly, you gotta sense of humour sometimes, you really do.

Polly   So I'll make fishcakes, haven't forgotten, just go through phases.

Henry   My mother made amazing fishcakes . . .

Polly   I know, you told me a thousand times about your mother's fishcakes.

Henry   You get old and repeat yourself, but I know I told you, I know that. You say these things 'cause it brings her back, like a refrain, or when you whistle a tune, it is pleasant to revive it, to bring it back . . . so if I say that Ma made amazing fishcakes – it's to bring her back – her face comes back.

Polly   OK, so your mother made amazing fishcakes?

Henry (*tad angry*)   Did my mother make amazing fishcakes!
She made fishcakes that made you tingle all over, that people
would travel far and wide to eat, just to nibble, that were
beyond any taste known to mankind. You could not believe
the flavour, it was more than just fish, it was the essence of
fish, the perfume of fish, the soul of fish . . .

Polly   Oy, that must have been some fishcake!

Henry   Beyond all flavour, like it was made to be served
at the table of God, made by angels and served on a silver
salver . . .

Polly   Well, well, well. You had an amazing mother, that's
for sure, I don't know how you could have left home . . . with
fishcakes like that . . . ?

Henry   Listen, we're talking a little bit *m'shiga* 'cause your
fishcakes are as good as hers, there's no question, it's just that
from time to time I like to pay a little tribute to Ma, that's all,
no big deal, I'm not comparing you. How can I compare
anyway, but no one makes chopped liver like you, *no one*, not
even Ma, God bless her soul. No you, yes you are the master
of chopped liver, what you make out of a simple chicken liver
is beyond belief, it's almost satanic. It is . . . a little dribble of
chopped liver spread on a little piece of matzo is the closest
thing I can imagine to going to paradise.

Polly   So now you want chopped liver . . . ?

Henry   No, I'm happy tonight with chicken soup and
dumplings, yes, that would suit me real fine . . . chopped liver
. . . maybe tomorrow . . .

Polly   OK.

Henry   So you think Les is dropping in? I don't think the
loving son is so loving lately!

Polly   He's busy. He's always busy. Whenever I speak to
him he's going off somewhere.

Henry   I gotta tell you . . .

Polly   Noo? Whatcha got to tell me . . .

Henry   Sometimes, sometimes when I'm eating one of your wonderful meals . . . sitting here eating one of your simple delicious, delightful dishes . . . I feel . . . really sad that it's only for me . . . it's so wonderful. Yes, Polly, it's so special that I wish others could partake of it . . . I really do . . .

Polly   Ahh, that's nice . . .

Henry   No, Polly, it makes me really sad sometimes that all this trouble, all this shopping and shlepping, and washing and cutting and chopping and mixing and baking and seasoning and waiting and lifting and sweating and testing and tasting, and preparing, and cleaning, and laying the table, and setting and heating and cutting and scooping . . . that all this is just for me and sometimes I can't bear it, Polly . . . I just can't bear it . . .

Polly   To share is nice . . .

Henry   Yeah, that's what I'm saying, I want the world to experience it, to share it with . . . a friend!

Polly   Well, sometimes your son comes round, sometimes Les comes over.

Henry   Les? Yeah, sometimes . . . When he can be bothered or if he's in the area . . . It's not nice the way he neglects his own parents . . . not nice . . . shame, *and* he loves your cooking . . .

Polly   Listen, he's got his own life, he comes when he's got the time, he's a grown man . . . he's got other obligations, other friends, things to do, what does he want with a couple of old *cuckers* like us?

Henry   You calling us a couple of '*alter cuckers*' – us, like we're finished, no use to the world, not even worth a visit?! Just a couple of rotting carcasses . . . sitting, waiting, worthless.

Polly   So give him a ring and see when he can come, and listen, he's not a child, he's an adult, so be nice and respectful . . .

Henry   No, you phone him, he'd rather hear from you, you're his mother, he's the apple of your eye. By you he can do no wrong . . .

Polly   Henry, he'd like it if *you* rang, 'cause you never call him, never say, just once, 'It would be lovely to see you. We miss you, so when you coming round?' . . . He'd love that.

Henry   How can I talk like that? I haven't talked like that to him in years . . . not in years!

Polly   So you should start. Start now, never too late to break a bad habit . . . He'd love it. You know, Henry, you've always been too critical of him, too judgemental!

Henry   Me?

Polly   Yes, Henry, you . . . You should have been a little patient with him when he was a kid, been a bit patient, a bit understanding, then maybe he wouldn't have got into trouble, wouldn't have mixed with the wrong people.

Henry   That's my fault that he took up with lowlifes and *ganuffs*, thieves and *drek*, my fault?! Please!

Polly   No, not your fault, it's the time, it's how we live today but we should have been a bit calmer.

Henry   OK, it's my fault . . .

Polly   It's nobody's fault, but ring him, show him a bit of love, that you miss him, that would be wonderful, he'd love that, he would. Course he would . . . Tell him we're making chicken soup, that's his favourite, and to come round, if not tonight then tomorrow . . . Please, Henry . . .

Henry   I should beg my own son for company . . .

Polly   You can't beg from your children, only from a stranger or lukewarm friends.

Henry   I should say we're lonely and beg our own son to keep us company?

Polly   No, tell him you're lonely for *him*, for him, for your beautiful son you're lonely, that's all you have to tell him, that you miss your lovely boy, your handsome son, that he should be well and that we miss him and that his mother misses him from the bottom of her soul and what a mitzvah it would be to have him here, to see his lovely face, his handsome face again and to know that he's well and thriving and to hear his voice again since it's been too long, oh God it's been far too long, and that we miss him so much, he would really love that, for you to tell him that, because I know he misses us, and how painful it is not to hear from him . . . And tell him you really didn't mean those harsh words you said to him, and you've been hurt over ever since, when he left us, and please, darling son, forgive us . . . Say that . . . it would be wonderful . . . Henry . . . Henry, that would be a mitzvah.

Henry   Polly, Polly, I can't say that . . . I just can't, can't, not now.

Polly   Henry. You're his father . . . is that so really difficult to do?

Henry (*in pain*)   Yes, Polly . . . for me . . . it's difficult.

Polly   Poor Henry! Is it such a difficult thing – to talk to your son?

Silence.

Then if you can't then don't . . .

They remain silent for a while.

So what time do you want your supper?

Henry   When you like, like when we always have supper . . . Sixish – sixish, OK?

Polly   OK, sixish, I'll go to the shops.

Henry   Tell you what Polly, I'm really looking forward to my chicken soup . . .

Polly (*who hasn't moved*)   Well, good, 'cause that's what you're going to get.

Henry   With dumplings?

Polly   Of course . . . with dumplings . . .

The lights fade, they remain seated, staring out, frozen in their thoughts.

'Ere

Characters

Bill, *fat, sluggish, morose, mid-forties*
Doreen, *fat, optimistic, slushy, sentimental, mid-forties*
Gas Inspector, *debt-collector, nice-looking*
Jesus, *tall, fair, beautiful*

Set

London. Now. Grungy slum. Kitchen. Lounge.

Bill So what's up . . . eh? What's up your nose, eh? Go on
. . . cough up your phlegm . . . spit it out! I hate it . . . I really
fuckin' hate it when you sit there like an old dog turd . . . a
dried-up miserable doggy turd.

Doreen Shut it! Oh shut it! You great fat honking piece of
pig shit . . . !

Bill Hey . . . hey, fuckin' watch it . . . That's not very
fuckin' nice . . . I don't like that . . . I fuckin' well bollocking
don't like it one stinking arse'ole bit . . . Your fuckin' pissing
attitude at the start of the day . . . That fucks my fucking day
up, that do . . . So what's up, go on, heave it out your filthy
gob, ya miserable dried-up slit . . . !

Doreen What's today, cunt? Eh? What's to-fucking-day?

Bill What?

Doreen Today.

Bill What . . . today?

Doreen Now . . . today, this minute, yeah . . .

Bill Fuckin' Friday innit, yeah? Slimebag . . . fuckin' Friday
. . . end of the working week!

Doreen What's it to you, you bone-lazy fucking parasite . . .
You don't fucking work . . . So what's it to ya, ya fuckin'
ponce . . . ?

Bill What's it ta me, you suppurating slash – what's it ta
me . . . ? Yeah . . . I worked once, didni? Yeah . . . so ah still
get that fuckin' little frill . . . The Friday fuckin' frill!

Doreen The Friday thrill, ya cunt, ya pathetic fuckin'
limp-cocked cunt . . . If you could only hear ya fuckin' self . . .
What a pathetic heap of shit ya become . . .

Bill What's got up your arse then, eh . . . ? Got the fuckin'
jam rags on . . . ha ha!

Doreen 'T's ma birfday innit!

Bill Fuuck!

Doreen Yeah, ya forgot, ya clapped out fuckin' wanker . . .

Bill Fuuuuck . . . Oh fuuuuuck!

Doreen Yeah!

Bill Fuck oh fuck!

Doreen Yeah!

Bill Fuck me!

Doreen Yeah, that's right . . . You leftover drip that ran down ya muvver's leg.

Bill You got me there . . .

Doreen Pig-faced bollockin' arsehole . . .

Bill I fort it was next fuckin' week . . . I swear . . .

Doreen Sure, you slow-witted, fat-gutted lump of garbage . . .

Bill I'm out of order . . . Yeah, I'm definitely outa order . . . No, she's right . . . I'm outa fuckin' order . . . Right . . . Ya got me . . . It's a fair cop . . . So make me a fuckin' cuppa tea, eh . . . there's a dear . . . and we'll get it sorted . . .

Doreen Yeah, ya fuckin' bettah . . .

She exits.

Bill (*to audience*) Yer! Forgot her shitty birfday . . . oh fuck, ha ha ha! But fair's fair . . . she 'ad me there . . . I mean the old rancid tard 'ad me ova a barrel din she . . . fuck it, I'll take the tub a lard to the Chinese and stuff her great gob with a few tubs of noodles . . . and some chop suey chow mein. I mean that'll go down a treat . . . she'll stuff 'erself silly and I'll put the nose bag on and all . . . yeah, while I'm about it . . . Fuckin' birfdays . . . tarts make yer laugh, don't they? . . . I mean they all get up their draws 'bout fuckin' birfdays . . . don't they? . . . I mean, it's a tart fing innit . . . ? Like they always wanna be fussed over, right . . . always banging ya on

the 'ead about fuckin' wedding anni-fuckin-versaries, birfdays,
'member when we met . . . ? Hey, hang about . . . it's the
cunting semi-final tonight . . . shiiiit! And I still can't work
that fuckin' video to record the cunt! Oh fuckin' bollockin'
dogshit!

Doreen *enters.*

Doreen   So 'ere's ya fuckin' tea, shit-for-brains . . . So get it
sorted, eh? So wha' we gonna do fer my birfday . . . ?

Bill   Darlin', we're gon' order a big fuckin' noshup from the
chink house. Get a crate of plonk from Asda's an' have
ourselves a right old feast . . . Dija have to leave the tea bag in
the cup like a fuckin' Tampax floating abaht?!

Doreen   Wot! Stay in again on me fuckin' birfday . . . On
me birfday! You great glob of suppurating shit! On me
birfday . . . !

Bill   'Old on, don't frow yor nappies out the pram . . . We'll
'ave some mates round, right? A bit of a ding-dong . . . Party
night . . .

Doreen   Who . . . eh . . . who? You ain't got no mates, 'ave
ya? Wot fuckin' mates you got?

Bill   Wot fuckin' mates I got?!

Doreen   You ain't 'ad no one round 'ere for years . . .
'Cause nobody fuckin' likes ya . . . In fact, the word on the
street is that you're 'ated . . . I mean fuckin' 'ated . . . Ha ha
ha . . . Mates . . . Don't make me larf!

Bill (*stung*)   *I* got a stack of mates, you fuckin' alligator
mouth . . . a stack . . . Yeah!

Doreen   How come we don't see any of 'em . . . eh?

Bill   How come?

Doreen   Yeah . . . how fuckin' come we don't see any of
your glorious fuckin' mates?

Bill   I'll tell you how come, you ugly cunt!

Doreen   Ooh, 'e's getting all upset and shitty . . .

Bill   'Cause I'm ashamed of this shithole you keep . . . This stinking, dirty filthy fuckin' slum you call home . . . So I see my mates outside . . .

Doreen   Oh sure . . . You got no mates . . .

Bill   Listen, you pox-ridden hag, why should I want my mates to clock this fuckin' lump of stink-gob I call a wife . . . Eh? I mean I'm still a man with some pride, and fuck me . . . I don't wanna shove it in their fuckin' faces . . . Yeah, 'Look what I ended up wiv' . . . Right?!

Doreen   What yor sayin then is that yor ashamed of me . . . Zat watcha saying?

Bill   Yeah, cloth-ears . . . You 'eard me . . . T' fuckin' fink, 'Poor Bill' . . . 'Ow'd he end up wiv such a fat fuckin' freak?' . . . You'd make them go all wobbly and sick . . . They'd pass out wiv the stink . . . They'd gas it round the neighbourhood . . . How does he sleep wiv it . . . ? Or does he put her in the kennel at night and bung her a few scraps . . . Ha ha ha!

Doreen   So d'ya fink you're a fuckin' oil painting, eh . . . I dunno how you can look in the mirror without wantin' to kill yourself . . . Pride . . . fuckin' pride . . . you got no pride or you wouldn't end up looking like an overweight sperm whale only wivout no sperm . . . only the fuckin' blubber . . . I mean, you make disgusting sound nice . . . It's lucky I'm short-sighted so I can't even see ya properly . . . You know why ya never go out? . . . In case the RSPCA mistake ya for the missing fuckin' link and haul you off to London Zoo!

Silence for a few seconds.

What yor sayin' then is that yor ashamed of me . . . zat watcha saying?

Bill   An' I was gonna take ya for a fuckin' Chinese . . .

Doreen   Wot, out?! You mean out . . . in the street and everyfing . . . Like going out?!

Bill   Yeah, like aaht . . . in the caff . . .

Doreen   But you said . . . you said to have it in . . . like a fuckin' takeaway in front of the fuckin' telly.

Bill   That was an option, that's all, just a fuckin' option!

Doreen   Oh, an option?

Bill   Yeah, a fuckin' option . . .

Doreen   Didn't sound like an option ta me . . . sounded like . . . that's it . . . sit in again and watch the boring fuckin' football . . . An I 'ate fuckin' football.

Bill   That's why it was an option . . . 'Cause it's the fuckin' semi-final tonight . . . But fuck it . . . It's ya birfday, right . . . And that's top fuckin' dollar ain't it . . . I mean, that's gotta take priority over a bunch of fuckin' pooftahs kickin' a ball abaht . . . right!

Doreen   Aah, aah! Nah that's better . . . that's a lot betta . . . I like it when ya a bit romantic . . . Then it's like the old Bill.

Bill   Ah, fuck it, don't go all sloshy and lose the fuckin' plot . . .

Doreen   Nah, nah, don't go all funny 'cause ya said sumfing nice for once in your life . . . Don't lose ya bottle . . .

Bill   I can be, ya see . . . I'm basically a bit of a romantic cunt at times, aint I?

Doreen   You can be . . . yeah, you can be and when ya nice I wanna play wiv ya willy!

Bill   Ged ahtovit, woman!

Doreen   No, Bill, I do . . . 'Cause when ya give me a bit of nice verbals it makes me go all a bit squelchy . . . Ooh, I'm feeling all squelchy squeezy . . .

Bill Fuckin' 'ell . . . Wot 'ave I brought on!

Doreen We ain't done nothing dirty fer years, 'ave we, darlin'?

Bill Oh fuckin' bollocks . . . 'S not my fault, is it . . . It goes off, dunnit, eh . . . Gets a bit boring so the frill goes, dunnit!

Doreen Yeah . . . But it's come back again . . . Just 'cause you were a bit nice. Ooh, it opened the floodgates . . . Ooh Bill, I'm getting all juiced up . . . !

Bill 'uckin' Jesus Christ!

Doreen 'Ere . . . Come 'ere, darlin' . . .

Bill Doooon't. Ya makin me fuckin' sick, ya fat old slag!

Doreen 'Ere . . . 'ere don't spoil it just when I'm getting all stirred up.

Bill I ain't even had my breakfast yet, ya fat old squelchy cunt!

Doreen Ooh, I'm feelin all slithery.

Bill Yeah, but I'm not, am I . . . 'T's all one side and I ain't 'ad my fuckin' breakfast . . . Wassa matter wiv you . . . Eh! Fuckin' leave it out . . .

Doreen Darlin, I'm horny fer ya big dick . . .

Bill Yeah, but it ain't big . . . It's sleepin', ainit?

Doreen Never mind, I'll get it big and fat again . . . Won't I? I'll pour some vegetable oil on it . . . Ya used to like that . . . And then I'll sit on ya cock . . . So all you 'ave to do is lay there . . . Eh? . . . Come on, Billy . . .

Bill Oh my gawd . . .

Front doorbell.

Oops, that's the door . . . Oo fuckin' calls 'ere?

Doreen   Maybe it the fuckin' postman wiv a parcel fer me birfday . . . Go on, Bill . . . So oo is it, eh?

Bill *exits.*

Doreen   'E's sweet really . . . I mean underneath all the shit and crap 'e comes aht wiv, underneath 'e's sweet and that makes me 'orny! Funny innit? You ne'er know when ya gonna suddenly fancy a stick of hard cock . . . It comes suddenly . . . the urge . . . like thunder . . . a trembling in ya knickers . . . Yeah . . . I suppose I could 'ave a wank but, 's not the same no matta wot the feminists say . . . as two of ya hacking away . . . Cor, my knickers are all wet . . . 'T's terrible . . . Oh come on, Billy boy . . .

Bill *comes in, flustered.*

Bill   Hey Dor, some cunt from the gas company says the gas bill's way overdue and the cunt's gonna cut us orf . . . Dintcha pay the fuckin' bill, ya mindless cuckoo!

Doreen   Course I paid the fuckin' bill you cross-eyed cunt . . . I bought a postal order and put it in an envelope for you to post . . .

Bill   Don't remember that . . . No I don't . . .

Doreen   Ya fuckin' brain's got rising damp and gangrene . . . I remember giving ya the fuckin' envelope ta post . . . When ya pick up the social security money at the post office . . . Where's ya brains? In ya dirty knickers?

Bill   Well, I musta posted it . . . Mustn't I?

Doreen   Look in ya fuckin' pockets . . . Look in ya fuckin' coat, ya cunt, maybe it's still there . . .

Bill   Oh fuck it! Awright . . . I'll ave a look . . . You see this geezer and explain.

Doreen   Oh fuck me . . . Now . . . When I'm in this state . . .

Bill   'E won't mind . . .

He exits.

(*Offstage.*) 'Scuse me, but wouldja mind 'avin' a word wiv the missus . . . She 'andles the household accounts . . .

Gas Inspector (*a youngish man*) *enters.*

Gas Inspector   Good morning . . .

Doreen   Oooh, good morning . . . You'll have a cuppa tea will ya? 'E's looking for the postal order in case 'e forgot to send it.

Gas Inspector   No, thank you . . . As I explained to your husband I am obliged by law to cut your supplies upon non-payment of bill.

Doreen   Oh no, that's terrible, 'cause I swear we paid it . . . I'm sure of it . . .

Starts weeping.

It's terrible . . . My old man can't work 'cause e's got emphysema from smoking himself to deaf, the cunt . . . So we try and cope . . . waa! We just struggling to survive, darlin' . . .

Gas Inspector   Look, 's not up to me, but you did get three warnings . . . According to the record book . . . You can appeal and request social security . . .

Doreen   Nah, be a nice boy . . . 'Ere, come ere . . . Sit dahn a mo . . . You gotta mum, aintcha?

Gas Inspector   Look, I'm sorry, but I need to cut the supply . . .

Doreen   OK, in a minute . . . I gotta tell you somefing . . .

Gas Inspector   OK, just a minute.

He sits.

Doreen   Look, I swear I paid . . . I always do, right, but my old man, 'cause he's got Parkinson's fuckin' Disease . . . he forgets . . . Like his brain's like fuckin' syrup . . . Right so, 'e's looking for it, right . . . So give 'im five minutes for the old cunt to find it, eh . . . There's a good boy . . .

Doreen strokes leg of **Gas Inspector**.

Gas Inspector   Excuse me . . . what are you doing?

Doreen   Nuffin, just admiring ya legs . . . Ya got nice strong thighs aintcha. I suppose ya do a lot of joggin', eh . . . ?

Gas Inspector (*getting aroused*)   I play a lot of squash . . .

Doreen   Ooh, squash, is it . . . Oooh, watcha got ere, eh . . . You naughty boy . . . It ain't alf a biggie, ain't it . . . Shall we give it a little squash . . . It's all hard innit . . . Let's ave a look at the old boy . . .

Opens fly.

Oooh, 'e's beautiful . . . and I'm gonna give him a little kiss 'T's awright . . . Don't worry, my old man don't give a toss, honest, so relax and I'll give him a nice gobble . . . You can do the gas anuvver time . . . Ooh, 'e's lovely . . . Go on, son, relax . . . Lay back . . . I luv suckin' cock . . .

Sounds of squelching, sucking, coming.

Gas Inspector   Ooooh! Ooooh! Ooooh! Luvly . . . Ooh . . . That's nice . . . Yeah . . . Smashing . . . Oooh . . . Bit slower . . . That's it!

He finishes.

Doreen   So 'ow was that, eh? Ja like that, my luvly sweetheart?

Gas Inspector (*dreamily, weakly*)   Yeah . . . luvly . . . Phew . . . That's one of the perks . . . !

Doreen   Oh, that one of the perks of the trade is it . . . you naughty boy . . . Well, by the amount of cum you shot out you ain't had a perk for a while, ave ya?

Gas Inspector   OK, so . . . er . . . when are you gonna pay?

Doreen   Oh darlin' . . . I just did it . . . Didn't I work it off for ya, sweetheart? Don't be mean, eh?

Gas Inspector   OK, just between us I'll strike it off . . . Just this time mind you.

Doreen   Oh, you're a luvly boy, you are. 'Ave a cuppa . . .

Gas Inspector   I'd better get on my way . . . Just this time. right!

Doreen   Yeah, darlin' . . . I won't take advantage . . . And fanks . . .

Gas Inspector *goes offstage and we hear him meet* **Bill**.

Bill (*offstage*)   Sod me up the khyber pass, but the old slag was right . . . found it in my fuckin' anorak pocket . . . the envelope . . . Here y'are . . . must have slipped my bonce . . .

Gas Inspector   Oh, er, thanks very much . . . Tada.

Slams door, exits.

Bill *enters room.*

Doreen   Oh fuckin' arseholes, Bill, we didn't need to now!

Bill   Wadja talking abaht . . . Cunt was gonna cut us orf, wan' 'e?

Doreen   Oh fuck it and shitarse!

Bill   Wot's fuckin' up! I found the fuckin' postal order didn' I . . . eh?!

Doreen   Well fuckin' done . . . But I just gave 'im a fuckin' free blow job for it . . . !

Bill   Wot!

Doreen   Yeah! I worked it orf, didn' I . . . And you come in and bung 'im the dosh! Fuck it!

Bill   You give im a blow job . . . ?!

Doreen   Like yeah!

Bill   Fuckin' shittin' bollox, and the cunt didn't say nuffin' but run orf with the money . . . Wotta cunt! Why dintcha say somefing, you old fuckin' slapper . . . Yer mouth got glued up?!

Doreen   Yeah, well, gotta bit shy and it all happened so fast . . . I couldn't get it aht . . .

Bill   Oh, never fuckin' mind . . . It'll be credit for the next bill . . . OK . . . O-fucking-K!

Doreen   Yeah, s'pose . . . Well, awright . . . Fuckit!

Bill   Yeah well . . . It weren't a fuckin' ordeal for ya . . . S'pose you even liked sucking his cock . . .

Doreen   'T's awright . . . Yeah . . . Mind you, 'e 'ad a big one, a real jaw-breaker . . .

Bill   Oh great . . .

Doreen (*dreamy*)   Yeah, a nice silky big pink one . . .

Bill   'Ere, give it a fuckin' break, will ya . . . I'm not one of yer girlfriends that you can unload your filth on . . .

Doreen   Well, it came in 'andy, don't it? I mean, having a pussy and a mouth do come in 'andy at times . . .

Bill   Yeah, well, some men will stick it in anyfing . . . But not to give it for free, you fat stupid slagheap!

Doreen   You said it'll be credit for the next bill.

Bill   Yeah, well, OK . . . I 'ope so . . . So 'e 'ad a big cock, did 'e?

Doreen   Nah, not too big . . . Don't want to wind you up . . .

Bill   Wind me up . . . You gotta be fuckin' jokin' . . . I don't give a shit! In fact, you can do that for *all* the bills . . . Do some graft for a change! . . . So, 'ow big was it?

Doreen   I dunno, wasn't paying that much attention . . . But it weren't nearly as big as yours, Bill!

Bill   Oh sure, yeah, like I give a fuck about the fuckin'
gasman . . . I don't give a monkey's fucking toss if it was as
big as King fucking Kong . . .

Doreen   Nah . . . It were a bit thin . . . Like a scrawny
carrot . . . Not a big juicy thicky like your, Bill . . . Yours is a
whopper . . .

Bill   Yeah, so why ja say it were a silky pink big one . . . ?
Eh . . . ?

Doreen   Just ta wind you up, ya silly fat cunt . . . Where's
ya humour . . . eh? Was winding you up! Silly fuckin' sausage.

Bill   Yeah . . .

Doreen   Course!

Bill   Ooh, I just got a bit of a twitch in my corry just nah . . .
It's stiffening up a bit . . .

Doreen   Oooh, you ain't said nuffin' so romantic fer
yonks . . .

Bill   Don't be a stupid shitpot . . . I ain't romantic . . . Just
finking of that tart on page three wiv the big tits . . . Was
finking of her and then the talk of cock . . . Made me fink of
her on page three sucking me off . . . Not you, you bloated
scummy hag.

Doreen   Don't matter . . . you can fink of her while I suck
your cock . . . Don't mind if you 'ave ya fantasy . . . You can
imagine that I'm 'er . . . Just close your eyes and imagine it . . .

Bill   Fuckin' 'ell . . . My imagination ain't that fuckin'
powerful . . . But on the other hand my cock's getting a bit
wriggly . . . Yeah . . . Maybe it needs some attention . . .

Doreen   Let's go ta bed, darlin' . . .

Bill   Fuck all that . . . Bollox . . . Nah I tell you wot . . . You
can give me a blow job 'ere on the sofa . . .

Doreen Oh Bill . . . I'd love to give you a blow job . . . It's been so long!

Bill Oh, yeah, don't get all fuckin' sloppy . . . Just git on wiv it, ya slag . . . 'Ere, wait a tick, I wanna fag . . .

Doreen Go on then . . .

Bill (*lights a fag*) Yeah, now turn the telly on . . . That's a good girl . . .

TV shows wars, fighting, bombs, deaths.

Doreen So you're be wantin' a cuppa next . . . !

She unzips his fly.

Bill Yeah, fuckin' after . . . A nice dark brown strong sweet cuppa . . . Ooh that's nice . . . nice one . . . Oooh shit and piss that's fuckin' awright that is . . . Yer, I forgot how good it can be . . . Oooh . . . you don't half know how to gobble dontcha . . . Ya see . . . ya can do something wiv yer gob that's useful instead of using it ta moan all the fuckin' time . . . a bit faster, darlin' . . . You old cunt . . . That's better . . . Squeeze my balls, luv . . . that's a dear . . . Oops, somefing's happening . . .

He leans in to the TV.

Another fuckin' bomb in Baghdad . . . I mean, I don't fuckin' get it . . . I mean, wiv all o' our firepower . . . I mean, fink about it . . . how much fuckin' firepower we got . . . we could wipe these evil cunts out in fuckin' seconds . . . but nah . . . we gotta respect the holy places . . . A bit slower, love, and squeeze 'arder . . . that's better . . . That ain't war . . . that's fuckin' wanking . . . war's fuckin' war . . . . Ooooh lovely . . . ooh . . . If I was the fuckin' president . . . you know what I'd do . . . nuke the fuckin' lot . . . then you get rid of the fuckin' problem . . . yeah! Yeah! Yeah! . . . Then start afresh. yeah . . . be a bit bold . . . I tell you . . . they wouldn't fink twice abaht fuckin' doin it to you, mate . . . Ooh fuck, now faster, yeah faster . . . go on ya big fat juicy pig . . . ataagirl! Ooh

KEBLAM! KEBLAH! KEBLOO! YA! YA! YA! OOOOH!
SHIT! PISS! AND FUCK! YAAAAAAAA!

Bill *lies there exhausted.*

Doreen   Wasat nice for you?!

Bill   Phew! 'T's awright . . . yeah, weren't bad . . . So
where's my cuppa . . . ?

Doreen   You liked that, dintcha . . . I could tell . . .

Bill   Yeah, 't's awright, course I thought of the tart on page
three!

Doreen   Don't care, 'cause I was the one that did it. not
her . . . She wouldn't come near you wiv a hundred-foot
bargepole fer a million quid . . .

Bill   I wouldn't be so sure if I were you . . .

Doreen   Ha ha ha! You gotta be fuckin' jokin . . . but to tell
you the truth I don't mind . . . it's still your spunk in my
mouth . . . Anyway, I fantasise too . . . !

Bill   Oh yeah . . . oo you fantasise about then, you soppy
old spunk bag?

Doreen   Well, I use you . . . to fink of Paul Newman . . . an'
I got such a vivid imagination that I can really see 'im . . .
yeah. I fink of 'im and his strong thighs and nice strong cock
and his lovely blue eyes . . . So I don't feel ya big ugly fat belly
no more or ya smelly dick . . . It all goes aht the winda and
I got Paul in my arms . . . and in my gob!

Bill   So why ya getting all poxy nasty . . .

Doreen   Not nasty . . . 'cause ya couldn't even say it was
nice or nuffin' . . .

Bill   Awright . . . 's nice . . . Ya wanna fuckin' medal . . . ?
Was nice . . . yeah . . .

Doreen   Just ta show a bit of appreciation . . . that's all . . .

Bill   I just did . . . yeah . . . 's teriffic!

Doreen   OK then, that's better . . . 't's all you 'ave ta say . . .

Bill   Yeah . . . to tell ya the truth it was fuckin' awright!

Doreen   Bill boy . . .

Bill   What's up? What's fuckin' up now?

Doreen   I'm a bit shy sometimes to say . . .

Bill   Nah, go on . . . spit the fuckin' fing outcha big gob . . .

Doreen   Jafink . . . like . . . you could give me one . . . ?

Bill   Wot?

Doreen   A blow job . . . like you use ta . . . eh . . . Billy . . . darlin' . . . ?

Bill   Give you one . . . Yeaaaaaaah!

Rushes out screaming.

Doreen (*turns off TV*)   'E's a right selfish arsehole cunt . . . Finks all women is just spunk bags . . . that's all . . . Mind you 's not every day he lets me do it . . . I mean, it's been years . . . so 'e must fancy me a bit . . . Maybe I gotta get myself a bit more sexy . . . 'cause if ya don't get poked ya tend to neglect yaself, dontcha . . . Get a thong maybe . . . yeah . . . for starters . . . go aht and get a sexy thong for me birfday . . . snaz up a bit . . . Nah . . . I got a feeling I'm being used . . . yeah . . . Mind you, 'e's got a nice big donk when 'e uses it . . . Cor . . . it's made me all juicy now . . . so I'd better have a wank or I'll be jumpy all day . . . 'S not a bad life really . . . and two blow jobs is a kind of birfday present innit? I mean when ya fink abaht it . . . I mean, there's not a whole lot left is there . . . eh . . . And if ya not getting it . . . watcha gonna do wiv all that spunk! Eh! I mean fink of all those geezers walking abaht wiv their balls hanging low wiv spunk . . . 'S why they's always getting mad wiv road rage . . . killin' people . . . leaping up and down . . . it's all that spunk wiring them all up!

Bill *enters.*

Doreen (*aside*) I mean, look at his face . . . it's completely changed after I siphoned out the spunk . . . See . . . 'E's like a little kid . . . so . . . ya taken me aht for a wog noshup tonight?

Bill Yeah . . . I said I would, didn'I . . . and if I said I would . . . I would . . . wouldn't I?

Doreen Hey Bill . . . Do ya really fink this place is a 'pisshole' . . . like a slum . . . ?

Bill Nah, I'm not gonna tell ya no fuckin' pork pies am I? Right . . . well, I fink it's like the 'Ilton fuckin' 'Otel . . . s'luverly . . . Ha ha! 'T's OK . . . I was just pulling your pubes 'cause ya upset me . . . dintcha? So I was havin a bit of a nause . . . dat's all . . . Nah . . . it's 'ome innit . . . ? Cosy . . . yeah, fuckin' crunchy . . . It's got wot ya call character . . . and ya don't see the filth after a while, do ya . . .

Doreen I try to keep it nice but it gets all upset so fast . . . and ya always around . . . ya never go aht 'cept for the social security money and ya fags . . .

Bill I said it's fuckin' nice and it fuckin' is! I mean, it's us, innit . . . 'omely, relaxed . . .

Doreen If we 'ad a few people round I'd really clean it up . . .

Bill Wadja mean, like ya saying again that I got no mates? Ya fink I got no fuckin' mates. You clean up this fuckin' poxy shithole and you'll have an army in 'ere!

Doreen Nah, I was teasing ya . . . ya got loadsa mates . . . only I don't see 'em cause ya too ashamed to bring 'em home. Aren'tcha . . . Ya ashamed of me. That's watcha said . . .

Bill 'Ere, shut the fuckin' moanin', ya sour-faced old poxy tub of shit . . . Listen, you old cunt . . . you're my mate . . . ain'tcha . . . eh? You're my fuckin' soddin mate!

Doreen Am I? Am I ya fuckin' mate . . . ?

'Bill   Yeah, that's wot I fuckin' said, didn'I?

Doreen   I'm ya best mate if the truth were told . . . ya best fuckin' china, I am . . . in't I?

Bill   Yeah . . . yeah . . . you're my fuckin' best china plate . . . O-fuckin'-K . . . for fuck's sake . . .

Doreen   I am . . . I know I am . . .

Bill (*defensive*)   Got loadsa mates . . .

Doreen   Course you 'ave . . . 'course! You 'ave loadsa mates! Hee hee . . . loads!

Bill   You want me to feel like I'm a fuckin' leper . . . an outcast wiv no fuckin' mates – dontcha?

Doreen   Nah. Didn't mean it – 'cause you said our home was like a shit hole – that wot you said, an' it hurt me! Yeah! Anyway, I'm ya fuckin' mate, ya silly old cunt! . . . Ain't I? Eh?

Bill   Well . . . nah . . . not . . . really . . . more like a slag that keeps the 'ouse looking like a fuckin' Bangkok brothel, I mean a blow job once a year don't really qualify you as a mate! Do it? You're me slut-bag . . . 'Owever . . . 'owever, we get wot we fuckin' deserve, I s'pose . . . and if all I could get was you, then fuck me . . . yeah . . . s'pose you're my mate!

Doreen   Oh ta! I just drank your spunk! So you should be all playful and 'appy . . . not a sour-faced streak a' piss!

Bill   I is 'appy . . . I is . . . an' I got a ton of mates!

Doreen   That fucked you up the arse didnit? I mean, that really gotcha!

Bill   Fuck no! Got wot? You old needling bitch fartbag and dog shit . . . got fuckin' wot?!

Doreen   Don't matter . . .

Bill   Go on . . . got fuckin' wot?!

Doreen   I says it don't matter. Don't wanna row on my fuckin' birthday . . .

Bill (*muttering*)   Got plenty of mates . . .

Doreen   'Oo's ya mates then . . . ?

Bill   'Oo's my mates?

Doreen   Yeah – 'oo?

Bill   'Oo?

Doreen   'Oo?

Bill   Well . . . just got a new fuckin' mate didn' I?

Doreen   Oh yeah? 'Oo's that?

Bill   The geezer from the gas board 'oos cock you sucked . . . we was both in the same gob . . . so in a way we're mates! I mean his spunk an' mine is probably stuck swimming abaht in one of your cracked teeth . . . right now, and makin' mates . . . !

Doreen (*feeling teeth with her tongue*)   Yer . . . you could be right!

Bill   The geezer in the Paki shop . . . that dump down the road where I get me fags an booze . . . 'e's a mate . . . always asks me 'ow I yam . . .

Doreen   Wot's 'is name?

Bill   'Oo gives a fuck . . . 'E's a Paki . . . most of 'em got the same name so it don't matter! 'E looked at me after I picked up my change . . . an' said . . . 'Thanks, mate.'

Doreen   Oh well . . . I can see now . . . you gotta lotta mates. Ha ha ha! Ooh . . . I'm gonna piss myself in a minute . . . ooh fuck!

Bill (*riled*)   Ah tell ya 'oo's my fuckin' mate! Yeah . . . me! That's 'oo . . . me! Me! Me! Me! Me! Me! Course I look after me! No one else gives a fuck aboutcha . . . except me! Me!

Me! Me! Me! Me an' Jesus . . . 'E's my fuckin' mate . . . 'e's up there watchin' aht for me, yeah? When ya in ya fuckin' grave ya got no mates but 'im.

Doreen   Yeah, but y'ain't in ya fuckin' grave, are ya?

Bill   Give it up! Will ya! Will ya fuckin' give it up!

Doreen   Shh! You'll wake the rats.

Bill   Ooh no! Dear God . . . why hast thou afflicted me . . .

Doreen   Don't get so fuckin' wound up . . .

Bill   So don't fuckin' wind me up!

Doreen   'K! Not on my birfday . . .

Bill   Jesus is my mate. Don't fuckin' need mates anyways! Fuck 'em! All they fink abaht is their fuckin' selves . . . greedy fuckin' pigshit . . .

Doreen (*pondering*)   Ya right . . . Yer . . . you are right . . .

Bill   Don't lift a fuckin' finger when ya fuckin' skint! Like when ya really fuckin' in shit street . . . right?! Where are they then, eh? Where fuckin' are they . . . ya mates!

Doreen   Yer right . . . yer right . . . yer right . . . !

Bill   Like when you 'ad yer left tit orf. In the 'ospital . . .

Doreen   Ooh, don't remind me!

Bill   You were in the 'ospital, yeah . . . and where was ya cuntin' family . . . eh . . . ? Where . . .

Doreen   My sister came . . . she did . . .

Bill   Yeah . . . like fuckin' once . . . wiv a tiny box of chocolate creams!

Doreen   But she did come . . .

Bill   Like wot I'm trying to get through ya fuckin' lug-holes is that ya can't depend on ya fuckin' mates . . . when you's in fuckin' need! So, best not 'ave too many . . . so you won't be disa-fuckin'-ppointed.

Doreen   I'm ya mate!

Bill   Oright . . . you's my mate, Jesus is my mate and I'm my fuckin' mate . . . so that's three! That's not bad for starters!

Silence.

Doreen   Jesus is ya mate!

Bill   Course . . . too fuckin' right!

Doreen   'E neva let ya down!

Bill   Nah! 'E's there for ya . . . at the death . . . no matter wot you got!

Doreen   'E's there for you

Bill   Yerp!

Doreen   Always!

Bill (*bit tearful*)   Yerp!

Doreen   'E's worth a hundred mates!

Bill   Tell me abaht it!

Doreen   'E'll be there when you drop off the perch . . .

Bill   'Sright . . . ya too fuckin' right!

Doreen   'E'll be there, waitin' for ya in heaven . . .

Bill   Too right 'e fuckin' will! For sure!

Doreen   'E'll be watchin over ya in ya sleep.

Bill   'E do!

Pause.

Doreen   But 'e don't like it when ya call me a fat old cunt . . . do 'e?

Bill   Nah . . . 'e don't mind . . .

Doreen   'E don't mind . . . our Jesus?!

Bill   'E makes allowances when 'e sees wot I gotta put up wiv.

Silence. Light changes – gets dusky.

Doreen   The days is getting shorter.

Bill   Yeah . . . I fink they're shorter than they used to be.

Doreen   I fink so . . . yeah . . . So we really goin aht to 'ave my birfday dinner?

Bill   Ah said ah would . . . didn' I? That's what ah said and yor gonna 'ave it! Even if I miss the semi-fuckin'-final on the box.

Doreen   Why dontcha record it on the video that you bought an' never use?

Bill   Fuckin' 'ell. Ya see the fuckin' manual . . . it's a fuckin' nightmare . . . you try it!

Doreen   Can't ya get one of yer mates to show ya! Hee hee hee!

Bill *looks, scowls.*

Doreen   Ask Jesus to show ya 'ow to work the video? 'E's ya mate! Hee hee hee hee hee hee!

Bill   That's a fuckin' diabolical fuckin' shitcunt thing to say. To take the piss out of the Lord's name. You're a real slag to utter that . . . fuckin' mental case!

Doreen   Joookin'! 'Ave a sense of humour for fuck's sake. Billy . . . I giv ya a nice fuckin' blow job . . . It's ma birfday . . . The gas ain't cut off . . . Let's enjoy life, eh . . . Don't fuck it up when it's goin so well!

Silence. Lights fade.

So when we goin' aht . . . aht for me birfday dinner?

Pause

'Cause I'm looking forward to it now! An' I didn't eat nuffin'
since breakfast 'cause I really like wanna look forward to me
fuckin' dinner aht . . . aht wiv people! Others! All aht and
noshing away 'appily . . . 'S nice that, yeah, that you fink of
celebrating my birfday . . . that way I can remember wot I did
on my birfday . . . we celebrated it in the chink 'ouse . . .
triffik! 'S not raining so we can walk there . . . 'T's only a ten-
minute walk . . . 'S nice, and maybe the stars will be aht . . .
some nice wine to go wiv it . . . yeah . . . We ain't been there
fer yonks . . . I like it there . . . there's a big picture on the
wall of a great fuckin' dragon! And we sat under that . . .
That's how I remember, I remember the fuckin' dragon,
remember, Bill . . . ? I remember last year . . . we went last
year and some skin'eds threw a fuckin' brick through the
fuckin' winda . . . oooh! That was a shocker, but it didn't spoil
it . . . nah . . . we just carried on noshin' . . . wouldn't let
anything spoil our night aht, 'cause we don't have many,
right? So I relish it . . . ah do . . . ah really do . . . I mean, you
gotta celebrate ya fuckin' birfday ain'tcha?! I know your
tummy was upset last time 'cause you 'eaved up on the
pavement . . . you 'eaved up the fuckin' lot! Poor fing! I fink
it was those skin'eds got under your tits! But didn't spoil it
fer me . . . I liked it . . . an' I got a nice memory from that
night . . . nice . . . going aht . . . all the people noshing 'appily
. . . yeah, like a big family . . . 's nice, yeah. An' you know
wot? I imagine . . . yeah . . . that they're all there for me
birfday. Hee hee! Ya know . . . just imagine it . . . fun.

Pause. **Bill**'s *face expressing nothing. Dead.*

Bill   Gonna miss the fuckin' semi-final . . . Don't mind . . .
nah . . . don't fuckin' mind . . . 'cause it's ya birfday, so I
don't fuckin' mind . . . but ah fink to meself . . . wot's it all
abaht? Wot do I fuckin' get, eh? Like itsy-bits of pleasure
conked on the head . . . Don't matter, 't's only football and
it's ya birfday! So that's awright! But ah fink . . . ah fink a lot
. . . don't matter, 'cause I'm a fuckin' bloke . . . don't fuckin'

matter, yeah . . .'cause blokes s'pose to be above all that slosh
. . . yeah, tougher . . . aht in the world . . . an' slush is fer tarts
yeah . . . but yeah . . . maybe I'd like a birfday . . . celebration
. . . maybe, yeah. Who gives a fuck wot I like?!

Doreen (*amazed*)   You neva wanted a birfday dinner or
nuffin'! You neva wanted it . . . didja . . . we can do it next
birfday . . .

Bill   Nah . . . nah . . . it don't matter, nah . . . it's gone outa
my system . . . so fuckit! Yeah.

Doreen   Jawanna birfday treat, Billy?

Bill   Nah! Nah! Nah! But ah got needs, don't I . . . I got
needs . . . a bloke's got fuckin' needs . . . but don't matter.
www.dotcom! Yeah. Wot's all that abaht, eh? Like the world's
gorn fuckin' barmy . . . I used to collect conkers . . . ya know,
those beautiful fat shiny brown conkers, and put one on a
string and bash another geezer's conkers . . . and that was life!
That was fuckin' life . . . yeah, I know it's kids' shit an' all that
. . . but those bootiful orange-brown shiny hard conkers were
like fuckin' jewels . . . they felt in ya pocket like treasure and y
'ad to pick em up off the ground like precious gems . . . I used
to luv my conkers . . . Yeah, fuckin' kids' stuff, but I ain' 'ad
a fuckin' moment in my fuckin' life . . . as a grown-up . . . not
one fuckin' cuntin' moment . . . that can ever come close to
my fuckin' time of collecting conkers . . . Dot-fuckin'-com!

Silence. Light slowly fades. Top light stronger.

Doreen   Is it 'cause you can't work the video? Eh?

Bill   'T's all part and parcel . . . 'T's all shit to keep ya from
putting ya fuckin' 'ead in the fuckin' gas oven . . . Yeah, ah
mean, wot's life? Knowin' how to get the cuntin' video goin'.
Yeah . . . then, OK . . . you get ya 'ead round that cunt an
they fling somefing else atcha . . . dot.com. Dot-fuckin'-com.
I mean, wot the fuck is that! Wothefuckisthateh! Ya fink I'm
a cunt? Zatwachafink . . . I ain't no cunt . . . Dor, I ain't no
fuckin' cunt . . . dot-fuckin'-cunt!

Doreen   'Oo said yer a cunt? 'Oo's said?! Eh? No one said
yer a cunt! No one.

Quiet

. . . Bill, wadja mean put your 'ead in the gas oven . . . ya
wouldn't do that, wouldja . . . eh, Bill? Hey . . . I gived ya a
nice blow-job an you wos 'appy . . . yes, you wos, so wotja
mean abaht the gas oven . . . why say that about putting your
'ead in the fuckin' gas oven?! Eh! Y'd leave me all alone . . .
and yo're all I got in the world . . . y'are, Bill . . . ya all I got . . .
an that's enuff fer me . . . 'onest . . . If I got you I'm 'appy . . .
'cause I got somefing ain't I . . . that's my reason fa livin' . . .
So ya my reason . . . so you got somefing to live fa an dat's me
innit . . . Course I needja . . . ya my reason to breathe . . . you
is . . . so don't be a cunt, Bill . . . We got a lot, yeah, we do.

Bill   A lot . . . yeah . . . Wez my conkers then?

Doreen   Bill . . . y'are a cunt sometimes . . . ya gotta leave
the conkers for the next lot . . . the kids . . . I'm ya conkers
now! In't I?

Silence

I betta get ready fa dinner . . . so I'm gonna change me
dress . . . Wadja want me to wear, eh? I wanna wear
somefing nice fa ya . . . fa me birfday . . .

Bill (*weary*)   Ooooh fuck!

Doreen   Yeah . . . ah do . . . make a fuckin' effort will ya,
Bill . . . eh! Eh!

Bill   Yeah! Yeah! Yeah!

Doreen   Soon . . . it'll be time to go aht. So I'm gonna get
ready.

Bill   Go on.

Doreen   An' you . . . ain't ya gonna get ready to go aht . . .
eh? Y'aint gonna go like that . . . like that, wiv ya old smelly
trousers on wiv old stains down the fly and crusty soup stains

on ya shirt. I mean, you don't half look like someone dragged you aht the dustbin . . . ya do!

Bill   Wot?! Dress fa the chink 'ouse? Fer the fuckin' oo-flung-dung merchants! Wosup widju . . . you gone bonkers ya cow?!

Doreen   Ya bonkers! Ya not dressin' up for the chinks . . . ya doin' it fa me . . . ya fat cunt. Fa me . . . ya reason in life . . . fa me . . . me! Me! Me is someone too, ain't I . . . Me is a human, ain't just a fuckin' blob in your eyesight that washes yer filthy knickers and feeds ya fat gut and cleans the fuckin' 'ouse. Ain't just a moving blob. I am a human being, mate!

Bill (*pained*)   Jesus, come to me, mate! Jesus save me . . .

Doreen   'E'll come to ya . . . don't worry . . . 'E'll come soon enuff . . . when ya clean up your act . . . 'E don't like dirty people . . . 'E's clean and spotless so 'e ain't gonna come when you is all filthy lazy dirty . . . you gotta make an effort!

Bill   Jesus don't care what I fuckin' look like . . . 'E cares what I fuckin' am!

Doreen   OK. 'E don't care that you're a lazy dirty scumbag . . . so while ya waitin fer Jesus, I'm gonna put on somefing nice for me birfday, OK . . . so make a fuckin' effort and Jesus ya mate will come, hee hee hee hee hee!

Exits.

Bill   Fuckin' birfday . . . that's wot got the whole house in a right fuckin' state . . . the slag's birfday . . . Every year the same fuckin' bollox . . . then, ya no sooner get over that than it's fuckin' Xmas! Oh fuck, that's coming up . . . then it's fuckin' New Year . . . shit . . . sa ya no sooner get over one than the next crock a' shit's starin' ya in the face . . . it's one fuckin' drama after another . . . each one loomin' up like a fuckin' plague . . . Oooh fuck! It wears you aht . . . it do . . . wivaht all that, life would be peaceful . . . nice . . . just roll through the day . . . cosy like . . . shop at Asda's, eat, watch the telly, get pissed, shit, sleep, wake, shit, pick up the dole

money, there's lots to do . . . I mean ya don't 'ave to get
bored . . . and when I cop hold of how to use the fuckin'
video . . . fuck me the days won't be long enough! Sometimes
it's 'orrible, but like, it's life . . . ain't it . . . so you sit back and
wait fa the horrible to pass . . . but it's life . . . Like sometimes
there's a fuckin' war . . . right . . . or a right nasty murder case
. . . famine in some scumbag banana state . . . it's part of
life . . . an' . . . well . . . I tolerate it . . . I mean, wot can ya
do? . . . I mean, today was an exception, yeah? So I let her
fulfil her female needs . . . makes 'er 'appy don't it? Makes 'er
feel like a female . . . yeah . . . hee hee hee! But she didn't used
to be a big fat ugly slob of blubber . . . nah . . . she was 'alf
that size . . . yeah . . . when we met she was a little cracker!
'Ard to believe it nah, ain't it . . . I'm mean, it takes the cake!

Doreen *enters. She's wearing an outrageously ugly outfit far too
small – tight mini-skirt, etc.*

Doreen   Baboom!

Bill *looks up. Stares open-mouthed, speechless.*

Doreen   Zat awright then? Eh? Don't just sit there like a
freshly laid turd . . . wiv ya gob open . . . wadjafink?

Bill   I fink I'm dreaming . . . yeah . . . that I died and woke
up in hell!

Doreen   OK – I don't dream I'm in hell . . . I don't 'ave
ta . . . 'cause I'm in it!

Bill   Well, I must say, yer dressed fer it . . . I mean, that's
the right clobber . . .

Doreen   Yo're a right fuckin' wanker Bill . . . It's ma
birfday . . . and I'm tryin' to make somefing special, 'cause it's
a special day . . . so this day ain't like all the other days
clumped together . . . when each fuckin' day's like the one
before, like turds in the loo . . . and all ya can do is fuckin'
abuse me, you dumb cunt, just 'cause you ain't got nuffin' to
sing abaht and I'm tryin to make it nice, and ya like a fuckin'
weight round my ankles dragging me down to your stinkin'

hell . . . Look at cha! If I visited hell they'd all look like you!
That's death . . . ya look like fuckin' death . . . The door is
closing on ya life, mate . . . and I'm keeping a crack of light
open on ya! Just a tiny crack to keep it goin' . . .

Bill   Then shut the fuckin' door . . . go on . . . shut it!

Doreen   Don't tempt me, ya cunt, or one day I just might!

Bill   An' make sure y'are on the other fuckin' side of it when
ya shut it!

Doreen   Wot? Ya want me fuckin' aht?

Bill   One way or another . . . fuckin' bliss.

Doreen   You want me fuckin' out of me fuckin' ouse? Me
own 'ouse . . . you ungrateful cunt

Bill   'T's my 'ouse. 'T's my 'ouse! Ya fuckin' parasite, ya
fuckin' vacuum cleaner . . . suckin' my life aht . . . you
cocksuckin' cockroach!

Doreen   Ya dirty, lazy scumbag . . . ! If I shut the door
they'd find you in a heap of shit and beer cans . . . dead and
rotten on the dirty armchair wiv ya filthy skid marks on it!
'Cause ya rely on me ta keep ya shit together! An' 'oo's gonna
bury ya when ya drop orf the perch . . . eh? No one! 'Cause
no one knows yar alive . . . so no one's gonna miss ya . . . no
one . . . no fuckin' one! No one's gonna say, 'Oh, where's Billy
boy?' dahn the pub . . . No one's gonna miss ya at work . . .
No one's gonna say, 'Wos 'appened ta Bill?' . . . No one . . .
'Cause to them ya dead already . . . ya fuckin' dead – nah,
except the geezer in the Paki shop might scratch his head one
day and say, 'Wot happened to that fat fuckin' unwashed
smelly sod that used to come in 'ere for 'is fags and the fuckin'
paper?'

Bell rings.

Nah, wot the fuck is that?

Bill   Maybe the gasman for a second helping . . .

Bell rings again.

Doreen   Oh fuckin' wait, ya cunt!

She exits.

Bill   I don't know what to do wiv it . . . but killin 'er is the only sensible option . . .

Doreen (*voice offstage*)   Ooh! Didja say Jesus? Cor, sod me, and we was just talking 'boutcha . . . Oh, you wanna see Bill . . . yeah, sure, OK, 'e's just rottin' in the livin' room . . . I'll make you a cuppa tea . . . OK . . . No bother . . .

She re-enters.

Bill, look 'oo's come to see ya! Jesus . . . 'E wants to chat to ya . . .

She exits.

Jesus *enters. He's dressed in white, with long black hair, and looks beautiful and radiant.*

Bill (*gobsmacked, few seconds of silence*)   Fuckin' 'ell! I don't believe it! It's you . . . oh, Jesus . . .

Falls to his knees.

Jesus! I wus finkin' abacha all day . . . I wus . . . I wus needin' ya . . . and sod me, yer 'ere!

Jesus (*gently*)   Bill . . . Bill . . . get off your feet . . . stand up . . . No need for that . . . sit . . . we'll both sit . . . That's better . . . I felt your pain . . . I felt it so strongly . . . I had to come.

Bill   Jesus! Jesus . . . but there must be thousands of people in pain . . . millions of 'em!

Jesus   I will get to them . . . when they call for me . . . when they call with a full heart . . . then I come.

Bill   I can't fuckin' Adam and Eve it! It's incredible . . . I'm gobsmacked . . . Dor! Come 'ere, ya fat bitch . . . see 'oo's ere!

Jesus   I saw your wife . . . she's fine . . . she's a good woman.

Bill   Oh?! Oh, good . . . ya really fink so?

Jesus   I know she is . . . she takes care of you . . .

Bill   Yeah, well, in a way . . . yeah, but between you and me Jesus, it's a bit dodgy . . .

Jesus   But if her will is good . . . you must be more accepting . . .

Bill   Ya righth Jeez, ya absolutely right . . . I see what ya sayin' . . . I mean, she's 'avin' a go . . . 'Ere, Jeez, ja mind if I get a photo of us two?

Jesus   You may take a photo if you wish . . .

Bill   Dor! Dor! Fuckin' 'urry up . . . I wantcha to take a photo . . .

He goes to a drawer and takes out a cheap camera.

Doreen (*offstage*)   Waitin' for the fuckin' kettle ta boil!

Jesus   Don't worry about that . . . worry about your pain . . . why it's there . . .

Bill   It's fuckin' diabolical . . . horrible . . . But ya know . . . now that yer 'ere . . . don't feel so bad . . . in fact, I feel good . . . yeah, really good!

Jesus   That's because you let me into your life. I'm your mate, Bill . . . I know you feel a loss from the world, but know that I am with you.

Bill   Aah, Jeez . . .

Jesus   And you're my mate too . . . you are, and I love you . . . Yes, with all my heart Bill . . .

Bill   Ya do! Oh Christ Almighty, that's triffick! I mean me! A soddin' nobody!

Jesus   Why should I not . . . you're God's creation and he made you in his image . . . so how could I not love you . . .

Bill (*tearful*)   Oh Jeez . . . I dunno wot to say . . .

Jesus   I'll tell you, Bill, you'll say 'I love you, Jesus' and all the pain will leap out of you . . . Satan put the pain there, Bill . . . 'I love you Jesus and know you're my beloved mate,' that's what you say . . . and when your heart is full of me, Satan will be spat out . . . and then your heart will open to Doreen, and then she will love you even more, and everything will fall into place. Everything, believe me!

Doreen *comes in with the tea.*

Doreen   Ah fink this is the best birfday present I could ever 'ave . . . I still can't believe it!

Bill (*proud*)   'E came ta me, Dor . . . cause 'e felt my great pain . . .

Doreen (*defensively*)   An' to me too! Right?

Bill   Yeah, of course fer you . . . but yer so lovely and scrumptious, so smashin' and generous, so kind and compassionate, so sweet and lovi''n that 'e knows . . . Jesus knows you already 'ave Jesus in ya heart.

Doreen   Oooh! Bill!

Bill   So 'e came to be my mate! Hey, that's fuckin' triffick . . . 'Ere, Dor, take a quick pic, 'e ain't got all day.

Doreen *takes the camera.*

Doreen   OK . . . smile . . . nah, a bit more than that! That's a bit glum . . . say 'shiiit'. Go on . . .

Bill *and* **Jesus**   Shiiiiiit!

Doreen   Nah, it's betta, but a bit wanky . . . Like, relax, Jesus. Yeah, that's betta. Go on, put yer arm over Bill . . . yeah . . . 's lots betta. Oops, ya lost ya nice lovely smile. OK! 'Shit' again!

Bill *and* **Jesus**   Shiiiiiit!

Doreen   OK, Bill, you take one of me and Jeez!

They swap positions. **Doreen** *now sits with her arms around* **Jesus**.

Bill   OK! Nah, Jeez . . . sorry my mate, but could you put your arm round Dor . . . yeah . . . ah . . . come on, don't be shy, Jeez . . . she won't bite cha! She ain't got no teef! Ha ha! Hey, put ya cheeks together.

They do. **Doreen** *puts her hand on his knee.*

Doreen   Oooh! He ain't alf lovely . . . ain'tcha . . . Yer a doll, Jeez!

Bill   OK . . . Oh, shit . . . wot fuckin' button do I press?

Doreen   The red one on top, ya cunt . . . Oh come on, Bill, don't be such a thicky!

Bill   OK, OK! Keep ya dirty draws on, ya fat smelly cunt! Oh! I got it!

Jesus   You must listen, because the pain you show was once a love . . . that died . . . it rots within . . . So grow new love from the seeds of the past . . . You show too much pain . . . when you abuse each other, you hurt me and you hurt creation . . . since the Lord's purpose in creating you is to love each other.

Bill   'E's right . . . 'E's fuckin' right . . . Sorry, Jeez . . . I'll watch out in future . . . yeah . . . I know watcha talking abaht . . . Forgive me, Jeez . . . We just got excited . . . like you being here is like a miracle and I got overcome . . . Nah, we gonna love each uvver from now on . . . and Jeez, thanks for being my mate!

Jesus   It's good what you're saying . . . hold on to it . . . I must go now . . . I have others to comfort.

Doreen   Oh! Finish ya tea luv . . .

Jesus   Very well . . .

Doreen   Ya wanna biscuit?

Jesus   I wouldn't say no . . . I have a little hunger . . .

Doreen   Oh! Shitty bollox . . . My beloved husband has scoffed the effin' lot! 'Ere, Bill, be a doll . . . run down to the corner wog shop and get us a packet of raisin biscuits . . .

Bill   Take me all of two minutes!

Jesus   Please don't . . .

Bill   Just drink ya tea and back in a snap . . .

He exits.

Doreen   Ya know, Jeez . . . yer ever so nice . . . ya are.

She puts her hand on his thigh.

It's been all like a dream really, and I feel ever so good inside . . . like pure and clean and everything.

Jesus   That's good. It means your heart is opening . . .

Doreen   Oh Jeez. Can I confess somefing to ya! It's terrible, but I feel I just gotta confess . . .

Jesus   Of course you can . . .

Doreen   Well . . . I have to tell ya . . . and I am, as you say, a creature of God . . . just a poor soppy tart . . . But when I sit wiv you . . . I get . . . a funny squelchy feeling . . . in my pussy . . . is that evil?

Jesus   Nothing in the eyes of God is evil if it comes from the heart . . . Feelings are natural, and those feelings you describe are provoked by love . . . So that can't be evil!

Doreen   Ooooh! Good!

Pause.

Jeez, d'ya mind if I touch your willy?

Pause.

Jesus   If it helps to make you happy . . .

She slowly moves her hand to his crotch.

Doreen   Ooh! You've got a lovely hard-on, Jesus!

Jesus   I share the same feelings as most men . . .

Doreen   You certainly do . . . Oooh . . . It's so nice and big . . .

Jesus   It's love, made manifest . . .

Doreen   Ya don't fink it's just lust, do ya, Jeez?

Jesus   Lust is just a word meaning hunger, desire, and longing preceding love . . .

Doreen *pulls up his robe and starts gobbling him.*

Doreen   Oooh! Oooh! Oooh! Jeeez!

Jesus   Hmm! Hmm! Hmm! Oh, that's so good . . . ooh! Slow down a bit . . . hey! That's really getting wonderful . . . Yeah . . . yeah . . . ow . . . ow . . . . Ooh fuck, ooh fuck.

He climaxes. Sound effects.

Oooh, that was nice . . . it's been a long time.

Doreen *finishes.*

Doreen   Ooh! You taste so nice, Jeez.

Jesus   Well, that's certainly relaxed me up a bit . . .

Doreen   Then obviously you really needed it . . . It'll make ya work a little more relaxed . . .

Jesus   Thanks for your love.

Doreen   Ooh Jeez, thanks for yours!

Jesus   And so I had better be on my way . . . you and Bill will be fine . . . I am sure of that.

Doreen   OK, OK, Jeez. Ya don't wanna wait for the biscuits?

Jesus   Tell Bill I have faith in him . . . God bless both of you.

Jesus *exits.*

Doreen   Cor blimey, it's like a fuckin' weird, wonderful dream . . . I can't believe it . . . 'E made me feel all funny, and horny, and squelchy, and lovely, that's 'cause 'e spreads love . . . Wot a diamond geezer . . . I can't believe it . . . Three in a day! 'T's amazin' . . . ma birfday! '' came ta ma birfday . . . Why? 'Cause we needed 'im . . . yeah . . .

Bill *enters, puffed out.*

Bill   Phew, I ran . . . Got cream biscuits . . . 'T's all the cunts 'ad . . . Hey! Where's 'e gone?

Doreen   'E 'ad to go . . . 'E's got a million people to see . . . we wos just lucky.

Bill   Cor! I ran all the way . . . I'm knackered!

Doreen   But 'e said God bless ya . . . he said that. Tell Bill, he said.

Bill   Aah! Yeah, he said we was real muckers . . . Sod me, I'm shattered!

Doreen   I mean, Bill, no one's gonna believe this . . . no one! 'S amazing innit?

Bill   Aah. Shame 'e's gone . . . 'E's really lovely 'e was . . . a real upright geezer. Ah well . . . That's a once-in-a-lifetime that is . . . but we got the pics!! Yeah! We'll get them developed . . . He said 'e's my mate!

Doreen   Shame ya didn't ask him how to work the video while 'e was 'ere . . .

Bill   Ya can't fink of everyfing . . . 'ind you, 'e would 'ava shown me . . . 'cause 'e knows everyfing . . . and you know wot? 'E's picked me . . . or us, OK . . . 'cause 'e knew I need 'im! Like a sudden guided missile 'e zoomed right into my pain!

Doreen   Course! 'E heard ya, Bill! 'E 'eard ya callin' to 'im . . . 'Eard ya cryin' in the night fer 'im!

Bill Awright . . . awright! Don't overdo it, Dor . . . don't go fuckin' potty!

Doreen Can't 'elp it . . . it's so wonderful . . . I can feel 'im . . . still feel 'im 'ere in the 'ouse . . . like 'e's inside me . . . Oooh, Bill, I'm in a quiver . . .

Bill Fuckin' 'ell, take it easy, mate . . . 'E came to me, right! Fa my pain 'e came . . . like a doctor . . . 'e came for my pain . . . ta 'elp me get rid of it . . . yeah . . . Oh, I'm knackered Dor . . . ran all the way to get the biscuits.

Doreen Ah! Yar a good boy, Bill, y'are!

Bill Ain't run fa years! I'm fuckin' pooped!

Silence. Darkness.

Doreen Sa wot now . . . ya gonna get ready for me birfday dinner at the wog shop, eh, Bill?

Bill *is still silent.*

Doreen Eh? Gowon . . . get nice and ready . . . put on that nice red pullover I got ya last Xmas . . . Come on Bill . . . eh . . . ? Ya look good in that . . . then we'll go aht and 'ave some luvley sweet an' sour chicken . . . Ooh I can't wait to get my mouth round that . . . Wot a day, eh? Topped wiv Jesus . . . sa wake up Bill . . .

She prods him. He flops over. Dead. In her euphoria she pays no attention.

Ah don't fink nuffin' on earth can top that . . . I mean that's the tops . . . and I gobbled 'im . . . 'E let me gobble 'im! I still can't believe it . . . sa nuffin' matters no more, nah! All those little fings that use ta bovver me . . . that's 'cause I didn't 'ave love. So everyfing bovvers ya . . . 'cause all the shit things slip in the empty space . . . and I don't really care 'bout the birfday dinner . . . 'cause nuffin' can top that . . . so you can watch the semi-final . . . yeah . . . but yeah . . . I fink I wanna go aht . . . I fink I'll go aht to the corner pub and celebrate all the luv inside me wiv a quick lager all by meself . . . yeah, and ponder the world . . . That feels real good . . . and I'll tell someone that Jeez visited us . . . an how 'e looked . . . how beautiful he was, an 'e made ya feel nice, luvly inside just ta gaze on 'im . . . an 'e smells lovely, yeah, like roses . . . course 'e was full of luv . . . 'e was, bursting wiv it . . . and 'e came to deliver some of it ta us . . . yeah . . . Now that's a one-orf . . . that is . . . that's special . . . oooh, I'm dyin' to tell someone that . . . 'S better than telling them 'bout ya operation . . . an ya neighbours getting on ya tits . . . Can't wait . . . just can't wait to get aht . . . well, I'm all dressed up an' all . . . so don't waste life, Doreen . . .

She exits, singing 'There's a Song in my Heart'.

Light slowly fades on dead **Bill***.*

Exit

Characters:

Anne, *young, alert, intelligent*
Ben, *bored, frustrated, and feels hard done by*

Anne I can't stand it . . .

Ben What can't you stand . . . Hmm . . . What?

Anne I can't stand the way you spit in the sink . . .

Ben I did that . . . I did that . . . Spit . . . ?

Anne I clean the sink and *yuk*! I see that gob . . .

Ben Sorry . . .

Anne Yuk, I can't stand it!

Ben Sorry . . .

Anne Our stuff in the sink . . . *yuk*!

Ben I said, I'm sorry!

Anne OK, but please . . . you know . . . just don't . . .

Ben OK, but leave off . . . alright?

Anne It's disgusting . . .

Ben All right, give it a rest . . .

Anne Where did you get that habit?

Ben I'm sorry, it just happened . . .

Anne Like a bachelor you live . . . an old bachelor . . .

Ben It didn't go down?

Anne Yuk!

Ben It didn't go down 'cause all your hairs block up the plughole . . .

Anne Mine?

Ben Well, hardly mine!

Anne So don't do it!

Ben So clear your hair out . . . Your hair blocks up the sink . . .

Anne   Hair is normal . . . It's normal . . . It's clean.

Ben   So is spit!

Anne   Yuk, resting on my hair . . .

Ben   Leave it out . . . will you just . . .

Anne   OK, I finished . . . Just so you know . . . You don't live alone . . .

Ben   I know.

Anne   You have to be considerate . . . to others . . . you know . . .

Ben   As long as you know . . .

Anne   Believe me, I know . . .

Ben   Then don't leave your hair to block up the plughole . . .

Anne   That's from washing my hair . . . That's what the sink is for . . . For washing . . . not spitting . . .

Ben   OK, don't make a sermon out of it . . .

Anne   I know you lived like an old bachelor for years . . . With your one-night stands . . .

Ben   What?!

Anne   I bet for them you never spat in the sink . . .

Ben   I never did one-night stands . . .

Anne   For them you were Mr Romantic, with clean knickers . . .

Ben   Meaning . . . ?

Anne   With familiarity you lose respect . . .

Ben   Who says I lose respect?

Anne   Your habits speak louder than your words . . .

Ben   Oh, leave it alone, will you?!

Anne   After a couple of years you don't change your knickers . . .

Ben   Who don't . . . ? I changed them only last month . . . Ha ha!

Anne   Yeah, you think you're joking . . . I clean them . . .

Ben   As long as you don't study them . . .

Anne   Sure, I take them to the fortune-tellers!

Ben   Anyway, you're no idol of purity . . .

Anne   Oh really . . .

Ben   You're not such a Madonna yourself . . .

Anne   And you're the one to talk . . . With your one-night stands . . .

Ben   I told you at the time, I was lonely . . .

Anne   And experimented . . .

Ben   Experimented . . . To find the right woman . . . Sometimes sex is the quickest way to cure loneliness . . .

Anne   So when you're feeling lonely you go out for a one-night stand . . .

Ben   It's possible . . . Yes . . . It's distinctly possible . . .

Anne   God knows what that thing has caught . . .

Ben   I caught nothing . . . I was careful . . .

Anne   I bet!

Ben   I was.

Anne   Yeah, if it moves . . . stick it in . . .

Ben   Not quite . . . You can find intimacy in a woman that might take for ever in a man . . .

Anne   So women are like fast food . . .

Ben   That's how we met!

Anne   Never!

Ben   Sure.

Anne   You came over with a hard-on and said, 'Look at this!'

Ben   I was fooling around . . .

Anne   I couldn't believe it . . .

Ben   It was a joke!

Anne   Is that how you meet your women?

Ben   That's how I met you . . .

Anne   Yeah . . . I was shocked . . . I couldn't believe it . . .

Ben   For some reason I felt comfortable with you . . . I'd never done that before . . .

Anne   God knows where that thing has been!

Ben   I never caught anything . . . I swear . . . Never . . . Not a thing . . .

Anne   Then you were lucky . . .

Ben   Maybe . . .

Anne   You were lucky, if you take it out like American Express . . .

Ben   Takes you anywhere . . .

Anne   I was really shocked . . .

Ben   But you like it . . .

Anne   I put up with it . . .

Ben   You liked it . . . You dropped your pants . . .

Anne   I felt sorry for you . . .

Ben   Hah!

Anne   You wriggled around a bit like you felt obliged . . .

Ben   But the room was freezing . . .

Anne   So you thought you'd warm it up?

Ben   So *you* did it the first time . . . with me . . . maybe every time . . .

Anne   Never was I shocked . . . I swear . . . Never did it on the first time before . . .

Ben   But you did then . . . the first night . . .

Anne   I must have been crazy . . . or felt sorry for you . . .

Ben   That's what they all say . . .

Anne   Open your flies and oomph!

Ben   You liked it . . .

Anne   Let's say, I put up with it . . .

Ben   So why do it?

Anne   Must have felt sorry for you in your cold bachelor flat . . .

Ben   So you didn't like it?

Anne   It wasn't fantastic . . .

Ben   So why did you do it?

Anne   Who can read the future?

Ben   First times aren't great . . .

Anne   I liked the Indian meal after best . . .

Ben   That was nice . . .

Anne   Then we talked . . .

Ben   Enjoyed that . . .

Anne   Should have done that first . . .

Ben   The meal was good because we broke the ice first . . .

Anne   Oh, so that's what it was . . .

Ben   You need to get over the excitement . . .

Anne   What excitement?

Ben   The anticipation of the first time . . . the frisson . . .
Get rid of it!

Anne   It's in your head . . .

Ben   It's like . . . you never did it before . . . That's what a
first time feels like . . .

Anne   You felt that?! . . .

Ben   Yeah . . . I did . . .

Anne   Like it was for you the first time?

Ben   Yes, each time is like the first time . . .

Anne   Oh, thanks . . . How many times before it feels like
the second time?

Ben   It's mysterious, I can't explain.

Anne   Like an alcoholic discovering a new pub?

Ben   You have to get it over with . . . the first time . . . and
then you can get to know each other.

Anne   Uh-huh . . .

Ben   Like it's a wall you have to penetrate.

Anne   A wall?

Ben   And on the other side's a garden . . .

Anne   How very romantic . . .

Ben   But you see the wall's more tempting than what's
within!

Anne   Really?

Ben   I mean, the wall is only the first step but not the last . . .

Anne   Ahh!

Ben   Like some people make getting through the wall . . . the last . . . then it's over for them . . .

Anne   But of course you're different . . .

Ben   I'd like to think so . . .

Anne   What makes you different from the others . . . ?

Ben   I don't invest too much importance in it . . .

Anne   Oh really . . .

Ben   No, or you might get terribly disappointed.

Anne   That's a rule, is it?

Ben   Mostly yes . . . Most times it becomes the be-all and the end-all . . . But it's not . . .

Anne   What is it then?

Ben   It's not what it is . . . It's what they think it should be . . . the apotheosis . . . and then there's the come-down . . .

Anne   Not always . . .

Ben   Usually . . . When all you have to do is bide your time . . . Put it on hold . . .

Anne   Like to be nibbled later . . .

Ben   That's right . . . All this energy redirected until the decent time . . .

Anne   When's that?

Ben   When you're not a whore . . .

Anne   Oh, when's that . . .

Ben   Depends . . . For some it's a rule . . . don't fuck on the first night . . . But the second . . . is more decent . . .

Anne   Oh, really? How quaint your rules are!

Ben   I didn't make the rules . . . It's how people behave . . .
On the first night you're a greedy beast . . . Only one thing
on your mind . . . 'I'm not like that' . . .

Anne   And the second night?

Ben   She's doing a fair impersonation of a whore in a Hong
Kong brothel.

Anne   Funny how men equate sexuality with whoring . . .
When it's the men who behave like whores . . .

Ben   We've been conditioned by women . . . by playing the
game . . .

Anne   Rubbish . . .

Ben   But it's true . . .

Anne   For you . . . for you . . . the expert . . . Oh, you
know . . .

Ben   For everyone . . . The second, maybe the third time
out implies interest . . .

Anne   That she likes him, that's all . . .

Ben   No, that she feels fucking is somehow wrong . . .

Anne   Don't use that word . . .

Ben   Sorry, OK . . . that making love is somehow tainted . . .

Anne   That's better . . .

Ben   She . . . women love it and want to . . .

Anne   Oh yeah . . . Maybe she wants to get to know him
better . . .

Ben   On two nights!

Anne   Maybe . . .

Ben   So he's a deep friend the second time?

Anne   He respects her more . . .

Ben   Ah, so it's a symbolic celibacy for the first night or two?

Anne   What's symbolic?

Ben   The time between the first meeting and the second symbolises time . . . knowledge . . . understanding . . . love?

Anne   No, it demonstrates that he wishes to see her and not use her . . . not just have a quick one . . .

Ben   Ah, so he gets it if he invests one night . . . like an investment payment . . .

Anne   Don't be so callous . . . as if you think that's being smart . . . Men have a way of turning everything to dirt . . . the Midas touch in reverse . . .

Ben   I don't . . . That's palpably unjust . . . I'm just relating the facts of life . . .

Anne   The 'fucks' of life, did you say?

Ben   That's right . . . take it which way you want . . . It's the system . . . She feels it's wrong . . . Sex is wrong for its own sake unless it's related . . . You're a whore if desire is not related to something . . .

Anne   Like love, care, knowledge . . .

Ben   Couldn't it be just plain lust?!

Anne   Women don't desire on first sight . . .

Ben   They don't?!

Anne   Not like men . . . walking around like dogs . . . sticking it into anything . . .

Ben   They feel attracted on first sight . . . women . . .

Anne   Not like men . . . We're biologically different . . . more discriminating . . . We don't get instant hard-ons . . .

Ben   Men are walking spunk bags . . .

Anne   That's right, I feel sorry for them . . . They can't help it . . .

Ben   That's right.

Anne   Women need to know . . . have to be discriminating . . . need protecting . . . We want strong . . . seed . . . so we choose . . .

Ben   You dropped your drawers the first time!

Anne   I was crazy . . . felt sorry for you with your hard-on . . .

Ben   Oh yeah, you soon jumped on it . . .

Anne   A lot of good it did me . . .

Ben   That's not nice . . .

Anne   Anyway, you apologised after . . .

Ben   I did?!

Anne   For the performance . . .

Ben   I wasn't totally into it . . . it was just a 'hello' . . .

Anne   Cock-a-doodle-doo!

Ben   I wasn't trying to win a gold . . .

Anne   'Sorry, darling' . . . I thought you were going to come at me like a tank!

Ben   Hey! I liked you . . . I wanted to . . . you know . . . all men do . . . or think they do . . .

Anne   End up all wind and piss, so why start?

Ben   Natural desire . . . to get close . . .

Anne   Desire to fulfil the image of yourself . . .

Ben   Oh, what do you suppose that is . . . ?

Anne   A walking cock with the fire power of an M16 . . .

Ben   Now where did you learn that . . . an M16?

Anne   I saw it in *First Blood* with Stallone . . .

Ben   So?

Anne   He fires that because he's afraid of being impotent . . .
It makes him feel omni-potent . . .

Ben   Is that your pocket psychology speaking?

Anne   No, I think a lot of obsession about war films stems
from a concern about size and performance . . .

Ben   There could be an element of truth in what you're
saying . . . maybe . . .

Anne   Firing all those subliminal dicks . . .

Ben   It's a theory . . .

Anne   Steel's hard, infallible . . . right . . . no slack!

Ben   Macho man!

Anne   The gun gives off that feeling of power . . .

Ben   It's shaped like a penis when you think about it . . .
Yeah . . . I've never liked war films . . .

Anne   If you can't fuck it . . . then kill it!

Ben   What about Lee Harvey Oswald?

Anne   He probably was impotent . . . There are ways of
being impotent . . . not just between your legs . . .

Ben   Society didn't want him and so he killed society . . . ?

Anne   In a way . . . yes . . .

Ben   Your theory's too simple . . . Women also use guns . . .

Anne   Some women do . . . penis envy . . . compensation
for what they perceive to be weakness . . . So they emulate
men . . . stupid women . . .

Ben   Your sisters wouldn't like to hear you say that . . . !

Anne   Women who fire guns are not my sisters . . . They're the 'Weird Sisters'!

Ben   What about Italian lovers . . . hot-blooded Latins . . . They kill each other like flies . . .

Anne   That's different . . . they're betrayed . . . they kill the lover . . . they kill his firing power . . .

Ben   Oh, I see . . . They're killing his dick but have to take the whole body with it . . .

Anne   That's right . . . You know how some of these Italians keep their ego between their legs . . .

Ben   I suppose a great many men do . . .

Anne   So if you mess with his pussy you're fucking his brain . . .

Ben   Ah, he gets a headache . . .

Anne   Of course, and for him a woman isn't a person . . . She's a pussy . . . being supported by arms and legs . . .

Ben   OK . . .

Anne   OK what . . . ?

Ben   You've made your point . . .

Anne   Well, it's true, ain't it . . . ?

Ben   If you say so . . .

Anne   I mean women don't go out killing . . . do they . . . except the weird ones . . . but not the normal ones . . .

Ben   Oh sure . . . Let's go, boys, and kill a few tonight . . . Unless we can nail down some pussy, that is . . .

Anne   That's right, and if you're really bored and mind-fucked, go out and kill a few animals . . . that can't hit back . . .

Ben   Plenty of women hunt . . .

Anne   I told you, sick fucks . . . but I don't know any . . .

Ben   There are plenty . . .

Anne   One in five hundred maybe . . . That would be a lot . . .

Ben   You've done a study I suppose . . .

Anne   Hunting's a way of life that's passed down through the generations . . . one sick fuck corrupting an innocent one . . .

Ben   A lot of respectable people go shooting . . .

Anne   Repressed neurotics . . .

Ben   Are you trying to tell me that all those hundreds of thousands of decent British men and women who peacefully marched in London to protest their right to hunt are all nutters . . . Are you seriously saying that?

Anne   Absolutely! Anyone who kills animals for sport has twisted values . . . Animals are like women . . . you can shoot them and then stuff them . . .

Ben   Oh, who's being vulgar now . . .

Anne   'Hunt some pussy' . . . 'Yeah, man, I gave her a good stuffing' . . . 'I banged her' . . . 'Shoot' . . . 'Fired my load' . . . You see, they're all hunting expressions . . . Are they not?

Ben   Man has always been semantically inventive . . . Metaphor is part of our rich literary legacy . . .

Anne   Animals are innocent creatures for idiots to murder . . .

Ben   Can you murder an animal?

Anne   What do you call it then?

Ben   I don't like it and I don't do it since my generative powers are still reasonably healthy so I have no subliminal need to screw animals via a gun . . . But you will admit that it's regarded as a sport . . . You know, to cull excess animals . . .

Anne   Oh, so it's altruistic . . .

Ben   In a way, you preserve the best . . . the fittest . . . and cull the old and mangy . . .

Anne   Oh, how kind . . .

Ben   In a way, yes . . . You keep the stock fit . . .

Anne   You keep your cock fit?

Ben   Stock fit . . . You heard me!

Anne   Then based on that philosophy why don't we cull a few million useless pensioners who are draining the assets from our state?

Ben   But human oldies are still spenders . . . they still help to keep the economic wheels turning . . .

Anne   A bit of culling wouldn't do any harm . . .

Ben   But you can't compare human beings with animals . . .

Anne   Easy bullshit for lazy-minded sadists who want to be gods . . .

Ben   I respect the true hunter who culls old or wounded deer to put them out of their misery . . .

Anne   I wasn't really talking about them . . . I'm talking about the other idiots who only hunt for pleasure . . .

Ben   Oh, back to the impotent ones I suppose . . . ?

Anne   Mentally yes, mentally sterile . . . They sadistically hunt animals just to get a bit of a thrill and some fresh air with their idiot wives . . .

Ben   Oh, now the women are involved again?

Anne   The idiot women . . . the shit that gathers round scum!

Ben   Oh heavy! Join the movement, sweetheart!

Anne   Why?

Ben   'Cause you're so anti-men . . . You hate them so much . . .

Anne   Only some, just as I hate some women . . .

Ben   Yes, but in the main it's men . . . Let's face it . . . Ordinary men hunt, right, but only weird women . . . So it's largely men . . .

Anne   I suppose they are the instigators . . .

Ben   Of course . . . yes . . . But you don't mind holding your hand out for a buck.

Anne   What?!

Ben   I mean, look at you . . . Complaining, whining, blaming, but you sit there like fat queens when the guy gets the bill . . .

Anne   It's your investment, you said . . .

Ben   Oh really, like it's nothing to do with me . . .

Anne   So you've got some temporary economic power . . .

Ben   I read somewhere that women spend forty-five million pounds a year just on mascara . . . In five years you could build a new sanitation system in Liberia!

Anne   Men spend billions on military hardware . . .

Ben   True . . . Much of it unfortunately on self-defence, while the men go out and get killed for you . . .

Anne   I suppose men have an innate need, a gene for self-destruction fortunately undetected in women . . .

Ben   You stuff yourselves and wrap fur round your fat necks, thus depleting the world's species and torturing the others . . .

Anne   Man-made propaganda for female wimps who can't resist narcissism . . . I loathe those women . . . Whores I'm not talking about . . . I'm talking about women! Real women! Shit-head!

Ben   Oh yeah . . . What about the mink stole in your wardrobe, arsehole . . .

Anne   That was a second-hand handdown from my aunt, you scumheap!

Ben   What about the trash you shove on your stupid face?!

Anne   Not mine!

Ben   With what you shove on your fucking faces, you could feed fucking India!

Anne   Not my fucking face . . . !

Ben   India! Do you know what you spend on that shit you shove on your face?!

Anne   Go on, tell me . . .

Ben   Well over twenty billion a year!

Anne   And whose fucking pockets does it go into . . . Huh?! Fucking men run the corporations . . .

Ben   Then fucking resist it . . . Resist . . . Say, 'Fuck it!' Accept it as a way of life . . . You're a fucking ecological hazard! Women!

Anne   So what do you think men spend on useless fucking wars to prop up their phoney ideology . . . You think women fight wars . . . ? Do women drop fucking atomic bombs . . . ? Did women invent Auschwitz . . . They couldn't . . . They couldn't begin to conceive the sickness in men!

Ben   Oh no, they supported Hitler, they loved the brute . . . They lined up on the streets with oily Nazi tears in their eyes and welcomed him in . . .

Anne   Stupid bitches fooled by propaganda, but not once they knew what he was about!

Ben   That's why some of the cruellest sadists in the camp were women warders . . .

There is a sound of knocking at the door.

Ben   There's a knocking at the door.

Anne   Best go and see . . .

Ben *goes offstage, or mimes a conversation onstage, apologising for the noise, etc.*

Ben   Upstairs . . . Keep the noise down a bit . . .

Anne   Walls here are paper thin . . . You can't even have a good row or a good fuck without someone knocking . . .

Ben   Charming . . .

Anne   Crap construction built by cheap builders . . . Women are always being ripped off by men . . .

Ben   You women . . . If you learned something useful like building, carpentry, car maintenance, maybe your sisters wouldn't rip each other off . . .

Anne   That's for sure!

Ben   Anyway . . . It's no use discussing it . . . I can't talk to you . . .

Anne   *Pourquoi?*

Ben   Because you turn everything into a war and start screaming . . .

Anne   You started it . . .

Ben   I?!

Anne   You wind me up, saying I hold my hand out . . .

Ben   No, of course you don't . . . I seem to pay the bills . . . Right . . . ?

Anne   If you had to pay someone wages to do what I do . . . !

Ben   Look, try and keep your voice low . . . OK . . . I know you're a woman, but try to reason about something you feel without screaming . . .

Anne   I keep your house in order . . . I look after you and your dump . . . Before I came it was a shithouse . . .

Ben   I dispute that it was a shithouse although you like to conveniently remember it like that so you can claim to have turned it into a palace . . .

Anne   Not a palace, but a home . . . a sanctuary . . . Before that it was a tired shag-nest . . . a squalid slum where you could indulge your sexual fix in the absence of friends . . . !

Ben   OK . . . you did . . . I am not arguing with that . . . You did make it into a home . . . where we entertained people for dinner parties!

Anne   Exactly . . . It was a strain for you at first, learning to communicate with your mind instead of your dick, but you did eventually get better at it . . .

Ben   Don't be so smug . . . I admit . . . You did make it . . . homely . . .

Anne   So you admit it was a poxy bachelor pad . . .

Ben   It was a home for me . . . My home . . . It was OK . . .

Anne   It took a month to clean it . . .

Ben   Well, you know that women make the best hausfraus . . .

Anne   No thank you . . . I've had enough bait for today . . . Yes, women make homes because they like balance . . .

Ben   That's nice . . . I love that . . . cooking beautiful meals . . . putting flowers around the place . . .

Anne   You liked that, you said . . .

Ben   I'm agreeing with you . . . I'm not denying it!

Anne   You said it was never a home until I moved in . . .

Ben   All right, it was a filthy cesspit . . .

Anne   That's right . . .

Ben   I love all the flowers . . . Sometimes it feels like a hospital!

Anne   It cleans out some of the bad odours . . . That's how it started . . .

Ben   Right, to clear out the stink of sour old bachelorhood! Like trees absorb carbon . . .

Anne   It helps . . .

Ben   Poor, neurotic, dirty, unwashed, stinking, fetid bachelors and then along comes a woman –

Anne   It's like you're unfinished without a woman . . .

Ben   – along comes a woman and saves us . . . Oh, thank you, thank you . . .

Anne   I'm glad you admit it . . .

Ben   Well, I've seen plenty of male homes without women around that are beautiful . . . elegant . . . clean . . .

Anne   Yes, gay men perhaps . . . They're good in the home . . . That's true . . . Because they have the instincts of women . . . So you prove my point.

Ben   Come off your soapbox . . . I've seen plenty of 'normal' men who don't want the hassle of living with women . . . That way they get to keep what's theirs . . .

Anne   Arrested adolescents like to live alone so they can play all their lives . . . but they miss out . . . big time!

Ben   Oh yeah . . . you know . . . Mrs Freud. Anyway, I know some very nice gays . . . very sensitive, educated people.

Anne   I'm not denying their sensitivity but they have to put their energy somewhere . . .

Ben   They don't have to do anything . . . They choose to put their energy somewhere . . .

Anne   Since they don't make children, they make lovely homes . . .

Ben   So what, it's better than dropping bombs . . .

Anne   Yes, they're not really into social violence . . .

Ben   So that's good, right . . . so maybe we should have a few more around . . .

Anne   I don't think they're doing too badly . . . They say one in ten are gay . . .

Ben   Oh God, more work for us boys . . .

Anne   Which boys?

Ben   Us boys of course!

Anne   Ahh! You've got more on your hands . . . more choice . . .

Ben   In a manner of . . .

Anne   That's why so many women mate beneath their status.

Ben   Not necessarily.

Anne   Yes, if men are turning into poofs . . .

Ben   One in ten you said . . .

Anne   So women get pot luck, and men get a good deal . . . There's more demand than supply so their value is artificially increased . . .

Ben   Maybe . . . Maybe men feel they're getting a raw deal from women . . . so they turn the other cheek . . . Ha ha!

Anne   You are so sickeningly witty . . .

Ben   You laughed!

Anne   'Cause it was pathetic!

Ben   Yes . . . So what are you saying?

Anne   Maybe that's why I got this really raw deal . . .

Ben   I didn't drag you here . . .

Anne   Maybe I just got used to less . . .

Ben   Like you weren't exactly lassoed . . .

Anne   We expect less, therefore we demand less . . .

Ben   Oh, so that's what you're saying . . . that I'm a bad deal . . . You've done really bad!

Anne   I just lowered my standards, that's all . . .

Ben   Oh, fuck you very much . . . There's an open door, Anny . . . I'm not forcing you to stay . . . I'm not forcing you . . . I might save some money . . .

Anne   That's all you think about – just throw down some money . . . There's more a woman wants . . . much more . . .

Ben   You never turned the filthy money away . . . didn't soil your hands!

Anne   You have more economic power . . . You work in money . . . You hold a few more strings . . .

Ben   Can't all be 'artistic wannabes' . . .

Anne   Even if the strings are dirty . . .

Ben   I work honestly and you never minded indulging yourself . . .

Anne   You're so brainwashed . . . It's like being with a male hustler . . . You've lost your humanity . . .

Ben   Ah, that's a mouthful . . .

Anne   You're out of touch with your own body . . .

Ben   Who is?!

Anne   You're so greedy and grasping . . . All you can think of is what you pay out . . . There're more ways of giving that have no price on it . . . Compassion has no price on it, decency has no price on it . . . respect certainly has no price!

Ben   But the rent that I pay has a price . . . My rates have a price, my car has a price, the clothes I buy for you have a price . . . All the bills that I pay have a price as well as the sushi that you stuffed down yesterday had a price . . . Seventy-five pounds, to be precise!

Anne   You wanted to go out . . . I was happy to cook . . .

Ben   And you're happy to eat when we go out . . .

Anne   Listen, mister, I don't need you to spend seventy-five quid on sushi . . . I'd be just as happy with a takeaway pizza . . . I'd rather have someone who really cares than an expensive indulgent meal . . .

Ben   I'll see the day when you're happy with that – sure . . .

Anne   Sure I would, since I don't need like you . . . You need things, for that's the criterion of your life – your work . . . *money*!

Ben   You love spending it, baby!

Anne   I accompany you . . . just to keep you company . . .

Ben   OK, well, eat at home . . .

Anne   That's fine by me . . . I like 'home' . . . You're the one who needs to go out . . . needs things . . . needs all the time . . .

Ben   That's a twist, as she shops in Armani with my American Express card!

Anne   You can have your fucking card back . . . !

Ben *is silent.*

Anne (*shouting*)   Do you want it back . . . ? You can have your American Express back . . . then you can buy the food, do the shopping, wash your own clothes, clean your loo, prepare the dinner, take the cat to the vet!

Ben   You can keep the card . . .

Anne   Anyway, you earn far more than me . . . So don't keep ramming it down my throat . . .

Ben   You brought it up . . . Ha ha! I made a pun!

Anne   Oh shut up . . . I can't endure it . . .

Ben   Listen . . . You know, maybe it's best . . . maybe we're not really suited any more . . . maybe you did get a bad deal . . .

Anne   I can't stand the war . . .

Ben   Look, I don't want to war . . . I just want a peaceful
life . . .

Anne   Yeah . . .

Ben   That's what I want . . . I really want a peaceful life . . .
Maybe I don't need what we've got . . .

Anne   I don't for sure . . .

Ben   It's like . . . it's gone very sour . . .

Anne   It has . . .

Ben   And maybe a lot of it's my fault . . .

Anne   Like we aren't really made for each other . . .

Ben   Who said we were?

Anne   Some men and some women are really made for
each other and when you find them it's like your world has
become complete . . . What a relief . . . No more searching . . .
Oh, sweet peace . . .

Ben   Keep looking . . .

Anne   I shall . . .

Ben   We came together . . . a bit of loneliness and we run to
the nearest . . .

Anne   Try to learn to be alone.

Ben   I was . . .

Anne   For a while . . . a few weeks . . . Then you get
panicked . . . run back to 'Mama' . . .

Ben   I didn't run . . . You ran here. You ran, did I beg
you . . . ? Did I . . . ? Did I go down on my bended knees . . . ?
I don't think so!

Anne   You whined with your lonely pathetic voice . . . 'You
coming over?' I heard that tone of desperation in your voice
and I yielded to you . . .

Ben   How kind you were . . . to move in with me . . . so
generous . . . so compassionate . . .

Anne   It was easier to live in one place . . .

Ben   But how you liked it . . . Oh yes . . . You loved it . . .

Anne   At the beginning you try to make something work . . .
something come to life . . . You try . . . even if at the time I
didn't really think or feel that we were suited to each other . . .
Something about coming home to a light on . . . You imagine
what it would be like . . . There's always a time to dream . . .
this may work . . . This time it could be good, since you
hold the ideal up in front of your eyes . . . like some pink
cellophane . . . enough of living alone . . . I want to curl up to
the same familiar smell . . . to make a home . . . That's what
I wanted . . . Something all humans want . . . above anything
. . . that word, 'home', that's what I wanted . . . to function
as a woman . . . to be loved and to give it . . . Strong certain
love . . . I try . . . I did . . . but there is a time . . . You get
taken for granted . . . used, too . . . Then you hardly touch . . .
I become like your need . . . your mother . . . there to blow
your nose . . . keep you company . . . because you can't face
yourself . . . It's terrible, and what's terrible is that because we
both want that thing . . . that elusive thing we don't admit
that we might not just have it . . . so . . . maybe live and die
alone . . . you and your book of numbers . . . anything to fill
the space of an empty night . . . doesn't matter who . . . just
fill them . . . You men . . . your kind of man is always alone . . .
aren't sure of who or what you are . . . so we help you find
yourself . . . and become your mirror, but you can only see
how glamorous you are . . . how wonderful . . . but eventually
it all turns sour, the relationship becomes fake . . . You just
want someone to wipe your arse . . . You use us like Kleenex
. . . So I will go . . . I will . . . to be alone may be the only way
to truly find out who I am and who you are . . . I can't
comfort you, so don't run to me any more . . . I'm going, so
get used to it . . . I will . . . To fight is just another way to

cover up the emptiness . . . It's a background noise . . . 'cause there's nothing else . . . So good luck . . . I'm going . . .

Ben Hey, come on . . .

Anne No, I am . . .

Ben Don't be so dramatic . . .

Anne I'm not, I swear I'm not . . .

Ben Take your mind back . . . Go on . . . You always seem to start things off . . . right from the word go.

Anne I did not, I made a comment on your disgusting habits . . .

Ben Once! Once! I slip up . . . Big deal!

Anne No, your mind is saying, 'I don't care any more . . . I don't care or mind what she thinks . . . '

Ben Oh, come on . . . 'cause I care . . .

Anne You're just panicking a bit . . .

Ben The hell I am . . . Listen, if you really want out . . . there's an open door . . . But it's silly . . . You're being really silly . . . We get on!

Anne Oh, really . . . That's what you think . . . ? Deep in your heart . . . ? It's not panic speaking . . . ?

Ben No, no! Don't be silly . . .

Anne You can look into your heart and really believe that . . . ?

Ben (*not too convincing*) Yes, yes! Basically we do . . .

Anne You think that's what love is . . .

Ben Love, shmove . . . It's a convenience . . . We need each other . . . Right?! Men and women need each other . . . Of course it's love but it's also more . . . it's . . .

Anne   NEED, NEED! That's all you say . . . That's what
I mean . . . You need, that's why you find if difficult to give . . .
Needers are too busy taking . . . !

Ben   Shiiit! Will you stop preaching to me . . . I'm not one
of your kids in your class . . . You're the taker . . . I'm the
giver, but somehow you've managed to twist that around with
a little female cunning . . . I gave you a home . . . a sanctuary,
and you loved it, you fell in love with it and you came because
you wanted to and now you feel a little brave so go . . . Go . . .
Please . . . don't do me any favour with your love. I'm not
begging for charity . . . I'll survive, believe me I'll survive . . .
I did before . . . I'm a survivor . . .

Anne *doesn't move.*

Ben   I don't need you . . . I don't *need*! Yes, it's comforting;
yes, I admit that . . . It is . . . comforting . . . but a parasite . . .
a complaining, whining parasite I can do without . . . Go
on . . . bum off someone else . . . You women are always
searching for someone to feed off . . . You need a place you
can wriggle into and eat the heart out like a maggot. Because
alone you cannot cope . . . Alone you feel like a leper . . . and
so you use your sex to screw men . . . You use your pathetic
acts of helplessness to make men feel like heroes . . . You
make yourself weak and vulnerable to con men into looking
after . . . when really you're strong and poisonous like
tarantulas . . . You suck their core away and when you've had
enough, you search for a new victim . . . I'm on to you baby
. . . So there's the door . . .

Anne   OK, I'm going . . .

There is a short silence while **Anne** *pauses, having taken it all in.*

Ben   Don't . . . Look, I didn't mean it . . .

Anne   It's probably the first time you'd told the truth . . .

Ben   It's not . . . I say that 'cause you make me so angry . . .

Anne   Out of anger comes truth . . . *in vino veritas* . . .

Ben   I am not drunk!

Anne   Anger's your alcohol . . . You meant every word . . .

Ben   I get mad and I say the worst thing I can think of . . .
It burns up the poison . . . and then I'm rid of it . . .

Anne   Temporarily, cut the tumour out but it grows again
because the seed of hate is there . . .

Ben   What are you talking about . . . *Hate*? What hate . . . ?

Anne   I'm going.

Ben   Dooon't! Annie, don't . . . I'm sorry . . .

Anne   I have to . . .

Ben   Come on . . . Hold me . . .

Anne   Ben, you'll get over it, I swear, and find someone
better . . . much better for you.

Ben   You're being silly, really truly silly . . .

Anne   I'm not . . .

Ben   I swear, I didn't mean it! Come on, you know I didn't
mean it!

Anne   You did and it's OK . . .

Ben   I know what I meant . . . I didn't . . .

Anne   It'll feel bleak for a day or two, maybe three, and
then you'll be so glad . . .

Ben   Don't try to tell me what I'll feel! You're not leaving!

Anne   I am . . . sorry . . .

Ben   No!

Anne   You know deep in your heart that it's best . . .

Ben   You don't know what's in my heart . . .

Anne   I think I do and you still have your book of numbers . . .

Ben   They're out of date by now . . .

Anne   Then you can make a new book . . .

Ben   Don't be so fucking bitchy . . .

Anne   It's no use . . .

Ben   I'm sorry . . .

Anne   It's too late . . . You've said 'sorry' too many times . . .

Ben   I'll make it up . . .

Anne   Don't worry . . .

Ben   Where will you go?

Anne   I'll find somewhere . . .

Ben   I *love* you!

Anne   You *need* me . . . Goodbye . . .

Ben (*shouting*)   Hey, wait . . . ! Gimme my fucking Amex card!

Anne *hands him the card as well as her keys, then exits.*

Ben (*thumbing through his old 'book' of numbers*)   Dirty, lousy, stinking fucking bitch! I mean, talk about being fucking used!

He goes to the phone and dials.

Hello, this is Ben whom you may remember from a couple of years ago . . . And so I'm just calling to leave you a message . . . to say . . . I would really love to see you again . . . And if you'd like to meet for a drink –

The lights are fading.

– that would be great . . . It would be good to catch up . . . And you know something . . . I've missed you . . . Yeah . . .

Blackout.

Made in the USA
Las Vegas, NV
28 February 2021

18575677R00243